RICHARD WRIGHT

TWENTIETH CENTURY VIEWS

The aim of this series is to present the best in contemporary critical opinion on major authors, providing a twentieth century perspective on their changing status in an era of profound revaluation.

Maynard Mack, *Series Editor*
Yale University

RICHARD WRIGHT

A COLLECTION OF CRITICAL ESSAYS

Edited by
Richard Macksey and Frank E. Moorer

Prentice-Hall, Inc.

A SPECTRUM BOOK

Englewood Cliffs, N.J.

Library of Congress Cataloging in Publication Data

Main entry under title:

Richard Wright, a collection of critical essays.

(Twentieth century views)
"A Spectrum Book."
Bibliography: p.
Includes index.
1. Wright, Richard, 1908–1960—Criticism and inter-
pretation—Addresses, essays, lectures.   I. Macksey,
Richard (date).   II. Moorer, Frank E.   III. Series.
PS3545.R815Z815 1984   813'.52   83-19285
ISBN 0-13-780924-7
ISBN 0-13-780916-6 (pbk.)

We would like to express our sincere thanks to the editorial staff of Prentice-Hall for both patience and encouragement in the gestation of this volume. We are especially grateful to our copy editor, Bill Green, for the care, sympathy, and critical attention with which he responded to the manuscript.

Editorial/production supervision by Rita Young
Cover illustration by Stanley Wyatt

10 9 8 7 6 5 4 3 2 1

ISBN 0-13-780924-7

ISBN 0-13-780916-6 {PBK.}

PRENTICE-HALL INTERNATIONAL, INC. (*London*)
PRENTICE-HALL OF AUSTRALIA PTY. LIMITED (*Sydney*)
PRENTICE-HALL CANADA INC. (*Toronto*)
PRENTICE-HALL OF INDIA PRIVATE LIMITED (*New Delhi*)
PRENTICE-HALL OF JAPAN, INC. (*Tokyo*)
PRENTICE-HALL OF SOUTHEAST ASIA PTE. LTD. (*Singapore*)
WHITEHALL BOOKS LIMITED (*Wellington, New Zealand*)
EDITORA PRENTICE-HALL DO BRASIL LTDA. (*Rio de Janeiro*)

For Our Sons

Richard Alan, Jr.
Robert Reverdy Ransom
William Dougal Ormondé

Contents

III. The Existential Quest: Freedom and Enclosure

RICHARD WRIGHT

Introduction

by Richard Macksey and Frank E. Moorer

The crow flew so fast
That he left his lonely caw
Behind in the fields.

RICHARD WRIGHT, 1960

Richard Nathaniel Wright was born in the Mississippi cotton belt in 1908, forty-three years after the end of slavery; he was born during the era C. Vann Woodward has styled the "New South." These geographic and historical circumstances had a profound impact in shaping Wright as an individual and as an artist. The legacy of slavery was overwhelming in Mississippi. While blacks formed the majority of the population, they were still for the most part peasants on large plantations. They shared none of the economic benefits or rising expectations of the New South. In fact, blacks had lost most of the privileges of citizenship they had been granted in the 1860s and 1870s. This agrarian culture was a world of poor landless descendants of slaves, still effectively controlled by a small cadre of white landowners. The custodians of Mississippi politics during Wright's formative years were demagogues of the unreconstructed ilk of J. K. Vardaman and successors like Theodore Bilbo. This was the feudal world into which Wright was born and in which he came of age. It was hardly the kind of environment to nurture a writer. In fact, all the institutions of the larger society were carefully calculated to stifle any creative efforts on the part of its black subculture. If we are to believe Wright's testimony, most members of his own family did not understand or sympathize with his efforts to become a writer.

Such, then, were the constraints society had erected to discourage mobility or even self-expression. The majority of blacks, willingly or not, had accepted their status as a circumscribed caste in a world stubbornly resistant to change. They would not aspire beyond the narrow limits prescribed by that society. Not so with Richard Wright; from his earliest years he sought to escape the barriers and restrictions that would consign him to the traditional role of a docile black with a future as a sharecropper or a source of cheap day labor for the landed class. The paradoxical but

1

inevitable form of his strongest affirmations, from early childhood on, was to say no, to refuse to accommodate.

Wright's family moved often during this childhood, though always within the social and economic limits dictated by society, making it impossible for him to attend school on a regular basis. After his father had deserted the family, Wright, his ailing mother, and younger brother lived for a while in Arkansas and Tennessee, but because his mother had to work, school attendance was sporadic at best. It was not until Wright returned with his mother to Jackson, Mississippi, to live with his grandparents that he was able to attend school there. Thus, he was twelve years old before he spent his first full year in school, but the constant moving about between 1908 and 1919 had made him much more aware of his world than the average twelve-year-old. Such experiences also tended to make him a loner. He refused to accept the things that many people in his culture simply took for granted. His was a questioning mind, and as a result he challenged many of the received ideas of his grandmother's and mother's world—questioning the traditional comforts of evangelical religion, the prescribed ways of "staying out of trouble," and even his own racial inheritance. To be sure, such attitudes were not designed to endear the boy to his teachers nor to other adults nor even to many of his own classmates. Consequently, rather than be rebuffed or written off as "strange," the young Wright gradually learned to keep many of his ideas to himself. While his early years were assuredly difficult, they were probably not as unremittingly difficult as Wright later recreated them in *Black Boy* (1945). Michel Fabre in his admirable biography demonstrates that both members of Wright's family and even some of the whites whom he early encountered recognized his talent and offered some encouragement.[1] Such exceptions to the picture presented in *Black Boy* did not, however, alter the overwhelming pressures of his society.

Wright's formal education ended in 1925 when he graduated, as valedictorian, from the Smith-Robinson Junior High School in Jackson. He had completed only the ninth grade. Later he would with furious determination educate himself through reading. It was in Memphis, where the youth moved shortly after his graduation, that he began his serious reading of H. L. Mencken, Sinclair Lewis, and Theodore Dreiser. He discovered first in Mencken, then in the naturalists, that language could be used as a "club," a weapon to persuade or coerce assent. The southern city culture of Memphis, with its public library as well as its newer forms of economic and social oppression, was the first stop on Wright's journey to become a serious writer, which meant for him a continuing effort to understand what it meant to be black in America. In the self-education

[1] *The Unfinished Quest of Richard Wright* (New York: William Morrow, 1973).

of a rural boy, it was the first major urban center in a series of stops that led on to Chicago's South Side, to Harlem and Greenwich Village, and finally to Paris.

Very early in his life, Wright collided with the absolute divisions between white and black worlds. As a writer, from whatever vantage, one of his major themes would be the place of blacks in the American landscape, discovering that the harsh constraints of the cotton belt were in various ways replicated in the great cities of the North, which had traditionally offered the promise of escape. Wright was never able to find a completely satisfactory answer to his question about the "place" of the American black, but his steady commitment to address this question, from changing perspectives, made him a pioneer for the generation that followed and guarantees his own place in our history.

It seems to us that Wright ultimately came to the conclusion that it was almost impossible to be black and "fully human" in America simply because the society did not allow blacks the psychological space to develop and cultivate the human spirit. In the majority of his works, Wright hammers home the point that American society was designed to cripple its black citizens, whether disabled by their submission or by their inarticulate anger. This presiding obsession with the elided place of blacks on the American landscape is for Wright at once a source of his strengths and his weaknesses as a creative artist.

Wright was the first outstanding black writer to achieve truly national acclaim. There had, of course, been other successful black writers before him: Charles W. Chesnutt of Cleveland, Paul Laurence Dunbar of Dayton, Harvard's unquenchable W. E. B. Dubois, and the galaxy of brilliant young writers of the Harlem renaissance had all claimed a certain audience. None, however, had been able to command the financial rewards and national critical attention that Wright received. And some of the literary figures who had preceded him, like W. S. Braithwaite or—the most luminous talent and strangest career—Jean Toomer, had after the fashion of James Weldon Johnson's "Ex-Coloured Man" effectively "seceded" from the race question. Wright, on the contrary, founded his career and commanded the conscience of his readers by refusing to look away or to qualify the violence that his insistent question implied. From our present perspective we can safely say that with Wright literature by black Americans came of age and lost the invisible status to which it had been consigned by the keepers of the American cultural establishment. We are not, of course, suggesting that after Wright publishers, critics, and the mass public all aggressively cultivated the work of black writers. Rather, we are simply stating that black writers of talent could no longer be ignored. Irving Howe succinctly stated the case for Wright as a literary watershed: "The day that *Native Son* appeared, American culture was changed forever. No matter how much qualifying the book might later need, it made impossible a repetition of the old lies."[2] As Howe observed, the appearance of Wright's first novel brought fully into the open the hatred, fear, and violence that have crippled and may yet destroy our society; but it also marked the emergence of a voice that spoke for those who previously had neither voice nor face; speaking in part through his own experience, Wright articulated a question that had previously been historical but which could now command a literary audience.

Any discussion of Wright's literary development inevitably raises attendant questions about the use and abuse of autobiographical evidence: How valid is *Black Boy* as autobiography? Did Wright distort evidence in order to present himself as the only rebel in the black community? Did he fail to see available sources of strength within this same community? In what ways did he participate in the anger and violence of his fictional personae? These and other questions will be raised concerning Wright's image of himself in relation to his art and his presentation of the black community. Each of his works can be situated at a closer or further remove from critical events in his life. Each event, however, can also be interpreted as an adumbration of the predicament of the "outsider"—from the childhood incident of the house fire and beating in *Black Boy* to the polemics of the last days in Paris. It would, in fact, not be distorting the evidence to suggest that Wright's expatriation after 1947 was an effort of the native outsider to find a home in the world. This quest pattern in the career of the artist echoes one of the most recurrent themes in Afro-American literature: the search for a living space in both the physical and psychological senses.

One of the dominant concerns in the American experience has been the abundant space—cultural as well as geographic—that Americans have had in which to move and shape their destiny. Sidney Mead has suggested in *Lively Experiment* that it was this space that made the "real difference" for citizens of the new Republic: "Gone was the traditional sense of confinement in space, for space relative to people that mattered was practically unlimited."[3] Black Americans did not, however, share in this sense of the unlimited horizon. And Wright had an especially acute awareness of the "spatial" limitations of the black quest for fulfillment in the American landscape. Thus his movements, given their most positive interpretation in the last pages of *Black Boy,* mark the successive stages in a frustrating search for personal freedom and important steps in the evolution of his art, an art that is so close to the crises of his life as to put the conventional terms of "impersonal" formalist criticism in question. The materials of

[2] *A World More Attractive* (New York: Horizon, 1963), pp. 100–101.

[3] *Lively Experiment: The Shaping of Christianity in America* (New York: Harper & Row, 1963), p. 6.

the autobiography—quest and exile, violence and victimage—are early and late the stuff out of which the fiction is selectively woven.

From *Uncle Tom's Children* (1938) to *The Long Dream* (1958), Wright insisted again and again that because of the lack of space that mattered, black life was hopelessly stunted. The recurrent pattern in Wright's fiction is a diastole-systole of a striving toward spatial liberation followed by an often ironic reassertion of enclosure. Thanks to his study of folk history for *Twelve Million Black Voices* (1941), Wright early recognized the figure, with a tradition stretching back into the slave narratives, of crossing over from bondage into a place of one's own. Thus, in the first story of *Uncle Tom's Children*, Big Boy, literally in a hole, has to escape the condemned native ground because his life depends on it. (Early in the story the boys chant, "Dis train bound fo Glory.") Wright makes it abundantly clear that the spatial world of Big Boy and his friends is no prelapsarian Garden of Eden; rather, the whole landscape is fraught with danger (real as well as symbolic snakes), and because of the simple impulse to enjoy nature two of his friends lose their lives. Here as elsewhere the entire black community is narrowly limited in its options. They cannot save Big Boy but merely talk about escape. Ultimately he has to make his own escape, as the lone individual on the road north, seeking another place to grow— and significantly, in the final moments he lapses into unconsciousness.

Even in the North, the traditional goal of escape, the black man or woman finds his world still painfully constricted by the larger society. Bigger Thomas in *Native Son* (1940), who has achieved Big Boy's escape, still lives in the closed world of ghetto space. He and the members of his family are relegated to a one-room cagelike apartment on Chicago's South Side. His imaginative world is restricted to the movies, the pool room, and the street corner. He has no vocational options. The only sort of job to which he can aspire that breaches the narrow urban frontiers however briefly is that of a uniformed chauffeur. Insistently, Wright suggests that Bigger's world is hardly larger than the one that Big Boy fled. In fact, the first lines of the novel seem to yank Bigger back into the consciousness that Big Boy had escaped in the last lines of his story. And the action begins immediately with a struggle to the death for simple living space between the Thomas family and the "huge black rat" ("You sonofa*bitch*!") that attacks Bigger in a desperate attempt to escape down his hole. The cityscape that seemed to promise freedom proves to be just as constrained and controlled by social forces beyond Bigger's horizon. He inhabits a world where all avenues of self-expression and growth are as effectively barred as the rat's hole. Like other rural *and* urban blacks, he lives in a world that systematically denies his humanity. The only way he can find, less than consciously, to affirm this humanity is through a brutal act of violence against the society that confines him. He finds no comfort in the sort of stoic religious acceptance and escape that his mother invokes in the first chapter as she sings, "Life is like a mountain railroad . . ." (again echoing the "Glory Train" of the earlier story). Wright thus uses the violence always so close to the surface in his fiction to deconstruct the comfortable myth of America as a society of unlimited space for the individual. On the contrary, Wright's recurrent argument is that American society is so repressive that blacks will have to engage in an act of violence (actual or symbolic) to strike through the mask of coercion, or alternatively will have to flee the society altogether in pursuit of their potential. Bigger's abortive revolt—played out in the now familiar terms of political, racial, and metaphysical rebellion—demonstrates both the violence and the limitations of the available means of self-definition. If, as James Baldwin has argued, he is a "monster," he is clearly a "sign" (*monstrum*) marking the limits inscribed on its scapegoats by a nation blind to its own inhumanity. His author reserves his most unrelenting indictment for the philanthropists and reformers of Bigger's world who would refuse to recognize these limits.

Hence, *The Long Dream,* the last novel he completed, with all its flaws, was not an aberration in Wright's literary development nor was it a sign that he had lost touch with the course of race relations in the United States. Rather, *The Long Dream* restates the paradigm of escape, the author's belief that a black, in order to maintain the vital sense of self, has literally now to leave the country. Fishbelly cannot grow as long as he remains in America. The American landscape will not nurture him. For Fish to remain in America was to become like his father, Tyree, certainly the most powerfully rendered father in Wright's fiction of dominating women, but a crippled figure nonetheless. Paradoxically, both Wright and his persona, condemned to freedom, must carry with them their roots.

If the search for a viable space drives both Wright and his protagonists forward, it is toward irrevocable decisions. There is no turning back toward the abandoned ground. Return for Wright is even more difficult than escape, and only within the highly stylized frame of *Black Boy* does he come close to a controlled passage back. The most vivid scene in his neglected psychoanalytic thriller, *Savage Holiday* (1954), is one of sudden exclusion and panic. Erskine Fowler, the affluent white protagonist propelled into a midlife crisis, steps out into the hall of his apartment house to gather in the *New York Times* and by a sudden gust of wind is irrevocably *locked out* of his world, naked and frantic.

In *Black Boy,* Wright sought to analyze the impact of America on his own early development as a black man and as a writer. The account is thus a *Bildungsroman* in a double key: the picaresque narrative of survival and escape (with elements drawn from black folk tradition) and a more lyrical narrative of the making of an artist bound for exile. While most critics agree that *Black Boy* is one of Wright's most compelling and artful works, there are problems with any simple, monovalent reading of the persona presented in the text. The stance taken by both the protagonist and his narrative voice toward his environment is one almost as hostile to the black community itself as to the more distant forces of oppression. And yet, as Constance Webb observes, in writing his autobiography Wright uses "himself as a symbol of all the brutality and cruelty wreaked upon the black man in the Southern environment."[4] If such were indeed the case, Wright had a curious way of presenting his life as a symbol of an entire race's confrontation with the American landscape. Despite the "representative" character of some of Richard's experience, the dominant movement is undoubtedly not toward solidarity but toward isolation and greater distance. In *Black Boy,* Wright seems to picture himself as the only real rebel in the black community. His escape was perforce a solitary one, and his delineation of blacks was almost as unsympathetic as his presentation of most southern whites: they are docile; they use religion as an instrument of tyranny; they have no positive values and traditions; and, perhaps worst of all, they conspire in the system of oppression. By contrast, Richard reads, Richard thinks, and Richard aspires to be a writer (an ambition no other black could conceive of). Working with other blacks in a hotel in Jackson, Wright contends that the other hall-boys had willingly embraced the way of life designed for them. They *would* not aspire beyond the limits set for them by their environment: "I began to marvel at how smoothly the black boys acted out the roles that the white race had mapped out for them. Most of them were not conscious of living a special, separate, stunted way of life."[5] Long before his encounter with Jean-Paul Sartre, Wright had discovered the infernal mechanism of *mauvaise foi,* an autohypocrisy that infects the social role playing of the oppressed. Yet in his analysis the narrator always distances himself from this sort of self-deception; it is a question of "them," not "us": "Although they lived in an America where in theory there existed equality of opportunity, they knew unerringly what to aspire to and what not to aspire to . . ." (p. 172). These were lessons that Richard, as picaro and aspiring artist, had never learned. The narrator could not understand how any black person could accept the trammels placed on his life without nursing a constant anger; yet when he observed the people around him, he found that they had all made some kind of tacit accommodation to their environment. Wright and his persona could never conceive the possibility of such an adjustment. Because of what he presents as his lucidity and because of his correspond-

---

[4]*Richard Wright: A Biography* (New York: Putnam, 1968), p. 205.
[5]*Black Boy: A Record of Childhood and Youth* (New York: Harper & Brothers, 1945), p. 172. All subsequent quotations are from this edition.

ing inability to share in the experiences of the black community, he could write—in an often-quoted aside—that there was "an absence of real kindness in Negroes. . . . And when I brooded upon the cultural barrenness of black life, I wondered if clean, positive tenderness, love, honor, loyalty, and the capacity to remember were native to man. I asked myself if these human qualities were not fostered, won, struggled and suffered for, preserved in ritual from one generation to another" (p. 32). And yet he turned from these parenthetical indictments of black culture ("how lacking in genuine passion we were, how void of great hope, how timid our joy, how bare our traditions, how hollow our memories") to a wonderful evocation of Granny's house in Jackson, the fields beyond, and the yellow, sleepy Mississippi river. (It must be added, however, that the sense of enchantment and adventure that informs this second passage was something that Richard and his brother tried in vain to communicate to the "timid children of the neighbors.") For Wright, then, as he selectively represented himself in his autobiography, he was born a loner and there were no redeeming qualities in communal black life to draw him back. He sought to distance himself as far as possible from the larger black community; and he found himself intellectually identifying with whites rather than other blacks. Some of his critics would argue that he made this identification simply because whites manifestly had the power, for in this formulation to have identified with blacks would have been to accept constriction and defeat at the outset.

It is important to recall, however, that Richard Wright's "autobiography" (whether in *Black Boy* or in its extension finally published in 1977 as *American Hunger*) is a work of art and as such a strenuous effort to master, shape, and illuminate the rout of unaccommodated experience. Whether as the tale of a picaresque survivor or portrait of the artist as a young man, the narrative needs a hero who can both carry the tragic burden of isolation and stand as a representative figure. In this sense "Richard" is no more (nor less) Wright than "Marcel" of *A la recherche du temps perdu* is Proust. The protagonist of the autobiography must stand for every youth from the Black Belt who had the courage to say no and the imagination to affirm his own identity. For the communal vitality of black culture one largely has to look elsewhere in Wright's work, but perhaps the final word on the "cultural barrenness" passage should be that of his friend from Chicago days, his sometime critic, and an artist who struggled long and successfully to liberate himself from Wright's powerful presence—Ralph Ellison. Writing in 1945, shortly after the appearance of *Black Boy*, Ellison addressed the indictment of black culture and the vision of human qualities as something that had to be "won":

> But far from implying that Negroes have no capacity for culture, as one critic interprets it, this is the strongest affirmation that they have. Wright is pointing out what should be obvious (especially to his Marxist critics)[:]

that Negro sensibility is socially and historically conditioned; that Western culture must be won, confronted like the animal in a Spanish bullfight, dominated by the red shawl of codified experience and brought heaving to its knees.

Wright knows perfectly well that Negro life is a by-product of Western civilization, and that in it, if only one possesses the humanity and humility to see, are to be discovered all those impulses, tendencies, life and cultural forms to be found elsewhere in Western society.[6]

Wright would probably add, from his later perspective of voyaging to five continents in search of ways of reconciling past cultures with modern technology, that in "Negro life" are to be found all those potentials *without* some of the moral obliquities that threaten to cripple Western society. (This is a *position* of the 1950's, subject to radical review in the 1960s by Cleaver and others.)

As for his autobiographical persona, Wright's first profound intellectual identifications were solitary encounters with books, especially during the Memphis years of self-education. At first, it was the discovery of Mencken, who by language and indignation forced America to look at its own often absurd and hypocritical image; then it was the naturalist novelists who succeeded in dramatizing the indignities and defeats of the disenfranchised; and later there was the poetic realism of Dostoevsky, writing from a psychological underground deep within another oppressive society.

With the move to Chicago, which carried him beyond the narrative frame of *Black Boy,* there was, however, a change in the register of Wright's identifications. It was still a world circumscribed by menial jobs and decaying tenements, but, as the country slipped further into the grip of the Great Depression, there was enough "psychological space" to include the reaching out to form intellectual and political bonds with other would-be writers and artists. The John Reed Club, organized in 1932, became a natural arena for these associations. Wright soon found himself the executive secretary of the Chicago chapter, was publishing in the Club journal *Left Front,* and had begun to form some of his first enduring literary friendships. The move from the John Reed Club, the secular arm of the Communist Party, to actual Party membership was, as designed, almost inevitable. Wright actually received his Party card a little later than is often reported—probably in late 1933 or early 1934—and his membership was to end with a decisive break in 1942, but the sense of belonging at last to a *band* of outsiders was a tonic event for him. Even though he would later inveigh against the fetters that the Party and Stalinist "discipline" placed on him, Wright recognized that in spite of these constraints Marxism initially gave him a perspective from which to comprehend and shape his experiences. Perhaps more important, however, it gave him a sense of belonging to a group with shared values and a communal sense of outrage. Writing much later, long after he had discovered that the psychic "space" afforded by the Communist Party had for him become an intellectual prison cell, he observed that "many a black boy in America has seized upon the rungs of the red ladder to climb out of his Black Belt. As well he may, if there are no other ways out of it. Hence, ideology here becomes a means toward social intimacy."[7] Again, in a 1955 letter to his close friend and long-time editor at Harper's, Edward Aswell, Wright spoke of the importance of his experience in the Party in helping him to see beyond race:

> I was a Communist because I was a Negro. Indeed the Communist Party had been the only road out of the Black Belt for me. Hence Communism had not been for me simply a fad, a hobby; it had a deep functional meaning for my life. Therefore, when I left the Communist Party, I no longer had a protective barrier, no defenses between me and a hostile racial environment that absorbed all of my time, emotions, and attention. To me the racial situation was a far harder matter than the Communist one and it was one I could not solve alone. (Quoted in Fabre, op. cit., pp. 230–31)

The first ideology that Wright learned by heart was the ideology of racism, ironically reflected in the bourgeois doctrine of personal liberty, and it was this lesson that carried him to Marxism. Long after his Communist years he continued to seek ways to reconcile large collective solutions with the claims of individual freedom. His life-long hostility to the faceless power of totalitarianism was deeply rooted in his equally strong commitment to the inalienable rights of the individual. In his creative work the continuing tension between the search for "large answers" and the freedom of the individual to follow his own vision led to a recurrent struggle between the forces of rational organization and the power of the individual imagination. If the experience in the Party failed to satisfy his quest for a program of justice beyond the trammels of political expediency, it did at least satisfy some of his hunger for emotional engagement, fellow feeling, and intellectual solidarity. He was thus closer to his evolving notion of community in the John Reed Club than in the Party itself. And in his work, especially the best of the early stories and a few of the poems (like the haunted vision of "Between the World and Me"), he managed to bring together the two conflicting elements of his personality in writing that escapes the limits of the ideological cage.

The decade of the 1940s began for Wright with a number of dramatic changes in his personal circumstances: the appearance in March 1940 of *Native Son*, which brought wealth and critical acclaim; his marriage to Ellen Poplar and the birth of his first daughter; his break with the Communist Party; a growing international reputation; and, within a five-year

[7]*White Man, Listen!* (Garden City, N.Y.: Doubleday, 1957), p. 45.

period, the appearance of the other two works that, with *Native Son*, are commonly assessed as his masterpieces—"The Man Who Lived Underground" and *Black Boy*. He had moved from Chicago to New York City and had explored the radically different mores of Harlem and Greenwich Village. Although he had moved a long way from rural Mississippi and its constraints and had achieved in his early thirties extraordinary recognition and success as measured by most commonly received standards, he was still a profoundly restless man. His correspondence of this period, both public and private, reflects his efforts to enlarge the scope of the "race question" and to redefine many slogan-haunted political issues in terms of the "plight of the individual" and a more adequate conception of what it means "to be truly human." It was out of this unrest and questioning that he responded with enthusiasm when the French government invited him and his family in the spring of 1946 as official state guests. The Wrights spent several months in the Latin Quarter of Paris, meeting the survivors of the older generation of American expatriates as well as the new lights of the existentialist and *négritude* movements. Among the Americans, French, and Africans of the intellectual *tout Paris* he found the promise of a humane community and the acceptance on his merits as an *homme de lettres* that he felt he could never fully achieve in America. He and his family in August 1947 emigrated to Paris, which was to be his home—despite wide-ranging travels—until his death in mid-career on November 28, 1960.

Much has been made of Wright's French expatriation by his American critics. They have argued that in his quest for spiritual space he simply removed himself too far from his cultural roots. Saunders Redding has asserted that by leaving America Wright had cut himself off from the vital source of his art.[8] The late Nick Aaron Ford in a hortatory mood made much the same argument: "Wright must return to his native land, at least for another brief look, if he wishes to write with strength and insight. . . ."[9] James Baldwin, who had also tried the role of French exile (though before his talents were fully formed), emphasizes in the "Alas, Poor Richard" section of *Nobody Knows My Name* the psychic costs of his former mentor's expatriation. Comparison with testimony from others who knew Wright well during the Paris years seems to suggest, however, that Baldwin is involved in special pleading here (as in the earlier Wright essays in the significantly titled *Notes of a Native Son*); having followed Wright to France in 1948 and owing him a considerable debt for encouragement and support, Baldwin, whose touch is less sure here than in his finest essays, seems to be working out his own personal and artistic independence from

---

[8] "The Way It Was," *New York Times Book Review,* 26 October 1958; reprinted in *Richard Wright: The Critical Reception,* edited with an Introduction by John M. Reilly (New York: Burt Franklin, 1978), pp. 328–29.
[9] Ibid.

profound Oedipal tensions. Wright was, of course, hardly alone among American black writers in opting for a European vantage. In addition to Baldwin and William Gardner Smith already in Paris, Wright was joined by his friend Chester Himes in 1953, while William Demby and, for a time, Ralph Ellison settled in Rome. Wright himself may have responded on occasion to the charges of having "cut his cultural roots" with a little too much bravado. In the introduction to his collection of lectures, *White Man, Listen!* he claims, "I'm a rootless man, but I'm neither psychologically distraught nor in anywise perturbed because of it. . . . I declare unabashedly that I like and even cherish the state of abandonment, of aloneness; it does not bother me; indeed, to me it seems the natural, inevitable condition of man." While the existential overtones of such a statement are obvious, it is also clear that Wright cherished precisely the sort of acceptance by a cosmopolitan community that welcomed him in Paris—and that he had sought out earlier during the Chicago and New York years. In truth, however, as Harold T. McCarthy demonstrates in this volume, the exile of Richard Wright began long before he and his family took the boat for France; his long search for a human habitation began back on the Mississippi Delta.

Thus, we believe that the American critics who fault Wright's decision to settle in Paris miss a continuity in the author's career. His search for a "public space"—to invoke the phrase from Auden's *New Year Letter* cited by Nathan A. Scott, Jr., in this volume—was succeeded by a restless quest for an "inner space" as well. There were certainly personal as well as intellectual reasons for his expatriation. Despite the "enlightened" circles in which he could then move in New York City, he worried about the impact of unregenerate racism, always just a few yards away, on his (white) wife and small daughter, Julia. In addition, while he was under frequently vicious attack from his former comrades in the Party, he recognized the corresponding threat to any figure on the Left from the rising tide of red baiting in America that was to culminate in the "McCarthy era." Most important to his own development, had Wright remained in the United States longer he probably would not have been able to write at all. He would have been too painfully close to the problem of race as it weighed on him and on those he loved; and it would arguably have consumed most if not all of his creative energies. Paris gave him a certain distance from his own race problem, even though the lesson of this problem was to remain his presiding concern. Six years after the decision he wrote that "the break with the United States was more than a geographical change. It was a break with my former attitudes as a Negro and a Communist—an attempt to think over and redefine my attitude and my thinking."[10] In a sense to be confirmed by the enlarging concerns of

[10]*Ebony*, July 1953, p. 40.

the next decade, he sought in Paris to become a "citizen of the world."
Other Afro-American writers had earlier experienced in Paris something of the same liberation from native racism. James Weldon Johnson,
writing in 1933, testifies that his arrival in Paris twenty-eight years earlier
had given him a new sense of freedom:

> From the day I first set foot in France, I became aware of the working of a
> miracle within me. I became aware of a quick readjustment to life and to
> environment. I recaptured for the first time since childhood the sense of
> being just a human being. I need not try to analyze this change for my
> colored readers; they will understand in a flash what took place. For my
> white readers . . . I am afraid that any analysis will be inadequate, perhaps
> futile. . . . I was suddenly free; free from a sense of impending discomfort,
> insecurity, danger; free from the conflict within the Negro-Man dualism
> and the innumerable maneuvers in thought and behavior that it compels;
> free from the problem of the many obvious or subtle adjustments to a
> multitude of bans and taboos; free from the special scorn, special tolerance,
> special condescension, special commiseration; free to be merely a man.[11]

In contrast with the childhood and youth that Wright records in *Black
Boy,* Johnson's early years were immensely richer in cultural nourishment,
security, and freedom; and yet Paris could give Johnson a sudden sense
of liberation from the ever-present problem of race that remained vivid
over half a lifetime of achievement. Coming from so much narrower a
"ghetto of the soul," surely Wright must have experienced an even greater
access to freedom. Far from being the lonely country boy lost in the
cosmopolitan world of Paris, as some of his American friends would present him, Wright was at last able to deal with the challenge of being "just
a human being" in terms that transcended his specific historical situation.
This did not mean abandoning the hard lessons that his American education had impressed on him. He recognized in the predicament of the poor
rural black making his way from the feudal world of Mississippi to the
harsh exclusions of the industrial North a paradigm for the largest historical movements of the twentieth century: the often brutal rites of passage
that marked the revolutionary transition of the agricultural Third World
thrust into the industrial and technological legacy of the West. And,
through his friendships with African leaders like Diop and Padmore,
through his travels to the Gold Coast and Indonesia, through his exploration of the historical paradoxes of "pagan Spain," he found an increasing
involvement in generalizing his own experience to a much broader notion
of cultural politics. (Although involved in the founding impulse of *Présence
Africaine,* he remained too much of a rationalist not to keep a certain
characteristic distance from the more mystical aspects of the *négritude*

---

[11]*Along This Way: The Autobiography of James Weldon Johnson* (New York: Viking, 1933),
p. 209.

movement. "Black power" for him was an all too material concept. Yet, at the same time, he seemed increasingly to translate what he had earlier seen as political problems into questions of morality and to temper his insistence on rational organization with a deeper appreciation of the role of intuition in resolving social conflict.) If in this evolution he may have lost some of the anger that frequently seems to be the motive force of his most powerful work, he gained a larger sense of what his quest to be fully human might mean. Paris offered him a window on the world, but it also gave him a mirror for his own spiritual development.

Certainly the Paris years brought no flagging in his energy as a writer. The work may have been uneven, occasionally thesis-ridden, but as an artist he was still in motion. During the busy decade of the 1950s, in addition to his engagement with the cultural congresses and manifestoes that seem to punctuate French intellectual life, in addition to his continuing commitment to younger black talents, his quixotic expedition to Argentina to portray Bigger in the film adaptation of *Native Son*, and his guerilla warfare with his enemies (real and imagined) on the Right and the Left, Wright managed to publish seven books and prepare an eighth for publication: his "existential" novel, *The Outsider* (1953); the "psycho-analytic thriller," *Savage Holiday* (1954); the four challenging, prophetic books on cultural politics, *Black Power* (1954), *The Color Curtain* (1956), *Pagan Spain* (1956), and *White Man, Listen!* (1957); the first novel of a projected trilogy, *The Long Dream* (1958); and the posthumously published collection of his later fiction, *Eight Men* (1961). He had also tried his hand at a play in collaboration with a young Frenchman, had written several thousand haiku, and had left the manuscript of the second volume of the trilogy, a novel of the Paris world tentatively titled "The Island of Hallucinations" (only fragments of which have been to date published). Thus when death called for him so unexpectedly at the Clinique Gibez he was, at fifty-two, far from a burned-out case.

A related indictment frequently brought by Wright's American critics against the work of the expatriate years was that exposure to French existentialism—through his friendships with Jean-Paul Sartre, Simone de Beauvoir, and (until the Algerian crisis) Albert Camus—had somehow debilitated his native vision with "ideas." That Wright always had a large appetite for intellectual speculation and that he had an autodidact's tendency at points in his fiction to lecture his readers is undeniable. These were traits that marked his work throughout, whether the "ideas" came to him from the naturalists, the Marxists, the Freudians, or the denizens of the Paris cafés. More central to his work, he had already developed a strong line of "existential" concerns—a profound sense of alienation; a fascination with "limit situations" and the absurdity of the human condition; an awareness of the presence of anxiety, dread, and death; and a secular ethic grounded in choice. Some of this "native existentialism" came, as we have seen, from his earlier reading of the nineteenth-century precursors of modern existentialist thought—Dostoevsky, Kierkegaard, and Nietzsche. But an irreducible element in his psychological and ethical kinship with French thought came from his own bitter experience, from the constant "double vision" of being black in America, from the "bad faith" of living Jim Crow, and from his own radical point of departure as a life-long "outsider."[12] It was an emotional and increasingly moral stance that he had learned from his own alienations, which he recognized in his reading of the fiction of "the insulted and the injured" from Dostoevsky to Dreiser; so that his first coming upon Camus, during the New York years, in works like *L'Étranger* and *Caligula* (a kinsman of Bigger Thomas), was a little more like Monsieur Jourdain's discovery of "prose."

Wright was, of course, delighted to find in Paris an "engaged" intellectual movement that, like his own life, had been so clearly forged in the experience of oppression—the movement of German prison camps, the Nazi occupation, and the Resistance. His response on the personal level to the generosity of Sartre's "humanism" was immediate; he wrote in his journal for August 27, 1947: "Sartre is the only Frenchman I've met who has voluntarily made the identification of the French experience with that of the rest of mankind. How rare a man is Sartre!"[13] Although the encounter with Sartre and his circle was at best a partial one—Sartre moving from an ethic toward political commitment, Wright in the opposite direction—for Wright it seemed a confirmation of his own journey rather than a detour. As can be seen from a number of essays in this collection, critical opinion about the success of *The Outsider* is still deeply divided, but the novel does articulate existential themes that were native to Wright's work from its first stirrings. (And, perhaps borrowing the basic plot device of a hero encountering the difficulties of "inventing himself" after a fictitious "death" from Luigi Pirandello's protoexistentialist novel of 1904, *Il fu Mattia Pascal,* the book reminds us all of the emotional baggage that we carry with us from earlier incarnations.)

Seen in perspective, then, both the life and the achievement of Richard Wright are rich sources of paradoxes. Despite his claim of being "rootless," he carried his earliest experiences of the rural South close with him through the landscapes of the industrial cities that are the terrain of so much of his fiction. A "loner" by choice, he still sought to be accepted on his merits by an aristocracy of the mind. He was fond of insisting, "I am a very average Negro," and yet he constantly strove to be "representative" in a much more Emersonian sense of the term. An "established author"

[12]Cf. Michel Fabre, "Richard Wright and the French Existentialists," *Melus,* V (1978), pp. 35–51. His most overtly existentialist fiction, *The Outsider,* owes more to the German tradition than to the French. Despite the merely deceptive similarity of the title to Camus' novel, the plot does have some congruences to Sartre's 1947 film scenario, *Les Jeux sont faits.*

[13]Quoted by Michel Fabre, *The Unfinished Quest of Richard Wright,* p. 322.

at an early age, favored with awards, money, and a large public, he continued to encounter brutal reminders of his exclusion: traveling Jim Crow through the South shortly after the publication of his most successful novel, or, stopping in the nation's capital en route to the Broadway production of *Native Son,* having to eat his dinner (with his producer, John Houseman) on the curb outside a restaurant across from the White House. In later years he was an ornament of USIA cultural activities and on familiar terms with most of the major European writers of the Left, and yet he expended great energy in escaping the harassment of the CIA and the plots of the Stalinists. Many of the paradoxical contradictions were, however, not merely the twist of circumstances but were deeply rooted within Wright's own personality. The perennial émigré who was the hungry seeker for community was frequently caught between psychic isolation and humanist solidarity. He remained through most of his life a skeptic about the possibilities of a life-enhancing black culture in modern America, and yet he invested considerable energy in trying to articulate the lessons of that culture as a way of understanding the problems of the emerging Third World. He was a committed rationalist striving for systems of explanation in a radically desacralized world, yet he retained a deeply intuitive suspicion of the totalitarian possibilities of most systems. As an artist he drew his strength from an uncompromising secular naturalism that "told the truth," yet in his most powerful work he explored the human heart and became a modern mythographer.

If Wright was a congeries of paradoxes, so too on balance have been his critics. Since the appearance of *Uncle Tom's Children* in 1938, he has been claimed by many rival camps and contradictory doctrines. The critical response to his work has been one more exemplary chronicle of selective blindness and insight. His earliest partisans were doctrinaire Marxists who later became his bitterest enemies. Later yet he supplied, somewhat obliquely, the slogans for black nationalism, but revisionist criticism has found in his work an unrelenting rejection of the "black experience." The fortunes of his critical reception could, in fact, serve as a brief history of American cultural dogmas over the past four decades. His own intellectual itinerary took him from one ideological resting place to another, from the sureties of naturalist reportage and Communist Party doctrine to existentialist humanism and social Freudianism, and during his last years to some guarded exchanges with African *négritude* and Eastern intuitionism. While the earliest response to his work tended to be sociohistorical and political, the titles of his writings alone (with the recurrence of overdetermined words like "son," "children," "boy," and "dream") were an obvious and often reductionist invitation to psychoanalytic critics of various persuasions. The threads almost inextricably binding his life and his works have engaged other forms of biographical interpretation of the fiction as well, while his great gift for translating melodrama into myth has attracted archetypal and anthropological readings. His existential and phenomenological concerns have been subjected to philosophic analysis and source study. Beginning with Ralph Ellison's 1945 essay "Richard Wright's Blues," there have also been efforts to relate his work, however ambivalently, to traditional strains in black popular culture. While initially his fiction may have seemed too rough-hewn and vigorously personal to attract the sympathetic attention of formalist critics, the acolytes of Jamesean craft, increasingly thematic readings have revealed a texture of key images (sight, fire, dismemberment, beasts, enclosure, flight) in the fiction so rich that they have at times threatened to lose the figure in the details of the artful carpet. (Donald B. Gibson, in his essay in this collection, addresses precisely this problem in reading *Native Son*.)

More recent critical dispensations have only begun to attend adequately to Wright's work. Thus, feminist critics, represented here by an essay written for this volume by Maria K. Mootry, will confront obsessive texts in which the women are at once the source of primal authority and the locus of rebellion and often brutal violence. Joseph K. Skerrett, Jr., in a pioneer Yale dissertation ("Take My Burden Up: Three Studies in Psychobiographical Criticism and Afro-American Literature," 1975) has brought to bear Kenneth Burke's strategic theory of "symbolic action" and Harold Bloom's theory of "the anxiety of influence" to interpret both Wright's artistic strategies and the ways in which his most gifted successor, Ralph Ellison, declared his literary independence. As an author who directly challenges every reader in deeply personal terms, elaborating the declensions of guilt and fear, fantasy and desire, not only in his personae but in the response of the audience, Wright invites further study by "reader-oriented" critics. Reception studies and analyses insisting on the constructive role of the reader in the creative process could suggest new lines of approach to Wright's legacy, helping us to understand some of the radical shifts in the aesthetic and moral response to his texts. Wright himself had, of course, long ago recognized that all discourse that matters is inescapably "interested," and Sartre, addressing the question "For Whom Does One Write" in *Qu'est-ce que la littérature?* as early as 1948, used the "case of Richard Wright" for what could be a model of early reader-response criticism.[14] Of an even more recent vintage, the devotees of deconstructive criticism have yet to turn their vigilant linguistic gaze and hypertrophied skepticism on crucial passages in Wright, unraveling some deep internal paradoxes and dismantling received notions of his argument. They would no doubt, in liberating latent metaphors from their moorings, discover subtextually a powerful sexual strain in much of the social rhetoric.

Of all the major schools of interpretation that have recently claimed

---

[14]*Situations, II* (Paris: Gallimard, 1948), pp. 125–28.

the critical scene, however, it is René Girard's synoptic view of human culture founded in the violence of the "mimetic crisis" and regulated by the ritual mechanism of the scapegoat that would seem to have the most to offer for an innovative approach to Richard Wright. This as yet unconsummated meeting may at first seem perverse, because Girard's fascination with the ways of primitive religion appears so antithetical to Wright's desacralized view of the modern world. And yet both are in essential agreement about the nature of our own "postsacred" time, and both have rather similar ideas about the violence underlying religious or judicial sacrifice, about the terrible reciprocity that binds victim and executioner, and about the radical challenge to older sacrificial resolutions of mimetic conflict that is presented by the latest global technology of destruction. Girard's reflections on the near future sound very much like Wright's anxious view of the world from Paris twenty years earlier: "Today the reign of violence is made manifest. The idea of 'limitless' violence, long scorned by sophisticated Westerners, suddenly looms up before us. Absolute vengeance, formerly the prerogative of the gods, now returns, precisely weighed and calibrated, on the wings of science."[15] In the Girardian model violence and the ensuing disorder are contagious and always threatening to escape their bounds. Under the old dispensation, the scapegoat or sacrificial victim—at once inside and outside the community—is used to deflect this violence; and this mechanism of surrogate victimage explains as well the ambiguous status of the victims of persecutions, pogroms, and lynchings—at once feared and despised, treated as martyrs and monsters. Whereas Wright understood the role of the scapegoat intuitively from his identification with the victim, Girard, moving from literary to ethnographic material, has proposed a systematic anthropology of violence and ritual attempts to contain it. He argues that the sacrificial process constitutes "the major means, perhaps the sole means, by which men expel from their consciousness the truth about their own mimetic relationships; the crimes attributed to the surrogate victim are the hidden desires of all men, the secret origins of human conduct." And from this process he would derive the origin of differential patterns (few more obvious than those regulating black and white) in human culture; these patterns lead him, in turn, to the process of symbol formation itself. The only escape from this cycle of violence, for both Girard and the late Wright, and the only hope for a society no longer able to live within the old sacrificial myths, is the achievement of a place for "nonsacrificial humanity." From Girard's anthropological perspective, there is a con-

---

[15]*Violence and the Sacred* (Baltimore: Johns Hopkins University Press, 1977), p. 240; see also the later developments in Girard's *Des Choses cachées depuis la fondation du monde* (Paris: Grasset, 1978) and *Le Bouc émissaire* (Paris: Grasset, 1982).

tinuity between the cruel experiences of the past and the present moment. In all the great crises of our cultures it is always a question of trying to drive violence outside of the community, but in the religions and humanisms of the past, this expulsion of violence can never be achieved save by partaking of it, that is to say at the expense of victims and of a place of exclusion outside of all human society, the desert or ghetto into which the scapegoat is driven. Today it is a question of "something very analogous and very different." It is still a question of controlling violence and reconciling men, but it has become an imperative now of achieving this without any violence and without there being any "outside." The mechanisms of reciprocal violence and exclusion are no longer viable options for a human society that has become global. In the light of what he calls the "non-sacrificial reading of Scripture," Girard argues that "the present crisis is not less redoubtable but it has acquired a dimension of the future, that is to say a sense truly human. A new humanity is in gestation, at once very similar and very different from that of which our expiring utopias have dreamt."[16] This is a humanism not unlike the one at the end of Richard Wright's "great voyage," a community achieved only when the bitter lessons of exclusion and victimage have been fully comprehended. The political dogmas and ideological formulation of the past had become for him inadequate charts for undertaking this voyage of survival. Wright in his fiction explains in a uniquely vivid way the world that Girard is describing in his theory. The critical connections between the two are yet to be explored.

But the secondary literature surrounding Wright's work is already vast. (A recent bibliographic survey of scholarship in southern literature records for the period 1968–1979 a total of 193 articles and 20 books devoted to literary studies of Richard Wright, and an even larger number of studies that include some treatment of his work.[17]) The selection of essays gathered in this volume can only aim at giving a representative overview of the more significant criticism his work has elicited since the 1940s. The first group of essays, "Roots and Branches," addresses Wright's background, his growth as an author through the Chicago and New York years, and his exile in France. Margaret Walker Alexander's essay traces her own relations with Wright during the formative Chicago years, offering a discussion of the genesis of *Native Son* and the influences that shaped him as a writer. George E. Kent develops the notion of Wright's "double consciousness" in terms of his early years and tragic inheritance, while Harold T. McCarthy discusses the question of his expatriation. Horace A. Porter,

---

[16]*Des choses cachées depuis la fondation du monde* (Paris: Grasset, 1978), p. 467.
[17]"A Bibliographic Survey of Scholarship in Southern Literature: 1968–1975, 1976–1979," prepared by Jerry T. Williams (unpublished).

in another essay written for this collection, attempts to see the major autobiographical writings—*Black Boy* and *American Hunger*—as a single effort to present a "portrait of the artist."

The second group of essays, "Native Sons and Native Daughters," focuses on Wright's most famous novel from both social and aesthetic vantages, addressing such related questions as the alleged loss of control in its conclusion and the persistent issue of the author's presentation of women. The final group of essays, "The Existential Quest: Freedom and Enclosure," takes the adjective *existential* from several perspectives, relating the short fiction and the later work to some widely divergent assessments of Wright's achievement. Nathan A. Scott, Jr., in a justly famous essay, raises the question of whether stereotype has been confused with archetype in Wright's most famous novel and presents a case for viewing *The Outsider,* with all its flaws, as the most ambitious of his fictions and "the one emphatically existentialist novel in contemporary American literature." Most of the contributors to this section bring some existentialist concerns to their readings, but the late Edwin Barry Burgum, an independent Marxist, anticipates some of their critical insights into the short stories in an early essay that remains one of the benchmarks on the subject. Finally, Michel Fabre, Wright's French biographer, contributes a sensitive reading of his most Dostoevskian work, "The Man Who Lived Underground," a bleak text that is for many modern readers the author's most accomplished work of art.

As we have seen, the trajectory of Richard Wright's "unfinished quest" carried him to five continents and through many ideological encounters. That the record he left behind is uneven is beyond dispute; at times the writing can be labored, the symbolism forced, the arguments tendentious. But at its best, during all three decades of his creative career, his voice has a unique authenticity and power to engage his readers, a rare courage to grasp the fear and rage that the creator shared with the "many thousands gone" who suffered these emotions inarticulately—the courage, in short, to acknowledge himself in his creations. Wright was thus a great precursor, the conscience of a nation that almost succeeded in condemning him to silence. He was an uncompromising teacher who compelled his audience to look directly at suffering without blinking. He was also a poetic realist who persisted in asserting the claims of the human imagination in the face of those brute forces that would deny it. He opened to view a precinct of suffering, a confine of the human heart, that his countrymen tried to conceal. His flight in search of a habitable space—at first a "public space," but increasingly an "inner space" as well—carried him beyond the sympathies of most of his audience and his early critics. But in the words of one of his last haiku, which serves as our epigraph, "he left his lonely caw / behind him in the fields" of American letters, an accusation and a testament to future generations.

Richard Wright

by Margaret Walker Alexander

Introduction

I first saw Richard Wright on Sunday afternoon, February 16, 1936, in Chicago at the Old Armory Building where he was presiding over the Writers' Section of the First National Negro Congress. I last saw him on the evening of June 9, 1939, in New York City where I had gone to attend the League of American Writers' Convention, see the New York World's Fair, and hopefully sell my novel, *Goose Island*. During those three years I think we were rather good friends. Looking back upon that relationship, it seems a rare and once-in-a-lifetime association which I am sure was not merely of mutual benefit but rather uncommon in its completely literary nature. And by "literary" I do not mean "arty" or pretentious or any form of dilettantism which he despised. I believe now that we shared a genuine interest in writing, in books, and literature. Moreover, we were mutually engaged in those three years in a number of associations and undertakings that, given the perspective of thirty-five years since their inception, seem uncanny in their significance.

We were writers together on the Federal Writers' Project of the WPA in Chicago; we were members of the South Side Writers' Group; we were interested in the little magazine, *New Challenge*; we had mutual friends and associates who were also writers; and during those three years we were struggling to publish for the first time in national magazines and books. We had varying and unequal degrees of success, but both of our talents found shape during those years. I know I owe much to his influence and interest in my writing and publishing poetry at that time: I am not so sure how much he owed to me. One thing I do know, however, is that during this three-year period Richard Wright wrote "Almos' A Man," *Lawd Today*, "The Ethics of Living Jim Crow," "Blueprint for Negro Writers," all the five stories in *Uncle Tom's Children*, and *Native Son*. Prior to our friendship, although he had published poetry in left-wing magazines, he had not published one significant piece of imaginative prose. I had the privilege of watching the birth of each of these works and seeing them through various stages of conception, organization, and realization. His first scissors and paste job was the first I had ever witnessed, and I rejoiced with him as each of these works found publication.

Langston Hughes originally introduced us (and when Wright died in Paris, Langston wrote me from London the news of their last visit). Wright in turn had introduced me to Arna Bontemps and Sterling Brown, who were on the WPA. In our South Side Writers' Group were Theodore Ward, the playwright, and Frank Marshall Davis, the poet, who was working for the Associated Negro Press. On the Project were such writers as Nelson Algren, whose sole work at that time was *Somebody in Boots*, Jacob Scher, James Phelan, Sam Ross, John T. Frederick, Katherine Dunham, Willard Motley, Frank Yerby, and Fenton Johnson.

Wright and I went to some of the same studio parties, read the same books, spent long evenings talking together, and often walked from the North Side where the Project was located, on Erie Street, downtown to the public library, or rode the El to the Southside where we lived. He gave me books for presents: an autographed manuscript of "Almos' A Man," a carbon copy of *Lawd Today*, which I had typed gratis; a copy of Flaubert's *Madame Bovary*, of e. e. cummings' *The Enormous Room*, and an autographed copy of *Uncle Tom's Children*. For two years after he went to New York we corresponded, and for the most part I kept his letters. My gifts were invariably of food and wine and cigarettes, and perhaps, what he valued most, an exchange of ideas, moral support and a steadfast encouragement, because I had no doubt from the beginning that he would win fame and fortune. When I met him his apprentice years were over and in that last year of his ten Chicago years it was easy to see where he was headed.

I

Going back in my memory to that Sunday afternoon in February, 1936, when I saw Wright for the first time, I remember that I went to the meeting because I heard it announced that Langston Hughes would be there. I met Langston first in New Orleans on his tour of the South in February, 1932, when he appeared in a Lecture Recital reading his poetry at the college, New Orleans University, where my parents taught. He encouraged me then to continue writing poetry and he also urged my parents to get me out of the deep South. Four years later to the very month, I wanted him to read what I had written in those four years. Six months earlier I had graduated from College at Northwestern and I still had no job. I was anxious to stay in Chicago where I hoped to meet other writers, learn something more about writing, and perhaps publish some of my poetry. I tried to press my manuscripts on Langston but when I admitted I had no copies he would not take them. Instead, he turned to Wright who was standing nearby, listening to the conversation and smiling at my desperation. Langston said, "If you people really get a group together, don't forget to include this girl." Wright promised that he would remember.

A month passed and I heard nothing. I presumed he had either forgotten or they didn't get a group together. Meanwhile on Friday, March 13, 1936, I received my notice in the mail to report to the WPA Writers' Project directed by Louis Wirth and located downtown in the Loop on Wells Street. Six weeks later I received a penny post card inviting me to the first meeting of the South Side Writers' Group. Twice I left the house and turned back the first time out of great self-consciousness because I felt I looked abominable. I had nothing to wear to make a nice appearance and I was going to the far Southside where I felt those people would make fun of me. But my great desire to meet writers and end my long isolation conquered this superficial fear. I made myself go. At the address given on the card, I discovered I was very late. I thought the meeting was over and I heard people laughing as I blurted out, "Is this the right place or am I too late?" I heard a man expounding on the sad state of Negro writing at that point in the thirties and he was punctuating his remarks with pungent epithets. I drew back in Sunday-school horror, totally shocked by his strong speech, but I steeled myself to hear him out. The man was Richard Wright. Subsequently, as each person present was asked to bring something to read next time, most people refused. When I was asked, I said, rather defiantly, that I would. I left the meeting alone.

Next time when we met at Lincoln Center on Oakwood Boulevard, I read a group of my poems. I was surprised to see they did not cut me down. Ted Ward and Dick Wright were kind in their praise. I remember Russell Marshall and Edward Bland were also there. Bland was killed in the battle of the Bulge. I was completely amazed to hear Wright read a piece of prose he was working on. Even after I went home I kept thinking, "My God, how that man can write!" After the meeting Wright said he was going my way. He asked me if I were on the Writers' Project, and I said, yes. Then he said, "I think I'm going to get on that Project." I looked at him in complete disbelief. I knew it took weeks and months to qualify for WPA plus additional red tape to get on one of the professional or art projects. What I did not know was that he had already been on WPA for some time. He was merely transferring from the Theatre Project to the Writers' Project.

The next week when I went to the Project Office for my semi-weekly assignment Wright was the first person I saw when I got off the elevator.

He quickly came over and led me to his desk. He was a supervisor and I was a junior writer. My salary was $85 per month while his was $125. He hastened to explain that he was responsible for his mother, his aunt and his younger brother and he was, therefore, the head of a family though single, while I had only my sister as my responsibility. A year later I advanced to $94, but then he was getting ready to leave Chicago. Gradually a pattern established itself in our relationship on the Project. I went downtown twice weekly with my assignments on the Illinois Guide Book and afterward I spent most of the day in conversation with Wright. Sometimes I was there at the end of the day, but I never worked daily, as he did, in the office. I worked at home and went looking for news stories or covered art exhibits and made reports. And that is how I came to have a creative assignment after I had been on the Project about nine months. Wright, on the contrary, worked with the editorial group and sandwiched his writing in-between when there was a lull in office work. He had taught himself to type by the hunt and peck method and I was astounded to watch him type away with two or three fingers while his eyes concentrated on the keyboard.

The first writers' conference I attended was a Midwest Writers' Conference early in the Spring of 1936 shortly after I met Wright. He was speaking and asked me to attend. Afterwards in our South Side Writers' Group meeting I was recalling the incident and Frank Marshall Davis asked me if that wasn't a communist group. I was confused and said, "I don't know." Then I looked at Wright who only grinned gleefully and said, "Don't look at me!" The whole thing sank in gradually that he was a communist. I honestly didn't know what communism or Marxism meant. I had no courses in sociology, economics, nor political science while I was a student in college. I majored in English with emphasis on the European Renaissance and except for a few basic and general courses in mathematics, science, psychology, and religion, I concentrated on literature, history, and languages. My sister knew more about Hitler and Stalin than I did. I was even more puzzled when Jack Scher tried to give me some advice one afternoon leaving the Project. He said, "Margaret, I hope you will get to know all these people on the Project without getting to be a part of them and all they represent. You are young and you have talent. You can go far, so observe them but don't join them." Only years later did I begin to understand him. I thought he was seriously talking about the labor movement which was so exciting at that time. The C.I.O. was just being organized and I heard John L. Lewis speak several times. The A.F. of L. had never wanted Negroes in their trade unions. Wright seemed intensely interested in the labor struggle as well as all the problems of race and what he explained to me was a "class struggle."

One of the first books he handed me to read was John Reed's *Ten Days That Shook the World*. I was fascinated. That same summer Maxim Gorky died and I had never before heard the name. I read quickly his *Lower Depths* and *Mother* and then I read the so-called "Red" Archbishop of Canterbury's book, *The Soviet Power*. Having very little money to spend on books I bought them as I bought my clothes on lay-away and under the influence and partial tutelage of Wright I put five Modern Library Giant books in lay-away: Karl Marx's *Das Kapital*, Strachey's *The Coming Struggle for Power*, The Complete *Philosophy of Nietzsche*, Adam Smith's *The Wealth of Nations* and a novel by Romain Rolland. A whole year later and long after Wright was in New York, the books were mine. One afternoon Wright quoted from T. S. Eliot:

> Let us go then, you and I, when the evening is spread
> out against the sky
> like a patient etherized upon a table.

And he exclaimed, "What an image!" Something exploded in my head and I went home to find my copy of Untermeyer's anthology, *Modern American Poetry*, and re-read Eliot. I remember how dull he had seemed at Northwestern when the teacher was reading aloud, and even when I heard Eliot reading on a bad recording, "We are the hollow men . . ."

I began James Joyce with *Portrait of the Artist as a Young Man*; then read *Ulysses*. Wright used James Joyce as an example when he was writing *Lawd Today*, being struck by a book that kept all the action limited to one day, but he considered *Lawd Today*, which I retyped for him, as one of his worst works. I think it was actually his first completed novel. I remember that he regarded Melanctha in Gertrude Stein's *Three Lives* as the first serious study of a Negro girl by a white American writer.

Stephen Crane's *Red Badge of Courage* I knew, but not *Maggie, A Girl of the Streets* which was Wright's favorite. I think from the beginning we differed about Hemingway and Faulkner. Although I had read some of Hemingway, I had not read much of Faulkner and, despite Wright's ecstatic feeling about *Sanctuary*, I found it revolting, possibly because I was still strongly influenced by a moralistic and puritanical background.

I never worshipped at the altars of either Hemingway or Faulkner but Wright deeply admired both. I read James Farrell's *Studs Lonigan* at Wright's request, but I could not work up a passion for Clifford Odets' *Waiting for Lefty* which the WPA Theatre Project had produced while Wright was working for the Theatre Project in Chicago as well as Caldwell's *Kneel to the Rising Sun*. Caldwell's *Tobacco Road* was a nationally famous play and a Pulitzer Prize winner as was Paul Green's *In Abraham's Bosom* which I particularly liked. John Dos Passos' *The Big Money* and Sandburg's *The People, Yes,* were current favorites that we both loved. Reading Proust was an experience I associate completely with Wright. Wright's favorite D. H. Lawrence was *Sons and Lovers* rather than *Lady Chatterley's Lover:* I confess now that my understanding of *Sons and Lovers* was much better when I was much older, best of all after I became the mother of sons. But I am sure all this must have led to some discussions we had then of Freud, Jung, and Adler, especially of Freud. Also it is very important to remember when we read the later Richard Wright in a book like *The Outsider,* written after his association with Sartre, that way back there in the thirties he was intensely interested in Nietzsche, Schopenhauer, and above all, the novelist Dostoevski. Wright and I differed keenly on our taste and interest in the Russian writers. He believed that Dostoevski was the greatest novelist who ever lived and the *Brothers Karamazov* was his greatest novel. I never felt quite that extravagantly about him, even though I plunged into the book at that period for the first time. Turgenev and Conrad were two others on whom we differed. I had read some of both but now I found a renewed interest, but I have never felt as sympathetic toward Conrad as Wright did. I liked the element of adventure in his sea-tales such as *Typhoon* but I have never liked the short fiction; I realize now that I have deeply resented what I feel is ersatz in Conrad's treatment of Africa and the Negro. The two works Wright and I discussed most were *Lord Jim* and *The Nigger of the Narcissus.*

If there were two literary books that were Wright's Bible they were Henry James' *Collected Prefaces* on *The Art of the Novel* and Joseph Warren Beach's *Twentieth Century Novel.* It must have been James who first interested him in the long short story or the short novel which he correctly called by the Italian name, the novella. When we consider, however, that Wright was also familiar with the short fiction of Dostoevski, Flaubert, Melville, D. H. Lawrence, Joyce, and Mann as well as James, one cannot be too certain who first led him in this direction. I know, however, that he had been interested in the short story form for a very long time. I vaguely remember and realize now that he loved Edgar Allan Poe, A. Conan Doyle and Jack London, and that he talked of having read pulps, detective stories, and murder mysteries, long before his serious reading began with Mencken while he lived in Memphis. He was tremendously impressed with Mencken and I never read his essay on "Puritanism in American Literature" without thinking of Wright.

Suspended in time somewhere between the Writers' Project and the South Side Writers' Group, possibly in the parlor of the house where I lived, three forms of writing took place in our consciousness, conversation and actions. We sat together and worked on the forms of my poetry, the free verse things, and came up with my long line or strophic form, punctuated by a short line. I remember particularly the poem, "People of Unrest," which Wright and I revised together, emphasizing the verbs:

> Stare from your pillow into the sun
> See the disk of light in shadows.
> Watch day growing tall
> Cry with a loud voice after the sun.

Take his yellow arms and wrap them round your life.
Be glad to be washed in the sun.
Be glad to see.
People of Unrest and sorrow
Stare from your pillow into the sun.

Likewise we sat together and worked on revisions of "Almos' A Man"
and *Lawd Today*. We discussed the difficulties of Negro dialect, and Wright
decided he would leave off all apostrophes and the usual markings for
sight dialect. We discussed folk materials and the coincidence of our
interest in Negro spirituals and the work songs and what Wright called
the dozens (cf. the opening lines of "Big Boy Leaves Home"). I remember
both of us were working on a piece using the words of the spiritual "Down
by the Riverside." "Silt" was a forerunner of the long short story "Down
by the Riverside" which Wright wrote that same year. I felt hopeless
about my novel manuscript which became *Jubilee* and of which I had 300
pages in first draft written at that time. We both decided I should put it
away until another time.

I was pleasantly surprised to learn early in January of 1937 that I
would be granted a creative writing assignment and my novel chapters
could now be turned in as my work assignments. The day I was told,
Wright was absent from work and I learned he was at home ill with a
bad cold. When I went home that afternoon my sister and I decided to
buy some oranges and take them to him. Then I could tell him my
wonderful good news. We found him in the house on Indiana Avenue in
bed in a room that I could not understand because it had one door and
no windows. Imagine my shock when I later realized it was a closet. He
was very happy to hear about my good luck and both of us were embarrassed about the oranges.

One cold windy day in Chicago, walking downtown from Erie Street,
we crossed Wacker Drive, turning our backs to the wind, and went into
the Public Library at Washington and Michigan Avenue. I was returning
a pile of books and Richard said he felt tempted to teach me how to steal
but he would resist such corruption. I assured him that I felt no compulsion to steal books.

II

Wright left Chicago for New York on May 28, 1937. It was Friday
afternoon and payday on the Project. We generally went to the same
check-cashing place nearby and when we were standing in line for checks
Wright was behind me, so he asked me to wait for him. About that time
one of the silly young gushing girls on the Project came up to me (as
Nelson Algren used to say, "Dames who don't know the day of the week")

and she said, "Margaret, tell Dick he's got to kiss all us girls goodbye."
I laughed at her and told her, "Tell him yourself, I wouldn't dare!" When
I got my check, I looked around and sure enough all the young white
chicks were mobbing him with loving farewells—so I left. Outside on the
street I had walked a block when I heard him yelling and hailing me. I
turned and waited. "I thought I told you to wait for me?" He grinned
impishly. I said, "Well, you were very busy kissing all the girls goodbye.
I'm in a hurry. The currency exchange will close." We cashed the checks
and got on the El. Fortunately the car was not crowded and we got seats
on one of the long benches. He said, "When I go tonight, I will have forty
dollars in my pocket."

"Oh, you are leaving tonight?"

"Yes, I've got a ride and lucky for me, it's a good thing 'cause I surely
can't afford the railroad fare."

"Well, you'll make it."

"I hope I can get on the Writers' Project there. I've got to find work
right away, and I hope I'm not making a mistake, going this way."

"How can you say such a thing? Aren't you on your way to fame and
fortune? You can't be making a mistake."

"I knew you would say that. I guess you won't think again about
coming to New York too, and soon."

"No, I've got to help my sister. I can't leave now."

"I think together we could make it big." He was not being sentimental
and I didn't misunderstand him. I said, "I know you will make it big,
but I can't leave now. Later, perhaps I will."

"You know, Margaret, I got a notice to come for permanent work at
the Post Office, and I sat in my room and tore it up. Bad as I need money
it was the hardest decision I ever made in my life."

"Well, would you like to be a postman all your life?" He looked at me
and laughed. He didn't need to answer, for he had said more than once,
"I want my life to count for something. I don't want to waste it or throw
it away. It's got to be worthwhile."

His stop came first and suddenly he grabbed both my hands and said
goodbye. That was Friday afternoon, and Tuesday I received his first
letter. It was very brief, saying he had arrived Saturday and at first felt
strange in the big city but in a little while he was riding the subways like
an old New Yorker. He thought he had a lead on a job—in any case he
would try Monday—and meanwhile, I must write him all the news from
Chicago and tell him everything that was going on on the project; and
like every letter that followed it was signed, *As ever, Dick.* I was surprised
to get that letter. I never really expected that he would write, but I
answered. My letters were generally longer, and I felt sometimes silly and
full of gossip, but he continued to write often, if sometimes quite briefly.

In the Fall of 1937, he wrote that he was entering the WPA short story contest sponsored by *Story* magazine and Harper's publishing house. I was supposed to enter *Goose Island* myself but I didn't get it ready in time. Wright had written all four of his novellas before going to New York. When he left he was working on "Bright and Morning Star," which was first published in *New Masses,* but it was not ready when he submitted the manuscript for the contest. "Big Boy Leaves Home" was the only story that had already been published; it appeared first in *American Caravan* while he was still on the Project in Chicago. He had also published "The Ethics of Living Jim Crow" in *American Stuff.* Earlier he had published poetry in *International Literature* and it was in that Russian magazine that both of us first read Sholokhov's *And Quiet Flows the Don.*

I don't think Wright ever wanted to write socialist realism, and he chafed under the dictates of the Communist Party to do so. If he had any aspirations beyond that, as he indicated after *Native Son,* it was toward his own unique form of symbolism. I don't think it came as a surprise when Wright won the short story contest though he had written once that it seemed a long time since he had submitted the manuscript and he hadn't heard anything. His friends in Chicago and New York were pleased and excited, but not surprised. They took it as a matter of course that his work was the best from all those sent in from WPA Projects around the country.

In November I published for the first time in *Poetry* magazine. Wright wrote at once that he had seen the poem, "For My People," written in the summer after he left, and he liked it very much. Meanwhile, we were getting things together for *New Challenge* magazine. He wrote that I should send my manuscript of poems somewhere besides Yale. There were lots of other places, he said, and I should give up trying them, for after all they weren't likely to publish me or any other black person.

In the Spring of 1938, *Uncle Tom's Children* was published and Wright won the $500 prize. The book got interesting reviews, but all of them did not make us happy. He had moved to Lefferts Place and was staying with Jane and Herbert Newton. Then, on the wings of success came the news that he was getting married. I hastened to congratulate him, and he denied the whole thing. I learned later that the young, black, and very bourgeois girl he was dating thought Wright was even more successful in a financial way than he was. He had arranged to rent extra space from the Newtons and move his bride in with them but her family wanted her to have the best and if he couldn't provide that—no soap. Well, it was no soap. Regardless of financial status, in one year after his arrival in New York he had achieved national prominence. He remarked in a letter at the end of that year that he had set a goal for five years and one of those years was over. He wanted to write another book right away, a novel, before the first one could be forgotten. Then he wanted to go to Mexico and he wanted to go to Paris.

During the first week in June, 1938, I received in rapid succession two airmail special delivery letters. I answered one at once but before he could receive my answer he wrote again in great excitement. He said, "I have just learned of a case in Chicago that has broken there and is exactly like the story I am starting to write. See if you can get the newspaper clippings and send them to me." The case was that of a young black boy named Nixon who had been accused of rape, and when the police captured him they forced a confession of five major crimes, of which rape was only one.

I went at once to the offices of the five daily Chicago newspapers to get all the back issues; and I began what lasted a year, sending Wright every clipping published in the newspapers on the Nixon case. Frankly, there were times when the clippings were so lurid I recoiled from the headlines, and the details in the stories were worse. They called Nixon a big black baboon. When I went into news offices or bought papers on the stands, I listened to jeers and ugly insults about all black people.

Meanwhile, Wright wrote that if I had anything I wanted published to send it to him and he would push my work, as he was now in a better position to help me get published. He had already read many of my assignments on *Goose Island* before leaving Chicago; and he suggested that I might send him more.

Not until Wright visited in November did I learn how he had made use of the newspaper clippings. Actually, the case rocked on for about a year. In the fall of 1938, Wright wrote that he would have to make a trip home to Chicago before he could finish the book. One Sunday in November, when I entered the house, my landlady said, "There is a surprise for you in the living room." I said, "A surprise for me? What kind of surprise?" I had come out of a bright day outside and the living room looked dim and shadowy. I squinted my eyes to see and Wright laughed, "Poor little Margaret, she doesn't even know me."

He had only stopped in his mother's house long enough to put down his bag. He washed his hands and ate with us—a quick meal of chicken and biscuits, soup and salad. Then he went out into the streets, visited his friends, the Gourfains, and found a vacant lot to use for the address of the Dalton house in *Native Son*. I thought we were walking aimlessly when we found ourselves at a little tea-room and we went inside. It was late Sunday afternoon—twilight or dusk and the little bell on the door tinkled to let the keeper know we were entering. There were only two people inside—a man wiping cups and the proprietor; but one knew Wright and we sat down at a table. Soon other men entered; the room began to fill with white men. Gradually I felt acutely that I was the only woman in the room.

Wright explained a little about the new book and told about the clippings. He said he had enough to spread all over his nine by twelve bedroom floor and he was using them in the same way Dreiser had done in

American Tragedy. He would spread them all out and read them over and over again and then take off from there in his own imagination. The major portion of *Native Son* is built on information and action of those clippings. One of the men asked him where he got the clippings and he looked at me and said, "She sent them to me." A mutual friend, Abe Aaron said, "You ought to dedicate the book to her" and I quickly said, "I'd kill him if he did. He's going to dedicate it to his mother." Wright said, "How did you know that?" But of course he did. Later he wrote, and I quote:

> I felt guilty as all hell for not writing to you, inasmuch as you had done more than anyone I know to help me with my book. Nearly all the newspaper releases in the book were sent to me by you. Each and every time I sat down to write I wondered what I could say to let you know how deeply grateful I felt.

All in all, Wright was a man of great personal magnetism and charm. Women and men adored him. He could charm the socks off of anyone and everyone he bothered to notice.

He asked me that Sunday if I had a little time to spend helping him find things for the book and I readily assented. On Monday we did several things. First, we went to visit Attorney Ulysses S. Keyes who had expressed an interest in meeting Wright and had once asked me to let him know whenever Wright came to town. He was the first black lawyer hired for Nixon's defense. He had also written a fan letter to Wright and when we went to his office he was quite glad to see the author of *Uncle Tom's Children*. I asked him about the Nixon case and if he wasn't the defense lawyer on the case. He said, "I was until this morning. The family has hired an NAACP lawyer, and after I had written the brief and everything." I then asked him if he would give it to Wright. All this time Wright said nothing and when I asked for the brief Wright looked at me as if I were crazy and I guess I was, but when we were outside I said, "Well, wasn't that what you needed?" He said, "Yes, but I didn't have the nerve to ask that man for his brief." But of course he found good use for it.

Next we went visiting Cook County Jail where Nixon was incarcerated. I nearly fainted when I saw the electric chair for the first time. Outside, we snapped pictures, but I still felt weak. On the elevated train we looked out over Southside rooftops and Wright explained that he had his character running across those rooftops. I asked, why? And Wright said, "He's running from the police." I said, "Oh, that must be dramatic to the point of melodrama." He said, "Yes, I think it will shock people, and I love to shock people!" He grinned gleefully and rubbed his hands together in anticipation, and I couldn't stop laughing.

The next day we went to the Library and checked out on my library card two books we found on the Loeb-Leopold case and on Clarence Darrow, their lawyer. The lawyer's defense of Bigger in *Native Son* was modeled after Darrow's defense. Wright was so long sending those books back that I wrote him a hot letter reminding him that I had not borrowed those books permanently! He finished the book early in the Spring of 1939 and he wrote that he had never worked so hard before in all his life.

> Listen, from the time I left Chicago and got back to New York, I worked from 7, 8, 9, in the morning until 12, 1, 2 and 3 at night. I did that for day in and day out. Sometimes I worked so hard that my mind ceased to register and I had to take long walks. I never intend to work that long and hard again. If this book is published, then I'll delay getting my next one out, for two reasons: I'm making a new departure and I don't want to kill myself. But I had to get that book out and I wanted it out before the first was forgotten. Rest assured, that if this book is published, you'll *hear* about it. The liberals, the CP, the NAACP—all of them will have their reservations. Really, I don't believe that they are going to publish it. Really, I don't even though they've signed the contract. . . .

And again he wrote:

> Yes, I'm beginning another book, but sort of half-heartedly. I'm trying to wait and see what in hell they are going to do with the last one. The title is "Native Son." I don't like the title. They have had it for a week now and I have not heard what they are planning; that is, I don't know if they are going to publish it late Spring or early Fall. The new book will be a sharp departure in my work. I feel that I've gone as far as I care to go with Negro characters of the inarticulate type. Within the next ten or fifteen days I'll hear from Guggenheim. Also I'll know if I can stay at Yaddo, an artist colony, free for a few weeks of rest.

And according to my journal entries I note that he wrote a few days later that he had gotten the Guggenheim! He asked me again about coming to New York and this time, with *Goose Island* finished, I said I was considering it. I have forgotten to say that when he was in Chicago in November, I had discovered the plot of *Native Son* while I was cooking that Sunday afternoon, and I turned to him, stricken, and said, "Oh, we are doing the same thing. The only difference is your main character is a man and mine is a woman." He said, "No matter, there's room enough for both" and he buttered another hot biscuit. But I was quite apprehensive and told him so. My fiction was not nearly as well formed and advanced as his, and I felt from that moment that *Goose Island* was doomed. The goose was cooked!

Then, quite without notice, about the middle of May, he turned up in Chicago again for a few days. His younger brother, Alan, was ill with bleeding ulcers and Wright had come to see about him. He asked me then about my plans for the trip, and said he would be speaking on Friday evening at the League Convention and hopefully I would be there then. We even discussed riding on the train together, but I said I was not quite ready. I was having real money problems and I did not want to tell him I might not be able to make it. One of the things I promised to do was read the manuscript of *Native Son* as I had read everything else he had written in manuscript before that, but I never quite got the time. I know I would have violently protested against the end of *Native Son*, although my protests would probably not have helped. I'm sure that was a revised ending. I don't think it was in character for an unconscious character such as Bigger Thomas to analyze his circumstance or situation in such conscious terms. It was obviously a Marxist ending made for socialist realism and not for the naturalistic piece of fiction that *Native Son* is. I can't believe that Wright didn't also know that it was wrong, and too contrived an ending.

Wright wrote a piece in *Saturday Review of Literature* called "How Bigger Was Born," and perhaps that character did evolve in his mind for a long time from his childhood and youth in the violent South; but I have told you how *Native Son* evolved from the Nixon Case and sociological research done long before Wright began writing his story.

I sometimes ask myself if I had not made the trip to New York that June of 1939, would we have remained friends. I think not. Everything seemed destined toward an end of those three years, for whatever the relationship was worth. At first I was hurt deeply, and pained for many years. The memory of that trip is still too painful to discuss, but as I have grown older and look back in maturity over those three years I know what happened was best for me.

III

Wright's philosophy was that fundamentally all men are potentially evil. Every man is capable of murder or violence and has a natural propensity for evil. Evil in nature and man are the same; nature is ambivalent and man may be naturally perverse and as quixotic as nature. Human nature and human society are determinants and, being what he is, man is merely a pawn caught between the worlds of necessity and freedom. He has no freedom of choice; he is born to suffering, despair, and death. He is alone against the odds of Nature, Chance, Fate and the vicissitudes of life. All that he has to use in his defense and direction of his existence are (1) his reason and (2) his will. By strength of reason and will he can operate for the little time he has to live.

His philosophy developed as a result of his experiences: he turned against orthodox religion at an early age because of the religious fanaticism in his family and early home-life. He grew up in a South where lynching and Jim Crow and every egregious form of racism were rampant; and the fate of a Black Boy was not only tenuous or nebulous, but often one of

doom. To be poor and black in an hostile white world was his first knowledge of the human condition and he found that living in a rural area or
in an urban area made no difference. His piece on "The Ethics of Living
Jim Crow" drives this home long before the autobiography *Black Boy.* The
five novellas that eventually form the second edition of *Uncle Tom's Children*
were all of one piece: the tragic fate of a black man in the hostile white
world of a violent South land. The title *Uncle Tom's Children* is a misnomer
and misleading. It is an abominable title chosen as usual by the publishers.
That book should never have been associated with Uncle Tom. It bears
no resemblance to *Uncle Tom's Cabin,* the book or the minstrel play. Any
one of the stories would have made a better title for the book. But to get
back to the point, *Native Son*'s bitterness is even more intense because
Bigger is in a bigger bear trap than Bobo and Big Boy. He is in *big*
Chicago, poor, black, ignorant, and scared! He has no hope of being able
to cope with the big white rich man's world in the big city. He blunders
into crime. He is driven by such desperate fear he cannot imagine himself
as a human being of dignity and worth. He begs the question. He is
unconscious, inarticulate, and confused.

Wright developed a cautious and suspicious nature. He said it was part
of his protective coloring but that suspicion of everybody grew as he grew
older and it was not unlike that of many philosophers who hold secular
or materialist positions. They have no faith in anybody, God, Man, or
the devil. He was not nihilistic but he partook of some of its negativism.
He was completely a secularist and secular existentialism was his final
belief. It is best expressed in what I regard as his most autobiographical
piece, *The Outsider.* Cross Damon has a lot of Richard Wright in him that
Bigger Thomas was not big enough to understand.

All the forces influencing Wright were forces of the white world: he
seems to have been shaped very little by black people. As a matter of fact
black people were never his ideals. He championed the cause of the black
man but he never idealized or glorified him. His black men as characters
were always seen as the victims of society, demeaned and destroyed and
corrupted to animal status. He was the opposite of what the liberal white
man is called: a nigger lover. He probably never reached the point of
hating his black brothers, but he felt himself hated by many of them.
Every positive force he recognized in his life stemmed from white forces.
Intellectually his teachers and master-models were all white. He was
befriended by whites; he was admired and loved more by whites than
blacks. Hatred of the collective white man as a force against the collective
black man was nevertheless coupled with genuine admiration and regard
for many truly personal benefactors who were white. I sometimes wonder
if it is malicious to think he would have been happier if he had been born
white than he was as a black man. He seemed to feel and believe that all
his troubles stemmed from being black. Unlike Langston Hughes, who

loved all mankind and especially his black brothers, Wright often said that there was no kind of cruelty worse than black people could inflict on their own people. His favorite authors were all white. I cannot think of a single black author during the thirties whom he admired to the point that he considered him the equal of any white writer. He had no great respect for the literary achievements of black people, not even Langston Hughes or W. E. B. DuBois. Many black writers admired him, but when he picked his friends among writers they were all white. He certainly had no high regard for black nationalism despite his interests in Africa and Asia. He was not a nationalist but an internationalist.

Wright's greatest influence, however, has been on black writers. A new school of naturalistic novelists and symbolists, all black, came out of the thirties and the forties because of Wright. Those most often mentioned and their works are Ann Petry, Willard Motley, Chester Himes, James Baldwin, and Ralph Ellison. I think it is safe to say that at least in fiction of the Twentieth Century in Black America we can mark or date everything before and after Richard Wright. Like the Russians who say they have all come out of Gogol's "Overcoat," most of our writers have come out of Wright's cloak.

Re-reading the early fiction of Wright one is struck by the passion and the power that always come through. These were also in his early poetry, the remarkable "Between the World and Me" and "I Have Seen Black Hands," two poems he wrote before he turned to Haiku, a form I cannot conceive as being Wright's despite his experimenting in countless poems with it. In his short factual prose pieces, articles, book reviews, news articles, and pot-boiling bits of journalism and propaganda one is always aware of the curious almost mercurial vitality that his writing possessed. Wright really began his imaginative writing career as a poet, although he never in life published a book of poetry. He understood quite well the craft and technique of poetry, particularly free verse. He read and loved poetry purely for enjoyment and relaxation. Once, going on a train trip, he took along Whitman's *Leaves of Grass* to read for pure pleasure. He was quite familiar with the poets of the thirties such as Muriel Rukeyser and Robinson Jeffers. Once he invited me to go with him to hear Kenneth Fearing. He liked T. S. Eliot, Yeats, Sandburg, Masters, and even Ezra Pound. He wrote back once from New York how he was reading the *Road to Xanadu,* an adventure in the imagination, and also for the first time, *Alice in Wonderland*.

Wright would have been the last person to argue his gift of inner perception, for he also wrote this to me:

> You know, Margaret, writing does not mean that one has a masterful grip on all of life. After all, writing comes primarily from the imagination; it proceeds from that plane where the world and brute fact and feeling meet and blend. In short, a writer may exhibit a greater knowledge of the world

than he has actually seen. That may sound like a paradox. . . . This is not irony. Hence, the alertness which should be mine, the sharpness of attention which people say it takes to write, that depth which people find in one's books, well, it simply is not there. . . . I am not subtle, even though there might be imaginative subtleties in my work. Imagination is truer than life; that is the fact which every writer discovers and the fact which people usually concede to the conscious mind of the writer. . . . Frankly, Margaret, what you see and feel in my work is something which everybody has and which, for some reason I don't really understand, gets itself on paper somehow. So don't expect me in my daily relations with folks to have the same strength of vision and awareness you see or think you see in my work. I'm answering this from an odd angle but I feel it is the angle which settles things. I take the world at its face value far more often than you will ever know. Maybe I'll see you again this summer and we'll talk more at length; and I won't be so hurried and worried as I was last time. . . .

The white scholar today who finds Wright a fit subject for study says he cannot understand the apathy of black scholars toward Richard Wright. What he fails to say is that the black writer has been profoundly influenced by Wright, impressed with his success and made confident and bold because of his intellectual honesty. Many black scholars have in truth written interesting articles if not books about Wright, but the black scholar does not in truth subscribe to the belief that we should bow down before this black god and worship his black genius, for some of us have known the man and we know that all men are made of clay.

Richard Wright: Blackness and the Adventure of Western Culture

by George E. Kent

I shall try to focus upon three sources of Wright's power: his double-consciousness, his personal tension, and his dramatic articulation of black and white culture.

His double-consciousness and personal tension can be discussed at the same time, since one flows into and activates the other. His personal tension springs from a stubborn self conscious of victimization but obsessed with its right to a full engagement of universal forces and to a reaping of the fruits due from the engagement. This right may be called the heritage of Man. And *double-consciousness*—W. E. B. DuBois, in *The Souls of Black Folk,* described it as the black's sense of being something defined and imprisoned by the myths of whites and at war with his consciousness of American citizenship—his heir-apparency to the potentials announced by the so-called period of Enlightenment. The consciousness of American citizenship lights aspiration, but impels the artist to look worshipfully upon the general American culture, and to devalue his condition and that of his people, even when he is conscious of their beauty:

> The innate love of harmony and beauty that set the ruder souls of his people a-dancing and a-singing raised but confusion and doubt in the soul of the black artist; for the beauty revealed to him was the soul beauty of a race which his larger audience despised, and he could not articulate the message of another people.[1]

Frantz Fanon, in *Black Skins, White Masks,* says simply that the black is over-determined from without, and gives this dramatic picture: "I progress by crawling. And already I am being dissected under white eyes, the only real eyes."[2] In literature, the war of the two consciousnesses

"Richard Wright: Blackness and the Adventure of Western Culture" by George E. Kent. From *CLA Journal,* 12 (June 1969), 322–343. Copyright © 1969 by the College Language Association. Reprinted by permission of the College Language Association.

Note: This article is slightly adapted from a lecture, in a series, delivered at the University of Chicago, during the spring of 1969.

[1]W. E. B. DuBois, *The Souls of Black Folk* (New York: Fawcett Publications, 1963), p. 18.
[2]Frantz Fanon, *Black Skin, White Masks* (New York, 1967), p. 116.

sometimes drives for an art that is "only incidentally" about Negroes, if it is about them at all; in which case the writer carefully reduces his particularism (the tensioned details of the black experience) and hustles to the "universal" (usually the culturally conditioned Western version). Other choices: to portray the exoticism that satisfies the symbolic needs of whites; to plead the humanity of blacks before a white audience; and, lately, to dig out and address a black audience, regarding its condition and its beauty. Within the concept of double-consciousness, it will be seen that Wright was both the cunning artificer and the victim.

But first, his personal tension, without which he may not have created at all, a tension, not really separable from the double-consciousness, that is one great source of his creative power. A slight handicap here, from the angle of scholarly documentation. The main source for information concerning Wright's early youth is still *Black Boy*, a great autobiography, but one whose claim to attention is the truth of the artist, and not that of the factual reporter. Both Ralph Ellison and Constance Webb, Wright's biographer, have identified incidents which Wright did not personally experience, incidents from folk tradition.[3] I see no great to-do to be made over Wright's artistic license, since folk tradition is the means by which a group expresses its deepest truths. Thus the picture, if not all the pieces, is essentially true.

What *Black Boy* reveals is that more than any other major black writer, Wright, in his youth, was close to the black masses—and in the racially most repressive state in the union, Mississippi. Worse still, Wright received violent suppression without the easement provided by the moral bewilderment and escapism so available in black culture. Such institutionalized instruments of bewilderment as the otherworldly religion, the smiling side of the "good" white folks, sex, liquor, and the warmth of the folk culture, formed no sustaining portion of his psychic resources. Parents, whose complicity in oppression made for physical security in the South of the pre- and post-World War I periods, were ineffectual. Wright's father was a zero. His mother—a woman bearing up under tensions from the terrors of the daily world, abandonment by a shiftless husband, and painful and disabling sickness—was hard-pressed by Wright and her own tough-minded honesty. Under a persistent barrage of questions concerning black life, answers escaped her lips that merely confirmed the boy's sense of embattlement in a world of naked terror; first, for example, explaining that a white man did not whip a black boy because the black

---

[3]See Ralph Ellison, *Shadow and Act* (New York, 1964), pp. 134–135; Constance Webb, *Richard Wright* (New York, 1968), p. 205. See also notes to this Chapter (XIV). From Miss Webb's discussion of *Black Boy*, I deduce that he was still too close psychologically to his youth to give a rounded picture. [Michel Fabre's 1973 biography has filled some of the lacunae in the history of Wright's early development. *Eds.*]

boy was his son, she then sharpened a distinction: "The 'white' man did not *whip* the 'black' boy. He *beat* the 'black' boy."[4]

Constance Webb states Wright's conscious purpose: "to use himself as a symbol of all the brutality and cruelty wreaked upon the black man by the Southern environment."[5] By depressing his middle-class background, Miss Webb continues, he would create a childhood that would be representative of most Negroes. Both the power of the autobiography and its flaws develop from Wright's single-minded intention. Actually, for much of the work, his strategy is to posit a self-beyond-culture—that is, the self as biological fact, a very tough biological fact, indeed. A cosmic self, which reaches out naturally (though in twisted and violent patterns) for the beauty and nobleness of life. The self is battered by the white racist culture, and, for the most part, by a survival-oriented black culture, that counters the impulse to rebelliousness and individuality by puritanical repressiveness, escapism, and base submission. That is, black culture suppressed the individual, in order to protect the group from white assault. The dramatic rendering of these forces and the stubborn persistence of the outsider self comprise the major strategy of the book.

And out of that strategy comes an overwhelming impact. Tension, raw violence and impending violence, which evoke, psychologically, a nightmare world in the light of day. The autobiography's first great subject is the growth of consciousness, the stages of which are communicated by statements of the reactions of self to preceding events. In confronting a racist America the black boy's consciousness learns to hide its responses and to pursue its aspirations by secret means. It is damaged for life, but it has avoided becoming a natural product of the system: the stunted, degraded, shuffling black, almost convinced of its own inferiority and the god-like power of whites. In the latter part of the book, through reading rebellious books, the consciousness of that other self—the white-defined Negro-victim—loses ground to the consciousness of self as American: the heir to the energy releasing resources of the Enlightenment. A desperate hope is created.

Thus *Black Boy*'s second great subject: the disinherited attempting to reclaim the heritage of Modern Man.

Black Boy is a great social document, but it could easily have been greater. Its simple naturalistic form, at first, knocks the reader off balance, but then comes reflection. Its universe of terror is little relieved by those moments of joy that usually glide like silent ancestral spirits into the grimmest childhood. To account artistically for the simple survival of the narrator is difficult. Except for the "cultural transfusion" that the narrator

[4]Richard Wright, *Black Boy* (New York, 1945), p. 52.
[5]Webb, p. 205.

receives near the end, Wright gives little artistic emphasis to cultural supports. The careful reader will pick up, here and there, scattered clues. For example, the extended family, with all its short-comings, show a desperate energy and loyalty. Reading was an early feeder of his imaginative life, and the role of his mother in supplying imaginative and emotional help was crucial. In *Black Boy*, the dramatic form does not, in itself, give her a decisive role, but the beatings, teasings, grim love and sporadic periods of silent understanding, imply an unorthodox devotion. The narrator reveals something of the sort in stating the impact of her sickness upon him:

> Already there had crept into her speech a halting, lisping quality that, though I did not know it, was the shadow of her future. I was more conscious of my mother now than I had ever been and I was already able to feel what being completely without her would mean.[6]

There were important facets of ordinary black life, which Wright did not understand because he saw them as an outsider or from the point of view of embattled adolescence. His father was simply the peasant-victim, with a life shaped by the rhythms of the seasons—a classification very likely to have been derived from his Marxian studies. In Memphis, Wright (or the narrator) meets Mrs. Moss, a spontaneously warm and generous black woman, with an equally warm and spontaneous daughter, Bess. Bess likes Richard and, in no time flat, wishes to marry him. The narrator is aware of her qualities, but ascribes their source to what he was later to understand as "the peasant mentality."

Yet this warm spontaneity, as much as the warped puritanism of his own environment, was a value bulwarked and preserved by the embattled black cultural tradition—not by nature or the rhythm of the seasons. Thus the utter bleakness of black life, its lack of tenderness, love, honor, genuine passion, etc., which Wright in a now famous passage in the second chapter of the autobiography noted as general characteristics, were partly reflections of his immediate home life and surroundings: "I had come from a home where feelings were never expressed, except in rage or religious dread, where each member of the household lived locked in his own dark world, and the light that shone out of this child's heart [Bess's] . . . blinded me."[7]

Personal tension and the double-consciousness. In response to white definitions, Wright was able to say to whites that he formed an equation not known in their definitions. Regarding his people, he was able to say that they are much like you define them but you, and not Nature, are responsible. If today, this no longer seems enough to say, or even to be

[6]*Black Boy*, p. 73.
[7]*Ibid.*, p. 190.

free of a certain adolescent narcissism, we can at least concentrate upon what insights should have been available to Wright during his time. If Wright in *Black Boy* seems too much concerned with warfare upon white definitions, it is good to remember that our growing ability to ignore them exists because the single-minded assault of Wright and others shook up the confidence of a nation and impaired their efficiency.

What can be held against him is that he seemed to have had little awareness that black life, on its own terms, has also the measure of beauty and grandeur granted those who are often defeated but not destroyed. It would be good here to know more about his reading, especially works written by black men. How startling, for example, to learn from Constance Webb that at the age of thirty-two, in 1940, Wright had not read Booker T. Washington's *Up from Slavery*. In a footnote to Chapter 13 of *Richard Wright,* Miss Webb states:

> Wright was almost ashamed to admit that he had never read *Up from Slavery*. He had escaped being educated in Negro institutions and never got around to reading those books which everyone was supposed to read. He did know that the greatest split among educated Negroes of a generation or so ago was over Washington's proposals.[8]

Miss Webb is valiant, but the explanation is lame. That very boyhood which Wright was attempting to understand in *Black Boy* depends, for proper dimension, upon an intimate knowledge of Booker T. Washington and W. E. B. DuBois and of the issues with which they grappled. Ironically, by 1903, DuBois in "Of Our Spiritual Strivings," *The Souls of Black Folk,* had already defined the problems and the danger which Wright (born in 1908) would confront as a writer.[9] Aside from such considerations, it would hardly seem that a person as obsessed with black problems as Wright was would require an education in Negro institutions to put him in touch with the major figures in his history.

The truth is probably that having caught a breath of life from the literature of revolt against the American small town and from Marxian dialectics Wright was overimpressed with their efficiency as tools to explore the privacy and complexity of the black environment. Certainly, Ellison, in 1941, described a system that Wright used for mastering culture that was double-edged and required wariness. Ellison praised Wright for translating the American responses that he heard whites express into terms with which to express the life of Bigger Thomas in *Native Son*. Ellison credited Wright with thus building up within himself "tensions and disciplines . . . impossible within the relaxed, semi-peasant environs of Amer-

[8]Webb, p. 186. Hollywood had asked Wright to write a screen play of *Up From Slavery*.
[9]DuBois, pp. 16–18.

ican Negro life."[10] Now such a system can immediately broaden and deepen perspective, but it also carries an obvious payload of distortion. In this regard, it is interesting to note that Ellison, who, in 1945, was obviously disturbed by Wright's famous description of black life as bleak and barren, now says that it is simply a paraphrase of Henry James's description, in his *Hawthorne,* of "those items of high civilization which were absent from American life during Hawthorne's day, and which seemed so necessary in order for the novelist to function."[11] One might add that the hard and sharp articulate terms of the black narrator's individualism and rationalism in *Black Boy* seem occasionally to be imports from Northern urban middle-class culture. Neither the folk black culture of the 1920's nor the general Southern culture allowed a childhood to escape the compulsion toward an almost superstitious display of forms of reverence for its elders—even when "reality" gave no justification for them. The rebellion against such a compulsion would, if natively expressed, have been less confident and articulate, more in the forms of silence, sullenness, and guilty outbursts.

In *Black Boy,* the young Richard Wright's impulse to individuality has already begun to engage the dominant forms of Western culture. It promises arms for the freedom of both the black artist and his people. On the other hand, the forms have for him, their deadend streets. Individualism in Western culture ranges from rugged activity to imprisonment in one's own subjectivity. While enabling one to escape the confines of a survival-oriented folk culture and to take arms against the West's racism, Western culture forms threaten to subtly transform the emotional and psychic reflexes, so that while the black writer's status is one of alienation, his deepest consciousness is that of the exaggerated Westerner.

In successive autobiographical statements Wright's alienation was apparent. In "The Man Who Went to Chicago,"[12] the picture is one of alienated man trying to express impulses which the forms of Western culture are supposedly dedicated to promoting: the triumph of the human individual (as Fanon termed it), of curiosity, and of beauty. But in Chicago, the capitalistic culture was giving no public sanction to the possession of such qualities by black men, and "adjusted" blacks were themselves an obstacle, as they vied for status in their misery.

Within the Communist Party, as reflected in "I Tried to Be a Communist," Wright found the "triumph of the human individual" balked on ideological grounds.[13] As to the racial thing, one leftist writer confessed, while recruiting Wright, for a Communist front group, that "We write

[10]Ralph Ellison, "Recent Negro Fiction," *New Masses* (August 5, 1941), p. 25.
[11]*Shadow and Act,* pp. 119–120.
[12]Richard Wright, *Eight Men* (New York, 1961), pp. 161–191.
[13]Richard Crossman, ed., *The God That Failed* (New York: Bantam, 1952), pp. 103–146.

articles about Negroes, but we never see any Negroes."[14] When it came to getting Wright a room in the New York City of 1935, the Communists went through the same foot-shuffling affected by other white Americans, and, in order to attend the Communist-sponsored conference, Wright, himself, found a room in the Negro Y.M.C.A., miles from the site of the conference.

Wright, a very big man, was aware that the Communists had no understanding of the depths of the lives of black men. But Marxism was *the* dynamic philosophy for social change. Where else was he to go? Meanwhile, his life reflected, in an eighth grade dropout's mastery of world culture, the great Western ideal: the expression of the individual life as revolutionary will. The process jerked uptight his emotional and moral reflexes. When he confronted African culture in *Black Power* or met representatives of non-Western cultures, he was both the alienated black man and the exaggerated Westerner, and was at once sympathetic and guiltily sniffy.[15] The fit of the two is uneasy. In *Black Power, Pagan Spain, The Color Curtain,* and *White Man, Listen!,* non-fictional works, the personality behind the print ranges from that of a bright, but somewhat snippish Western tourist to that of a Western schoolmarm, although his ideas are more frequently interesting and provocative.

But Wright remained embattled.

And in the 1950's, in the novel *The Outsider,* he was raising the question as to whether the Western game had not lost all vitality.

II

For Richard Wright the job of writing was most serious and his struggle was very great. In "Blue-Print for Negro Writing," he saw blacks as essentially a separate nation, and felt that the job of the black writer was to create the values by which his race would live and die.[16] However, he argued that ultimately a nationalist perspective did not go far enough, and that having broadened his consciousness through an understanding of the nationalist folklore of his people, the black writer must transcend nationalism and transform his own personality through the Marxian conception of reality.

Now Harold Cruse in *The Crisis of the Negro Intellectual* has ably pointed out that the American imported and unadapted Marxism was a deadend street, since it had no conception of the black reality nor any real intention

[*Note:* This adapted article contained no subhead I. *Eds.*]

[14]Crossman, p. 108.
[15]Webb, pp. 320–322.
[16]Richard Wright, "Blueprint for Negro Writing," *New Challenge* (Fall, 1937), pp. 53–64.

of acquiring one.[17] As I have indicated, Wright was not unaware of the myopia of American Marxists. His positive gain was sufficient psychological distance from the American middle-class oriented cultural patterns to articulate perspectives and symbols of the black and white cultures. This gave him, at least, a version of the total American reality as it relates to blacks. Although Wright had qualified his Marxist stance by stating that Marxism was the bare-bones upon which the black writer must graft the flesh, he did ask that the writer mould Negro folklore "with the concepts that move and direct the forces of history today," that is, with Marxism. The negative effects of this Marxism, as well as the emphatic convictions that derived from psychology and the social sciences, were that the very lights they provided for gaining power over certain aspects of black humanity, by their very glare, blinded him to others.

Take that fine group of short stories that comprise *Uncle Tom's Children*. On a first reading, the reader is overwhelmed by the sheer power of naturalistic form, out of which several stories explode upon him. In "Big Boy Leaves Home," Big Boy and his gang are discovered by a Southern white woman bathing in the nude in a Southern white man's creek. (The black man and the white woman are a Negro folklore theme.) Startled when they come toward her to get their clothes, she screams. Her nearby escort shoots and kills two of the boys, and Big Boy wrests the gun from him and kills him. With the help of the folk community and his family, Big Boy escapes, but his friend Bobo is brutally lynched by a mob. From his hiding place Big Boy witnesses the deed. He escapes the following morning in a truck bound for Chicago.

The story has been very justly admired. In the 1930's when the story first appeared the very type of lynching it described was horribly so much more than a mere literary reality. Black men, remembering the wariness with which they stepped around such women in real life and that lingering dread of being trapped with them in some unstructured situation where neither "racial etiquette" nor rational chat would absolve, could read and feel the stomach gone awry. Also that high irreverence of boyhood smashed up against the System is so well pictured; the dialogue is so full of life, and the folk culture so carefully evoked—who could resist? Add to this powerful scenes, and narrative drive.

But then, a serious flaw. Wright's chief interest is in Big Boy—in his raw revolutionary will to survive and prevail. So that Wright forgets that youth does not experience the shooting down of two comrades and the horrible lynching of a third, without a sea change in its nature. But Big Boy remains simply pre-occupied with physical well-being, and casually

---

[17]Harold Cruse, *The Crisis of the Negro Intellectual* (New York, 1967), pp. 181–189. See also his *Rebellion or Revolution* (New York, 1968).

explains how it went with his comrade, Bobo: "They burnt im. . . . Will, ah wan some water; mah throats like fire."[18]

"Down by the Riverside" continues the emphasis upon the will to survive, although Mann, the main character, is killed by soldiers under emergency flood conditions. Mann is determined to get his pregnant wife to a doctor and his family to the hills away from flood waters that already swirl at his cabin door. In a stolen boat, he is forced to kill a white man. Mann pits his will against nature and whites. It is a brilliant but losing battle and he knows well before the events that he will be killed and captured.

He expresses will by determining the moment when he will die. In this way, he briefly affirms for the universe that Mann existed:

> Yes, now, he would die! He would die before he would let them kill him. Ah'll die fo they kill me! Ahll *die* . . . He ran straight to the right, through the trees, in the direction of the water. He heard a shot.[19]

Although he is killed by the soldiers, they have been forced to accept the time that he offers.

With "Long Black Song," the third story, the focus is shifted. Silas, the character representing individual will, does not appear until the second half of the story. Wright instead focuses upon Silas's wife, a person conceived of as sunk-in-nature or as undifferentiated nature. The shift destroys the simple story line which Wright has followed. Blacks, uncommitted to struggle, in the earlier stories, were backstaged or absent.

Sarah, on the other hand, as a black person not emerged from nature, requires a creative energy to lift her from the category of stereotype which Wright was unable to give her. One has to see her as earth goddess or as the stereotype of loose sexuality. Since Silas's violent war with whites and his obvious needs and heroic struggle claim the sympathy of the reader, the symbols that have given Sarah a tenuous stature as earth goddess, above the wars of black and white men, crumble, and she appears as mere mindless stupidity and sensuality.

In her actions Sarah resists Western clock time. The sole clock in the house is out of repair. In an obviously symbolic action, her baby is unpacified when she holds him up to the sun (nature's time), but quietens when she allows him to beat upon the clock (Western time). She declares that they need no clock. "We just don't need no time, mistah."[20] Wright gears her responses to images of the season and its rhythms.

Dreaming secretly of Tom, a man with a similar emotional structure,

---

[18]Richard Wright, *Uncle Tom's Children* (New York, 1940; Perennial Library Edition, 1965), p. 66.

[19]*Ibid.*, p. 102.

[20]*Ibid.*, p. 108.

Sarah is seduced by a white salesman, whose music and personality evoke her maternal feelings and a sense of harmonious nature. Silas, her husband, upon discovering betrayal kills the salesman and other white men. Again the choice factor of the stern willed: Facing a lynch mob, Silas insists upon determining the mode of his death by remaining in his burning house, which the mob has set on fire.

Silas breaks out in one powerful nationalistic chant against the way the cards are stacked against him as a black man in the universe. He has accepted the world of time, materialistic struggle, and manipulation of Nature. He has worked for ten years to become the owner of his farm. Yet the tone and terms of his chant imply that the dread of the day of reckoning had long been on his mind: "He began to talk to no one in particular; he simply stood over the dead white man and talked out of his life, out of a deep and final sense that now it was all over and nothing could make any difference."

> "The white folks ain never gimme a chance! They ain never give no black man a chance! there ain nothin in your whole life yuh kin keep from 'em. They take yo lan. They take yo women! N' then they take yo life."[21]

In addition, he is stabbed in the back by "Mah own blood," i.e., his wife. At bottom, Silas is concerned about the meaning of his life.

This nationalistic base is also a part of the two preceding stories. In "Big Boy Leaves Home" it is tacitly assumed. The folk elders' unspoken assumptions, the quickness with which they devise Big Boy's escape, and the white supremacy assumptions with which whites instantly and almost casually commit the most horrible violence, reflect nationalist stances. In "Down by the Riverside," a part of the same Nationalistic assumptions are operative, and Mann expresses a lament for the failure of himself and others to live up to the Nationalistic implications of their lives.

> For a split second he was there among those blunt and hazy black faces looking silently and fearfully at the white folks take some poor black man away. Why don they help me? Yet he knew they would not and could not help him, even as he in times past had not helped other black men being taken by the white folks to their death.[22]

In a vital creative formula, Wright has thus combined the idea of revolutionary will, embryonic nationalism, and Negro folklore moulded into a martial stance.

The pattern is continued in the last two stories, which differ from the first group by bringing the Communist movement into the picture and having the individual will relate to the group will. "Fire and Cloud" has

---

[21] *Ibid.*, p. 125.
[22] *Ibid.*, p. 97.

the black minister Taylor to lead black and white workers in a march upon a Southern town, which has refused to relieve their hunger. At first Taylor's motivations are religious impulses and a concept of nature as communal. The tilling of the land brings organic satisfaction of great depth. But the whites have taken the land and confiscated nature. Taylor's will is strong. He endures vicious beatings by whites and learns that he must get with the people, if the problem is to be solved.

The last story, "Bright and Morning Star," is superior to "Fire and Cloud," because it more carefully investigates the inner psychology of An Sue, a mother of communists, who gives up the image of Christ by which she has formerly shrunk from the world. Her nationalistic impulse is in her distrust for white comrades, a feeling which her son has enthusiastically transcended. An Sue, however, is all too prophetic. Booker, a poor white communist informer, tricks her into giving him the names of comrades, although her intuition sees him in the image of the oppressor, the "white mountain."

Now in order to see Johnny Boy, whom the mob has captured, and confirm her suspicions about Booker, she goes to the mob scene "like nigga woman wid mah windin sheet t git mah dead son."[23] In the sheet she conceals a gun. Defiantly refusing to make her captured son inform, she endures his being maimed; then as Booker begins to inform, she kills him. She and her son are then killed by the mob, although "She gave up as much of her life as she could before they took it from her."[24]

The nationalist impulse thus overrides both escapist religion and communism. She is between two worlds without the benefit of the "grace" that either might confer. The impulse that sustains her defiance is more than nationalist; it is that of revolutionary will, the demand for the right to give final shape to the meaning of one's life. In a word, like all the heroic characters of *Uncle Tom's Children,* her choice is existential. The device of the winding sheet, with which she asserts her will, will be recognized as a well known Negro folklore story.

As Wright's fictional scene moved to the urban ghetto, he encountered a new challenge because the forces that attacked the lives of black people were so often abstract and impersonal, unlike the Southern mob, sheriff, or plantation owner. Yet out of the urban area was to come the most prophetic images relevant to the ordinary black man in the ghetto.

Although *Lawd Today* was first published in 1963, a statement in the bibliographical section of Constance Webb's *Richard Wright* notes that it "was probably written sometime between 1935 and 1937."[25] Constance Webb speaks of his working on a novel about post-office workers during

[23] *Ibid.,* p. 207.
[24] *Ibid.,* p. 214.
[25] Webb, p.424.

the summer of 1935.[26] The book does have something of an exploratory air about it, and it certainly does not immediately connect its wires to ideology or resound in defense of blacks. I think that critics have been offended by the brutality and lower depth quality, which its black characters project. Wright's flaming defense of blacks and indictment of whites had filled the vision of even mild-mannered black critics and given them the benefit of a genteel catharsis; therefore, it was very easy to miss the more negative attitudes that he held in regard to black life.

Yet *Lawd Today* is very important in the study of Richard Wright for several reasons. It defines at least an essential part of black life, points up the importance of the inscriptions from other writings as aids to understanding his intentions, and enables us to see Wright examining a slice of black life practically on its own terms.

In addition to Wright's strictures on black life in *Black Boy*—cultural bareness, lack of tenderness and genuine passion, etc.—there had also appeared the statement that "I know that Negroes had never been allowed to catch the full spirit of Western Civilization, that they lived somehow in it but not of it."[27] *Lawd Today* addresses itself to this situation. The title *Lawd Today*, a folk exclamation on confronting the events of the day, is to express a people who have not been able to make their life their own, who must live "from day to day." And as Conrad Kent Rivers put it in his poem on Wright—"To Live from Day to Day is not to live at all."

To compound the problem: Wright was perfectly capable of seeing emptiness as characteristic of the life of the ordinary white worker. In "The Man Who Went to Chicago,"[28] his white female co-workers in a restaurant exposed "their tawdry dreams, their simple hopes, their home lives, their fear of feeling anything deeply. . . ." Although they were casually kind and impersonal, "they knew nothing of hate and fear, and strove instinctively to avoid all passion." Their lives were totally given to striving "for petty goals, the trivial material prizes of American life." To become more than children, they would have to include in their personalities "a knowledge of lives such as I lived and suffered containedly." Wright is on his way to describing a shallowly optimistic America, one that avoided the tragic encounter and the knowledge to be derived therefrom, one that excluded blacks from "the entire tide and direction of American culture," although they are "an organic part of the nation. . . ."

A similarity, yes, and yet a difference. Wright seems to see ordinary white life by its intrinsic relationship to Western technology, as pulled into some semblance of order—one that is sufficient for superficial living, elementary assertion of will and materialistic acquisitiveness. On the other

---

[26]Webb, p. 135.
[27]*Black Boy*, p. 33.
[28]*Eight Men*, pp. 168–170.

hand, Saunders Redding comments perceptively on one of Wright's objections to black life: Wright knew "that survival for the Negro depended upon his not making choices, upon his ability to adapt to choices (the will of others) made for him. He hated this. . . ."[29] In his introduction to the 1945 edition of St. Clair Drake and Horace R. Cayton's *Black Metropolis*, Wright more fully describes conditions which he feels deprive Modern Man of deep organic satisfaction, and programs the stunted and frenzied lives of blacks.

As an expression of this extreme frustration, *Lawd Today* deserves a separate and more careful analysis than I can here give to it. Its universe provides its chief character, Jake Jackson, a Mississippi migrant, and his friends no true self-consciousness. It is a universe of violence, magic, quack medicine, numbers playing and dreambooks, roots and herbs, cheap movies, tuberculosis and venereal disease, hard liquor and sex and corrupt politics. The relation between Jake Jackson and his wife Lil is that of warfare; the book begins with Jake's brutal beating of her, and it ends with Jake's drunken attempt to beat her again, an event that sees her, in self-defense, knocking him unconscious.

> "Lawd, I wish I was dead," she [Lil] sobbed softly.
> Outside an icy wind swept around the corner of the building, whining and moaning like an idiot in a deep black pit.[30]

The brutal relations of Jake and Lil provide the one-day frame for the book. The only real value represented is the rough and ready fellowship between Jake and his friends—Al, whose pride stems from his membership in a national guard unit that breaks up strikes and leftist gatherings; Bob, who suffers throughout the story from a bad case of gonorrhea; and Slim, whose body is wracked with tuberculosis. Jake knows that something is missing from his life, but he can't pin it down. So he and his comrades turn to whatever will jolt their bodies into a brief illusion of triumphant living.

Wright uses several external devices, in order to make his intentions apparent. For rather heavy-handed irony, he has the events to take place on Lincoln's birthday. The radio delivers a steady barrage of talk about the war that freed the slaves while Jake and his friends, spiritually lost and enslaved in urban society, fumble through the events of the day. Part I bears the inscription taken from Van Wyck Brooks's *America's Coming-of-Age*: ". . . a vast Sargasso Sea—a prodigious welter of unconscious life, swept by groundswells of half-conscious emotion. . . ." The inscription is obviously well-chosen, and is to be applied to the lives of Jake and his friends. Part II is entitled "Squirrel Cage," a section in which the charac-

---

[29]Herbert Hill, *Anger and Beyond* (New York, 1966), p. 209.
[30]Richard Wright, *Lawd Today* (New York, 1963), p. 224.

ters' actions are no more fruitful than those of caged animals. An inscription from Waldo Frank's *Our America* speaks of the lives of men and women as "some form of life that has hardened but not grown, and over which the world has passed. . . ." Part III takes both its title, "Rat's Alley," and its inscription from T. S. Eliot's *Waste Land:* ". . . But at my back in a cold blast I hear/The rattle of the bones, and chuckle spread from ear to ear." Thus the title headings and the inscriptions alert the reader to the themes of artificially stunted and sterile lives, half-conscious and inarticulate, and force a wider reference to their universe. Something very big and nasty is indeed biting the characters in *Lawd Today*, but it is part of the theme of the book that, though one character prays and most of the others beg, borrow, and "ball," they cannot name the water that would relieve their wasteland.

In concentrating upon simply presenting their lives and their surroundings, Wright displays gifts that are not the trademarks of his other novels. Sensational incidents do not threaten the principle of proportion, or make melodrama an end in itself. Of all things, Wright displays, in his opening portrait of Jake Jackson, a talent for biting satire! Humor, so limited in other works, is often wildly raucous. The gift for portraying extended scenes, apparent in other works and so important to the novelist, is still marvelously in evidence. So also is Wright's great talent for the recording of speech rhythms and color. In the character Al's narrative of a masochistic black woman, Wright even does credit to the tall story tradition.[31]

But his most astonishing performance in Section IV of "Squirrel Cage," in which, for thirty pages, all speeches are anonymous and the postal workers render communally their inner life and feelings.

> They had worked in this manner for so many years that they took one another for granted; their common feelings were a common knowledge. And when they talked it was more like thinking aloud than speaking for purposes of communication. Clusters of emotion, dim accretions of instinct and tradition rose to the surface of their consciousness like dead bodies floating and swollen upon a night sea.[32]

Despite the negative simile about dead bodies, the speeches form a poem, a device which breaks the novel's tight realism and gives its rendering power a new dimension. It is strange that Wright did not develop the technique further, since his naturalism, in order to fully encompass his reach, required the supplement of his own intrusive commentary.

Lawd Today enlarges our perspective on *Native Son*, for it creates the universe of Bigger Thomas in terms more dense than the carefully chosen

---

[31]*Ibid.*, pp. 158–161. See also an apparent reworking of the story in Eldridge Cleaver, *Soul on Ice* (New York, 1968), pp. 166–169.

[32]*Lawd Today*, p. 162.

symbolic reference points of *Native Son*. The continuity of Wright's concerns stands out with great clarity and depth. Running through all Wright's works and thoroughly pervading his personality is his identification with and rejection of the West, and his identification with and rejection of the conditions of black life. *Lawd Today* is primarily concerned with the latter.

In *Native Son*, Wright's greatest work, he returned to the rebel outsider, the character with revolutionary will and the grit to make existential choices. Bigger Thomas, like the heroic characters of *Uncle Tom's Children* finally insists upon defining the meaning of his life: ". . . What I killed for, I am," cries Bigger at the end of his violent and bloody life.

Wright early establishes the myth of the heritage of Man, Western Man, as a counterpoint to the disinherited condition of Bigger Thomas, a Southern black migrant with an eighth grade education. In the first section of the novel, Bigger expresses his frustration by violent and cowardly reactions, and by references to the rituals of power and freedom that he envies. What does he wish to happen, since he complains that nothing happens in his universe? "Anything, Bigger said with a wide sweep of his dingy palm, a sweep that included all the possible activities of the world."

> Then their eyes [Bigger's and his gang's] were riveted; a slate colored pigeon swooped down to the middle of the steel car tracks and began strutting to and fro with ruffled feathers, its fat neck bobbing with regal pride. A street car rumbled forward and the pigeon rose swiftly through the air on wings stretched so taut and sheer that Bigger could see the god of the sun through their translucent tips. He tilted his head and watched the slate-colored bird flap and wheel out of sight over the ridge of a high roof.
> "Now, if I could only do that," Bigger said.[33]

Bigger, himself, instinctively realizes that a job and night school will not fundamentally alter his relationship to the universe. To the white and wealthy Mrs. Dalton's query concerning night school, his mind silently makes a vague response: "Night school was all right, but he had other plans. Well, he didn't know just what they were right now, but he was working them out."[34] As to the job with the Daltons, it is but an extension of the System that holds him in contempt and stifles his being; the "relief" people will cut off his food and starve his family if he does not take it. Because of the resulting pressure from his family for physical comfort and survival, ". . . he felt that they had tricked him into a cheap surrender." The job and night school would have programmed his life into conformity with what Wright called the "pet nigger system,"[35] but would not have gained respect for his manhood.

[33]Richard Wright, *Native Son* (New York: Signet, 1961), pp. 23–24.
[34]*Ibid.*, p. 62.
[35]Webb, p. 205.

Bigger Thomas and Richard Wright were after the system—not merely its pieces.

A major source of the power of *Native Son* derived from Wright's ability to articulate the relevant rituals of black and white cultures—and Bigger's response to them. These rituals emphasize the presence in culture of rational drive, curiosity, revolutionary will, individualism, self-consciousness (preoccupations of Western culture)—or their absence.

Thus blindness (shared by white and black cultures), softness, shrinking from life, escapism, otherworldliness, abjectness, and surrender, are the meaning of the black cultural rituals from which Bigger recoils, and the counters with which blacks are allowed to purchase their meager allowance of shelter and bread. They contrast sharply with Bigger's (the outsider's) deep urges for freedom of gesture and spontaneous response to existence. Wright's indictment is that these negative qualities are systematically programmed into black culture by the all powerful white oppressor.

Having murdered the white girl Mary Dalton—thus defying the imprisoning white oppressor—Bigger Thomas feels a rush of energy that makes him equal to the oppressor. He now explains his revolt against black culture. Buddy, his brother, is "soft and vague; his eyes were defenseless and their glance went only to the surface of things." Buddy is "aimless, lost, with no sharp or hard edges, like a chubby puppy." There is in him "a certain stillness, an isolation, meaninglessness."[36]

Bigger's sister Vera, "seemed to be shrinking from life with every gesture she made." His mother has religion in place of whiskey, and his girlfriend Bessie has whiskey in place of religion. In the last section of *Native Son*, his mother's epiphany is her crawling on her knees from one white Dalton to the other to beg for the life of Bigger. In "Flight," the second part of the novel, Bessie's epiphany is a prose blues complaint concerning the trap of her life, and then in a terrible sigh that surrenders to Bigger her entire will, she betrays her life completely. Finally, after Bigger is captured, a black minister epiphanizes the version of religious passivity that insured endurance of aimless and cramped life, as he unsuccessfully appeals to the captured Bigger. The gestures and rituals of the black minister are rendered with masterly brilliance.

In contrast, the symbols, rituals, and personalities of the white culture express directness, spontaneous freedom, at-homeness in the universe, will—and tyranny. While Bigger concentrates upon avoiding answering questions from the communist Jan Erlone and the liberal Mary Dalton in yes or no terms, he is confounded by their ability to act and speak simply and directly. In a very fine scene that evidences Wright's great

[36] *Native Son*, p. 103.

novelistic talent, their very freedom and liberality dramatize his oppression and shame. Their gestures say that it is their universe. And the fact that Jan Erlone and Mary Dalton, in seconds, can, as individuals, suspend all racial restraints underlines the habitual racial rigidities ingrained in Bigger's life, which deprive him of spontaneous gesture. Oppressively, "To Bigger and his kind white people were not really people; they were a sort of great natural force, like a stormy sky looming overhead, or like a deep swirling river stretching suddenly at one's feet in the dark." The white world is the "white blur," "white walls," "the snow"—all of which place Bigger in the condition of the desperate rat with which *Native Son* begins.

The Jan Erlone–Dalton group of whites express the rituals mediated by a sufficient humanism to partially obscure their relationship to a brutal system. They inspire Bigger's hatred but also a measure of bewilderment. Even the elder Dalton can be nice because the System does the work. With one hand he functions in a company that restricts blacks to ghettos and squeezes from them high rents for rat infested, cramped apartments; with the other, and without conscious irony, he gives substantial sums to black uplift organizations. Although the Daltons' kindness cannot extend to sparing Bigger's life (since he has murdered their daughter—the flower of the system), he will prevent the ejection of Bigger's family from its rat dominated apartment.

The liberalism of the Communist Jan Erlone, his girl friend sympathizer Mary Dalton, and the rest of the Dalton family function as esthetic rituals that create an easy-going atmosphere for sullen submission and inhibition. In the militarized zone are the racial rituals of Detective Britten bouncing Bigger's head against the wall and spitting out definitions of blacks that deny their life. Then there are the agents of the mass media, the rhetoricians, the police, and the mob.

Bigger standing equally outside the shrinking black culture and the hard-driving white culture can only feel the existential choice demanded by his compulsion toward the heritage of man shoving upward from his guts, and sense that something very terrible must happen to him. Near the end he is tortured by the knowledge that his deepest hunger is for human communion, and by his lawyer's briefly raising it as a possibility. But the mirage is soon exposed and he must warm himself by the bleak embers of his hard-won and lonely existential knowledge: "... what I killed for, I am!"

It is part of the greatness of *Native Son* that it survives a plethora of flaws. For example, despite Wright's indictment of white society, he shows in his major fiction little knowledge that, while black life is stifled by brutality, the private realities of white life find it increasingly impossible to free themselves from the imprisoning blandishments of a neurotic culture. His failure to image this fact, although we have seen that he had some understanding of it, makes it seem that Bigger's problems would have been solved by his entry into the white world. The great engagement of the universe that rages through the first and second parts of the novel sputters, at points, in the third part while Wright scores debater's points on jobs, housing, and equal opportunity. The famous courtroom speech that the attorney Max makes in behalf of Bigger hardly rises above such humanitarian matters. Thus a novel that resounds in revolutionary tones descends to merely reformist modulations that would make glad the heart of a New Deal liberal.

As the theme and situations of the novel increase in density of implication, Wright is too frequently touching the reader's elbow to explain reactions and make distinctions that are too complex for Bigger to verbalize. The style, therefore, fails at crucial points. Melodrama, as in the murder of Mary Dalton, is sometimes very functional. At other times, it is unfortunately its own excuse for being.

And so one may go on, but when he finishes he will find *Native Son* still afloat and waiting for the next reader to make it a reference point in the fabric of his being.

Wright's vision of black men and women rendered in the four books that I have discussed stormed its way into the fabric of American culture with such fury that its threads form a reference point in the thinking and imagination of those who have yet to read him. Quickly downgraded as more art-conscious black writers made the scene, he seems now all too prophetic, and all too relevant, majestically waiting that close critical engagement which forms the greatest respect that can be paid to a great man and writer.

Thus, today, when we think that we know so much about black life, even down to its metaphysics and ambiguity, it is humbling to realize that the lifelong commitment of soul that was Richard Wright is of the essence of much that we think we know.

The Horror and the Glory:
Richard Wright's Portrait
of the Artist
in *Black Boy* and *American Hunger*

by Horace A. Porter

As the curtain falls on the final page of *American Hunger*, the continuation of Richard Wright's autobiography, *Black Boy*, he is alone in his "narrow room, watching the sun sink slowly in the chilly May sky." Having just been attacked by former Communist associates as he attempted to march in the May Day parade, he ruminates about his life. He concludes that all he has, after living in both Mississippi and Chicago, are "words and a dim knowledge that my country has shown me no examples of how to live a human life." Wright ends his autobiography with the following words:

> ... I wanted to try to build a bridge of words between me and that world outside, that world which was so distant and elusive that it seemed unreal.
>
> I would hurl words into this darkness and wait for an echo, and if an echo sounded, no matter how faintly, I would send other words to tell, to march, to fight, to create a sense of the hunger for life that gnaws in us all, to keep alive in our hearts a sense of the inexpressibly human.[1]

American Hunger (1977) is the continuation of *Black Boy* (1945). Wright initially composed them as one book entitled *The Horror and the Glory*.

"The Horror and the Glory: Richard Wright's Portrait of the Artist in *Black Boy* and *American Hunger* by Horace A. Porter. Printed by permission of the author.

[1]Richard Wright, *American Hunger* (New York, 1977), 135. It is unfortunate that *American Hunger* is such a late arrival. Its chief value is that it brings together for the first time in book form the second half of Wright's original autobiography, most of which was published in essay form in the *Atlantic Monthly* (August and September 1944), in the anthology *Cross Section* (1945), and in the September 1945 issue of *Mademoiselle*. Therefore, *American Hunger* is hardly new and surely not a lost literary treasure and fortuitously blown into public view by heaven's four winds. In any case, whatever the reason for its belated, posthumous publication, it has been effectively robbed of its capacity to affect significantly the public's mind. For despite the power of *Black Boy* and *Native Son*, they are now part and parcel of a bygone era. For a thorough discussion of this matter, see Jerry W. Ward, "Richard Wright's Hunger," *Virginia Quarterly Review* (Winter, 1978), 148–153.

Thus, a reading of the two volumes as one continuous autobiography is crucial for a comprehensive understanding of his portrayal of himself as a young writer. Wright achieves remarkable poetic closure by bringing together at the end of *American Hunger* several interrelated themes which he elaborately spells out in *Black Boy*. The passage cited above illustrates his concern for words, his intense and troubling solitude, and his yearning to effect a revolution in the collective consciousness of America through the act of writing. In a sentence, the end of *American Hunger* is essentially the denouement of *Black Boy*.

Although critics have discussed the effect of Wright's early life on his writings, none has shown systematically how *Black Boy* (and to a lesser degree *American Hunger*) can be read primarily as a portrait of the artist as a young man. Consequently, I intend to demonstrate how the theme of words (with their transforming and redeeming power) is the nucleus around which ancillary themes swirl. Wright's incredible struggle to master words is inextricably bound to his defiant quest for individual existence and expression. To be sure, the fundamental nature of the experience is not peculiar to Wright. Many, if not most writers, are marked by their experience with words during childhood. It is no accident that, say, Jean Paul Sartre, a writer whom Wright eventually meets and admires, entitles his autobiography *Les Mots*. What one sees in Wright's autobiographies is how the behavior of his fanatically religious grandmother, the painful legacy of his father, the chronic suffering of his mother, and how his interactions with blacks and whites both in and outside his immediate community are all thematically connected to the way Wright uses words to succeed as a writer and as a man.

The first chapter of *Black Boy*, the first scene, foreshadows the major theme—the development of the young artist's sensibility—of the book. Wright begins his narrative by recounting how he set fire to his house when he was four years old. His is a conflagration sparked by an odd combination of boredom, curiosity, and imagination. One day Wright looks yearningly out into the empty street and dreams of running, playing, and shouting. First, he burns straws from a broom; then, his temporary pyromania getting the better of him, he wondered how "the long fluffy white curtains" would look if he lit them: "Red circles were eating into the white cloth; then a flare of flames shot out. . . . The fire soared to the ceiling. . . . Soon a sheet of yellow lit the room."[2] Then, most terrifying of all, Wright runs outside and hides in "a dark hollow of a brick chimney and balled [himself] into a tight knot."[3] Wright's aim in hiding under the burning house was to avoid the predictable whipping by his mother. Moreover, his four-year-old imagination is so preoccupied with the effect

[2]Richard Wright, *Black Boy* (New York, 1945), 4.
[3]*Ibid.*, 4.

of his derring-do that he does not realize that his own life is on a burning line. Hiding beneath the house and thinking of the possible consequences of his actions—the death of family members—Wright states: "It seemed that I had been hiding for ages, and when the stomping and screaming died down, I felt lonely, cast forever out of life."[4]

Wright may not have been completely aware of the psychological import of his opening scene. For, it appears that we must interpret young Wright's act of arson for what it really may have been. Perhaps even at that early age he was trying to free himself from the tyranny of his father's house in which his fanatically religious grandmother ruled: "I saw the image of my grandmother lying helplessly upon her bed and there were yellow flames in her black hair. . . ."[5] The fact that young Wright has these thoughts while in "a dark hollow of a brick chimney . . . balled . . . into a tight knot," raises more profound psychological issues. Does this image represent a yearning to return to the womb? Does it constitute symbolic parricide? Does it symbolize the possibility of a new birth? When Wright sets his father's house aflame, he also makes an eloquent statement against the world the Southern slaveholders had made. Wright's later anxiety and guilt over having turned his back on his father's world drives him to write. His autobiography is an act of self-assertion and self-vindication in which he fearlessly confronts his father. Moreover, he demonstrates his love for his mother. And he pays homage to the anonymous, illiterate blacks whose world he fled.

In the process of moving away from his family and community, Wright began experiencing the problem (a consuming sense of loss and abandonment) that was to become central to his life and his work. In certain primary respects, he was surely cognizant of the problem, but it operated on levels sufficiently profound as to be unfathomable later in his career. Numerous passages in *Black Boy* illustrate the phenomenon.

What has been characterized as ritual parricide comes readily to mind when Wright's father is awakened one day by the meowing of a stray cat his sons have found. Wright's father screams at him and his brother: "'Kill that damn thing!'" His father shouts, "'Do anything, but get it away from here!'" Ignoring the advice of his brother, Wright does exactly what his father suggests. He puts a rope around the cat's neck and hangs it. Why? Wright explains:

> I had had my first triumph over my father. I had made him believe that I had taken his words literally. He could not punish me now without risking his authority. I was happy because I had at last found a way to throw criticism of him into his face. I had made him feel that, if he whipped me for killing the kitten, I would never give serious weight to his words again.

[4]*Ibid.*, 5.
[5]*Ibid.*, 5.

> I had made him know that I felt he was cruel and I had done it without his punishing me.[6]

Young Wright's cunning act of interpretation is the telling point here. If one were dubious about the meaning of the son's act of arson, the passage cited above demonstrates a full-blown hatred and contempt. But note how Wright focuses on his father's words, how he attempts to neutralize his father's psychological authority by a willful misinterpretation of his statement.

At the end of the first chapter of *Black Boy*, Wright banishes his father from the remaining pages of both volumes of his autobiography. His father eventually deserts his mother and she struggles to support her two sons. On one occasion when Wright and his mother pay his father and his "strange woman" a visit in order to obtain money for food, Wright's father hands him a nickel. Wright refuses to accept the nickel, his father laughs and puts the nickel back in his pocket, stating, "'That's all I got.'" That image of his father was indelibly etched in Wright's memory. Wright states that over the years, his father's face would "surge up in my imagination so vivid and strong that I felt I could reach out and touch it; I would stare at it, feeling that it possessed some vital meaning which always eluded me."[7]

Wright does not see his father for "a quarter of a century" after that encounter. His reunion with his father after a prolonged period leads to one of the more poignant and profound meditations of the autobiography. Staring at "the sharecropper, clad in ragged overalls, holding a muddy hoe in his gnarled, veined hands," Wright sees his biological father, but he also sees another man. The man standing before him is now both more and less than his father:

> . . . My mind and consciousness had become so greatly and violently altered that when I tried to talk to him I realized that, though ties of blood made us kin, though I could see a shadow of my face in his face, though there was an echo of my voice in his voice, we were forever strangers, speaking a different language, living on vastly different planes of reality. . . . I stood before him, pained, my mind aching as it embraced the simple nakedness of his life, feeling how completely his soul was imprisoned by the slow flow of the seasons, by wind and rain and sun, how fastened were his memories to a crude and raw past, how chained were his actions and emotions to the direct, animalistic impulses of his withering body . . . I forgave him and pitied him as my eyes looked past him to the unpainted wooden shack. From far beyond the horizon that bound this bleak plantation there had come to me through my living the knowledge that my father was a black peasant who had gone to the city seeking life, but who had failed in the

[6]*Ibid.*, 10–11.
[7]*Ibid.*, 30.

city, and who at last fled the city—that same city which had lifted me in its burning arms and borne me toward alien and undreamed of shores of knowing.[8]

In the foregoing meditation, Wright depicts his father as a "sharecropper," a "black peasant," whose actions and emotions are "chained . . . to the direct, animalistic impulses of his body." He and his father are "forever strangers, speaking a different language." Even in this passage which ostensibly has little to do with language, Wright reminds us that his ability to use and understand words has transformed him. His mind and consciousness have been "greatly and violently" altered. So Wright finally achieves the kind of authority he longed for as a kid. His father is no longer the threatening figure who told him to kill the kitten. From Wright's point of view, he has become something other; now, he is more phenomenon than person. Thus, Wright is simultaneously compassionate and dispassionate. On the one hand, he forgives his father; on the other, he clearly indicates that certain bonds between him and his father have been irreparably severed.

Wright's mother also plays an important role in this psychological scheme of reconciliation and vindication. Despite the fact that his mother whipped him until he was unconscious after he set the house afire, he expresses tenderness toward her throughout *Black Boy*; Wright informs the reader that his mother was the first person who taught him to read and told him stories. After Wright had hanged the kitten in order to triumph over his father, he explains that his mother, who is "more imaginative, retaliated with an assault upon my sensibilities that crushed me with the moral horror involved in taking a life."[9] His mother makes him bury the kitten that night and makes him pray.

Wright's mother not only instructs him in the high moral values of civilized society, but she also teaches him how to survive in a hostile and impoverished environment. She teaches him "the ethics of living Jim Crow." She frequently whips him because she knows that certain small gestures of self-pride and assertion would lead readily to brutality or death. Thus, if Wright's mother's arm is sometimes the arm of the oppressive social order, that same arm is, ironically, the tender, loving arm of the parent, nurturing and protecting her young. She instructs him in those traditions of black life that are sustaining—the necessity of learning to persevere, the ability to maintain grace under pressure, the practice of containing one's pain. Small wonder that Wright sees in his mother's suffering and in her will to live in spite of her rapidly declining health, a symbol of the numerous ills and injustices of the society in which they both live:

[8]*Ibid.*, 30–31.
[9]*Ibid.*, 11.

My mother's suffering grew into a symbol in my mind, gathering to itself all the poverty, the ignorance, the helplessness; the painful, baffling, hunger-ridden days and hours; the restless moving, the futile seeking, the uncertainty, the fear, the dread; the meaningless pain and the endless suffering. Her life set the emotional tone of my life, colored the men and women I was to meet in the future, conditioned my relation to events that had not yet happened. . . . A somberness of spirit that I was never to lose settled over me during the slow years of my mother's unrelieved suffering, a somberness that was to make me stand apart and look upon excessive joy with suspicion, that was to make me self-conscious, that was to make me keep forever on the move, as though to escape a nameless fate seeking to overtake me.[10]

Wright, the loving son, feels powerless before the seemingly vast impersonal forces which break his mother's spirit and ruin her health. His mother's life becomes a psychological and emotional charge to him; the "vital meaning" inherent in her suffering is the unstated psychological instruction to dedicate his life to the amelioration of the ills and injustices of society in whatever manner he finds appropriate and effective. Had Wright become indifferent toward the symbol of suffering his mother's life represents, his indifference would have been in effect psychological and moral betrayal of the first order. However, his reflections on his mother's suffering profoundly changes his whole attitude at the tender age of twelve. The spirit he catches sharpens the edges of his inchoate, artistic sensibility. We witness the writer's personality assuming self-conscious definition:

The spirit I had caught gave me insight into the suffering of others, . . . made me sit for hours while others told me of their lives. . . . It made me love burrowing into psychology, into realistic and naturalistic fiction and art. . . . It directed my loyalties to the side of men in rebellion; it made me love talk that sought answers to questions that could help nobody, that could only keep alive in me that enthralling sense of wonder and awe in the face of the drama of human feeling which is hidden by the external drama of life.[11]

Furthermore, the symbol of Wright's mother's suffering gives him hope. Long before he leaves the South he dreams of going North in order to "do something to redeem my being alive":

I dreamed of going North and writing books, novels. The North symbolized to me all that I had not felt and seen; it had no relation whatever to what actually existed. Yet, by imagining a place where everything was possible, I kept hope alive in me. But where had I got this notion of doing something in the future, of going away from home and accomplishing something that

[10]*Ibid.*, 87.
[11]*Ibid.*, 87.

would be recognized by others? I had, of course, read my Horatio Alger stories, and I knew my Get-Rich-Quick Wallingford series from cover to cover, though I had sense enough not to hope to get rich . . . yet I felt I had to go somewhere and do something to redeem my being alive.[12]

Note that Wright considers the writing of books or novels as the activity which would give his life meaning—"redeem my being alive."

In the preceding pages, we discuss the subtle psychological question of Wright's relationship to his parents. The task now is to demonstrate specifically how Wright uses words to remove himself from the oppressive community which tries to stifle his imagination. Over the years, Wright becomes increasingly defiant and articulate. And the members of his Southern community become suspicious of his goals and motives.

Words lead to Wright's salvation and to his redemption. From the first pages of *Black Boy*, the reader witnesses Wright at the tender, impressionable age of six becoming a messenger of the obscene. One day a black man drags Wright, who is peering curiously through the doors of a saloon, inside. The unscrupulous and ignorant adults give him liquor and send obscene messages by him back and forth to one another. Wright goes from one person to the next shouting various obscenities in tune to the savage glee and laughter of the crowd. Surely, the incident makes Wright, inquisitive as he is, wonder about the odd effects of his words.

He later learns his first lesson on the power of the written word. Returning home after his first day of school during which he had learned "all the four-letter words describing physiological and sex functions," from a group of older boys, he decides to display his newly acquired knowledge. Wright goes from window to window in his neighborhood and writes the words in huge soap letters. A woman stops him and drives him home. That night the same woman informs his mother of what Wright calls his "inspirational scribblings." As punishment, she takes him out into the night with a pail of water and a towel and demands that he erase the words he had written: "'Now scrub until that word's gone,' she ordered."

This comical incident may appear insignificant on the surface. Furthermore, one cannot know the nature or the degree of the psychological effect the incident had on Wright. However, it seems reasonable to assume that it had a significant psychological impact. As Wright presents it, it is the first occasion on which words he writes are publicly censored; the first incident during which family members and neighbors become angry, if amused, because of words he writes. Wright states: "Neighbors gathered, giggling, muttering words of pity and astonishment, asking my mother how on earth I could have learned so much so quickly. I scrubbed at the four-letter soap words and grew blind with anger."[13]

---

[12]*Ibid.*, 147.
[13]*Ibid.*, 22.

Wright's first written words are not the only words to get him in trouble. His first exposure to imaginative literature also causes a scene. One day a young school teacher, who boards with his grandmother, read to him *Bluebeard and His Seven Wives.* Wright describes the effect that the story has on him in visionary terms: "The tale made the world around me, throb, live. As she spoke reality changed, the look of things altered, and the world became peopled with magical presences. My sense of life deepened and the feel of things was different, somehow. Enchanted and enthralled. . . ."[14]

Wright's visionary, enchanted state does not last. His grandmother screams "'you stop that you evil gal!' . . . 'I want none of that devil stuff in my house!'" When Wright insists that he likes the story and wants to hear what happened, his grandmother tells him,"'you're going to burn in hell. . . .'" Wright reacts strongly to this incident. He promises himself that when he is old enough, he "would buy all the novels there were and read them." Not knowing the end of the tale fills Wright with "a sense of emptiness and loss." He states that the tale struck "a profoundly responsive chord" in him:

> So profoundly responsive a chord had the tale struck in me that the threats of my mother and grandmother had no effect whatsoever. They read my insistence as mere obstinacy, as foolishness, something that would quickly pass; and they had no notion how desperately serious the tale had made me. They could not have known that Ella's whispered story of deception and murder had been the first experience in my life that had elicited from me a total emotional response. No words or punishment could have possibly made me doubt. I had tasted what to me was life, and I would have more of it somehow, some way. . . .[15]

This passage dramatizes one of the central conflicts of Wright's autobiography. It shows, on the one hand, Wright's literary precocity and illustrates on the other how his days with his grandmother led to one psychological scrimmage after another. The grandmother loathes what she considers to be Wright's impertinence. No matter, given Wright's thirst for knowledge, his longing to achieve a self-conscious, independent manhood, his intense desire to live in a world elsewhere, he proves to be extremely vigilant in his fight against those, including his grandmother, his uncle, his aunt, and his high school principal, whom he calls his "tribal" oppressors. To Wright, theirs is at worst the path to poverty and ignorance and at best a path to what Mann's Tonio Kröger calls "the blisses of the commonplace." Wrights wants neither.

Reflecting on his grandmother's insistence that he join the church and

[14]*Ibid.*, 34.
[15]*Ibid.*, 36.

walk in the path of righteousness (as she sees it), Wright states: "We young men had been trapped by the community, the tribe in which we lived and which we were a part. The tribe for its own safety was asking us to be at one with it. . . ."[16] Moreover, commenting on how the community views anyone who chooses not to have his soul saved, Wright asserts:

> This business of saving souls had no ethics; every human relationship was shamelessly exploited. In essence, the tribe was asking us whether we shared its feeling; if we refused to join the church, it was equivalent to saying no, to placing ourselves in the position of moral monsters.[17]

It is important to keep in mind that Wright's mother is an exception. To be sure, she shares many of the views of the community, but out of love, she aids Wright in his attempt to escape the tribe. Speaking of his mother after the Bluebeard incident, Wright says: "I burned to learn to read novels and I tortured my mother into telling me the meaning of every strange word I saw, not because the word itself had any value, but because it was the gateway to a forbidden and enchanting land."[18]

Against the wishes of the community, Wright continues to read and develop as a young writer. His first real triumph comes when the editor of the local Negro newspaper accepts one of Wright's stories, "The Voodoo of Hell's Half-Acre." The plot of the story involves a villain who wants a widow's home. After the story is published, no one, excepting the newspaper editor, gives any encouragement. His grandmother calls it "'the devil's work'"; his high school principal objects to his use of "hell" in the story's title; even his mother feels that his writing will make people feel that he is "weak minded." His classmates do not believe that he has written the story:

> They were convinced that I had not told them the truth. We had never had any instruction in literary matters at school; the literature of the nation of the Negro had never been mentioned. My schoolmates could not understand why I had called it *The Voodoo of Hell's Half-Acre*. The mood out of which a story was written was the most alien thing conceivable to them. They looked at me with new eyes, and a distance, a suspiciousness came between us. If I had thought anything in writing the story, I had thought that perhaps it would make me more acceptable to them, and now it was cutting me off from them more completely than ever.[19]

Herein, Wright identifies another problem which menaces him throughout his writing life. The problem is the young artist's radical disassociation of sensibility from that of the group. In this regard, he is

[16]*Ibid.*, 134.
[17]*Ibid.*, 134.
[18]*Ibid.*, 135.
[19]*Ibid.*, 146.

reminiscent of the young artist heroes of Mann and Joyce, of Tonio Kröger and Stephen Daedalus. However, Wright's plight as a young artist is significantly different in a crucial way. His is not simply the inability to experience, by dint of his poetic sensibility, "the blisses of the commonplace." Not only is Wright pitted against his immediate family and community, the tribe, as he calls them. He must also fight against the prejudices of the larger society.

Wright wrote "The Voodoo of Hell's Half-Acre" when he was fifteen. He concludes:

> Had I been conscious of the full extent to which I was pushing against the current of my environment, I would have been frightened altogether out of my attempts at writing. . . .
>
> I was building up in me a dream which the entire educational system of the South had been rigged to stifle. I was feeling the very thing that the state of Mississippi had spent millions of dollars to make sure that I would never feel; I was becoming aware of the thing that the Jim Crow laws had been drafted and passed to keep out of my consciousness; I was acting on impulses that Southern senators in the nation's capital had striven to keep out of Negro life. . . .[20]

A telling example which brilliantly demonstrates what Wright means in the passage cited above involves his love for words and books once again. When Wright is nineteen, he reads an editorial in the Memphis *Commercial Appeal* which calls H. L. Mencken a fool. Wright knows that Mencken is the editor of the *American Mercury* and he wonders what Mencken has done to deserve such scorn. How can he find out about Mencken? Since blacks are denied the right to use the public libraries, he is not permitted to check out books. But Wright proves both ingenious and cunning.

He looks around among his co-workers at the optical company where he is employed and chooses the white person—a Mr. Falk—who he thinks might be sympathetic. The man is an Irish Catholic, "a pope lover" as the white Southerners say. Wright had gotten books from the library for him several times, and wisely figures that since he too is hated, he might be somewhat sympathetic. Wright's imagination and courage pays off. Although somewhat skeptical about Wright's curious request from the outset, Mr. Falk eventually gives Wright his card, warning him of the risk involved and swearing him to secrecy. Wright promises that he will write the kind of notes Mr. Falk usually writes and that he will sign Falk's name.

Since Wright does not know the title of any of Mencken's books, he carefully composes what he considers a foolproof note: "*Dear Madam: Will you please let this nigger have some books by H. L. Mencken.*"[21] The librarian

[20]*Ibid.*, 148.
[21]*Ibid.*, 216.

returns with Mencken's *A Book of Prefaces and Prejudices*. His reading of Mencken provides him with a formidable reading list: Anatole France, Joseph Conrad, Sinclair Lewis, Sherwood Anderson, Dostoevski, George Moore, Flaubert, Maupassant, Tolstoy, Frank Harris, Twain, Hardy, Crane, Zola, Norris, Gorky, Bergson, Ibsen, Shaw, Dumas, Poe, Mann, Dreiser, Eliot, Gide, Stendhal, and others. Wright starts reading many of the writers Mencken mentions. Moreover, the general effect of his reading was to make him more obsessive about it: "Reading grew into a passion. . . . Reading was like a drug, a dope."[22]

Mencken provides Wright with far more than a convenient reading list of some of the greater masters. He becomes an example to Wright—perhaps an idol—both in matters of style and vocational perspective or stance:

> I opened *A Book of Prefaces* and began to read. I was jarred and shocked by the style, the clear, clean, sweeping sentences. Why did he write like that? And how did one write like that? I pictured the man as a raging demon, slashing with his pen, consumed with hate, denouncing everything American, extolling everything European or German, laughing at the weaknesses of people, mocking God, authority. What was this? I stood up, trying to realize what reality lay behind the meaning of the words. . . . Yes, this man was fighting, fighting with words. He was using words as a weapon, using them as one would use a club. Could words be weapons? Well, yes, for here they were. Then, maybe, perhaps, I could use them as a weapon.[23]

A few months after reading Mencken, Wright finds the convenient opportunity to flee to the North. He closes *Black Boy* on an optimistic note.

American Hunger opens with Wright's arrival in Chicago and with the din of that windy city entering his consciousness, mocking his treasured fantasies. Wright had envisioned Chicago as a city of refuge. However, his first years are "long years of semi-starvation." He works as a dishwasher, part-time post office clerk, life insurance salesman, and laboratory custodian. Since none of these jobs lasts long, finding adequate food and shelter becomes extremely difficult. At one point, Wright shares a windowless rear room with his mother and younger brother. But good luck occasionally comes in the guise of ill. Many of the experiences he has while working odd jobs supplies revelations which subsequently form the core of his best fiction. Wright probably would not have written *Native Son* if he had not seen and felt Bigger Thomas's rage.

The first half of *American Hunger* is primarily devoted to a sociopsychological portrayal of Wright's life and work among the black and white poor. Wright shows how ignorance and racial discrimination fuel prejudice and self-hatred. He gives us glimpses of *les miserables*, who are corrupted, exploited, and destroyed. While working as an insurance sales-

[22]*Ibid.*, 218–19.
[23]*Ibid.*, 218.

man, Wright himself aids in the swindling of the black poor. Yet we are aware throughout that his is a form of predatory desperation. His is the hard choice between honesty and starvation.

Communists dominate the second half of *American Hunger*. As Wright tells his story, he has strong reservations about the party from the outset and gets involved indirectly. He becomes a member of the party primarily because he is a writer and he leaves it for the same reason. Lacking intellectual communion and meaningful social contacts, he joins Chicago's John Reed Club. The members enthusiastically welcome him, and he is immediately given a writing assignment for *Left Front*. After only two months and due to internal rivalry, Wright is elected Executive Secretary of the club. He humbly declines the nomination at first, but, after some insistent prodding, reluctantly accepts the position. Thus, though not a Communist, he heads one of the party's leading cultural organizations. Given his independence of mind, however, he raises too many troubling questions for party officials and they soon begin to wage a war against him. They try to harness his imagination and whip it down the official ideological path. But Wright is already at work on the stories of his first book, *Uncle Tom's Children*. He writes: "Must I discard my plot ideas and seek new ones? No. I could not. My writing was my way of seeing, my way of living, my way of feeling, and who could change his sight, his notion of direction, his senses?"[24]

Wright dwells rather tediously on the Communist party in the six brief chapters of *American Hunger*. However, he does devote limited space to the story of how he "managed to keep humanly alive through transfusions from books" and the story of how he learned his craft: "working nights I spent my days in experimental writing, filling endless pages with stream-of-consciousness Negro dialect, trying to depict the dwellers of the Black Belt as I felt and saw them."[25] And ever conscious of the need to refine his craft, Wright moved into other realms. He read Stein's *Three Lives*, Crane's *The Red Badge of Courage*, and Dostoevski's *The Possessed*. He strove to achieve the "dazzling magic" of Proust's prose in *A Remembrance of Things Past*: "I spent hours and days pounding out disconnected sentences for the sheer love of words. . . . I strove to master words, to make them disappear, to make them important by making them new, to make them melt into a rising spiral of emotional stimuli, each feeding and reinforcing the other, and all ending in an emotional climax that would drench the reader with a sense of a new world. That was the single aim of my living."[26]

Finally Wright was able to redeem himself with words. They moved

[24]Richard Wright, *American Hunger* (New York, 1977), 93.
[25]*Ibid.*, 24.
[26]*Ibid.*, 25.

him from Mississippi to Chicago to New York and eventually made Paris his home town. Using words, he hurled himself at the boundary lines of his existence. Goethe's saying that "Man can find no better retreat from the world than art, and man can find no stronger link with the world than art" sums up the conundrum of Wright's life.

Richard Wright:
The Expatriate as Native Son

by Harold T. McCarthy

> "Keep the habit of the observer, and, as fast as you can, break off
> your association with your personality and identify yourself with
> the Universe."
>
> RALPH WALDO EMERSON,
> *Journal*, October 2, 1837

I

Such American novelists as Henry James, Hemingway, and Henry
Miller did not discover how to cope as artists with their experience until
their sense of American life had been placed in a European perspective.
With Richard Wright the opposite was true. When he left for Paris in
1946, where he was to make his home until his death in 1960, his best
fiction had been written and exile was only to dilute his capacity for
dealing with American life in those works of fiction, principally *The Outsider*
and *The Long Dream*, which he wrote abroad. Critics of Wright's work
seem fully agreed that as a result of leaving America he lost touch with
the source of his strength as a writer, namely, his being a Negro, a man
immersed in the American Negro experience, and a spokesman for black
causes.

There are two fundamental conditions, however, which should qualify
this prevalent view of the relation of Wright to his American experience
and the part which his activities as an expatriate played in affecting his
thinking and writing. One condition is that in a very real sense Wright
may be said to have gone into exile from that moment in early childhood
when he began his long migration from the shack near Natchez, Mississippi, where he was born; so that all his fiction written from, and at times
about, the "alien" lands of Chicago and New York bore the mark of an

"Richard Wright: The Expatriate as Native Son" by Harold T. McCarthy. From *American Literature* 44 (March 1972), 97–117. Copyright © 1972 by the Duke University Press. Reprinted by permission of the Duke University Press.

outsider not responding to felt, personal experience, but consciously shaping an intellectual criticism of specific aspects of American life. A second condition is that only after he had left the United States was Wright able to acknowledge—in Africa, in Indonesia, and in Spain—the manifold ways in which, beneath the shifting facade of formal institutions, a people sustained its folk identity, the kind of folk identity he had responded to only as a monstrous caricature in the U.S.A. It was in "savage" and "pagan" lands and in the privileged role of neutral observer that Richard Wright finally "came home." In African, Asian, and Spanish life he found a universal significance for the Negro, which had been America's Metaphor. It is necessary, then, first of all to clarify Wright's relation to his American experience and the effect of this relationship upon his fiction; and secondly, to examine Wright's nonfiction of the 1950's in order to observe his recognition of the roots of separate cultures, and the implications this had for his sense of himself as a black American.

When he drew his self-portrait in *Black Boy* (New York, 1945), Wright went to some pains to make clear that his cultural alienation had begun in his black home and in a black community where, as a small child, he was scarcely aware of the existence of a white race. Writing in his early thirties, Wright insisted upon the fact that his family had tried to beat fear and submission into his nature years before interracial contacts made evident the rationale for a "nigger" identity. Creating the image of himself as a perceptive child, sensitive and imaginative and forever trying the conduct of his elders in the court of his innocent intellect, Wright seeks to demonstrate that from the start he was never able to accept the role being foisted upon him by the black community; that when the time came for participation in the Southern racist assumptions he could not make the instinctive adjustments which both black and white accepted as an inevitable way of life; and that his flight to the North was as much a flight from the black as from the interracial community. In fact he saw black and white as inseparably fused in their acceptance of a grotesque racial myth. What angered many black readers of Wright's autobiography even more than the disclosure of Negroes as leading shabby, empty, fear-ridden, tyrannized lives was his portrayal of them as yielding mindlessly to such degrading tyranny and positively insisting on preparing their young by what Ralph Ellison termed the "homeopathic method" for submission to such a mythos.

Possibly Wright believed in the truth of the picture of the culture presented in *Black Boy*; but it is more probable that even as he tried to reconstruct his early years, at a time when he was making his traumatic break with the Communist Party, his creative memory chose those events which reflected his own rational integrity in a world of irrational elders. Neither land nor race had ever held possession of his mind, he believed, as they had possessed the minds of his family and friends; so that in looking back he recorded, not the felt life itself, but the reasons why he had been an alien in his own home. The reasons, brilliantly dramatized, are those to which a northern, liberal mind would respond with an appropriate compassion and outrage. The portrait is of the artist as a black boy, but it is primarily the portrait of an artist.

If Wright was in individual exile in the South, flight to Chicago, while it greatly eased the conditions of his exile, did not change his analysis of, or his relation to, the racial condition. Black men in Chicago were still the children of Uncle Tom as the name-play "Bigger Thomas" suggested. In *Uncle Tom's Children, Lawd Today,* and *Native Son,* Wright made fewer cultural concessions to the blacks than to the whites. Victim and victimizer are locked together, the fear and violence of one inevitably producing the fear and violence of the other. Wright felt that his personal escape had not come from playing the racial game with greater skill, or from manipulating its centuries-old rules, but through the process of altering his own mind. With all but incredible tenacity he had held to an image of himself antecedent to the concept "American Negro" and largely by reading kept alive his ability to dream of possibilities in life wholly other than those which made up the reality in which he lived. He wrote in *Black Boy* (p. 218), "I hungered for books, new ways of looking and seeing. It was not a matter of believing or disbelieving what I read, but of feeling something new, of being affected by something that made the look of the world different." "Accidental" reading of fiction and criticism nourished his sense of possibilities, not simply in that they presented glimpses of other cultural worlds, but in that they persuaded him "that America could be shaped nearer to the hearts of those who lived in it" (p. 227). Literature, which had been so instrumental in enabling him to become a person wholly different from the being predicated by his environment, served, through the literary magnet of the John Reed Club in Chicago, to bring Wright into the organization of those whose commitment to political goals allowed no tolerance for the creative imagination of the individual artist. Wright never ceased completely to trust himself or to keep for himself the essential control of his identity; but he allowed himself to become further estranged from a sense of being part of a people, of a landscape, of songs and rhythms and gestures that make up the Negro American folk heritage.

In almost all of Wright's work, from *Uncle Tom's Children* to *The Long Dream* and *Five Episodes,* there are passages of dialogue, glimpses of river life, snatches of song, interior scenes, and perceptions of character that give a flickering sense of a folk heritage; but overwhelmingly his black characters are shaped to fit a literary strategy. The havoc worked on such promising stories as "Fire and Cloud" and "Bright and Morning Star" as well as on *Native Son* by the obtrusion of Party doctrine has been much lamented. But what is more lamentable is that Wright should have been so outraged by the black man's acceptance of the role defined for him by

American culture that he responded to no impulse to discover what was fine in the black culture, what was noble in its heritage, what brighter side of generosity and love might exist on the coin which bore the image of poverty and despair, or what meaning there might be in the special responsiveness to things not of this world. Faulkner wrote, "They endured." The words summed up a long history which he had evoked aesthetically. Wright, however, was caught up in a hideous present moment, the Great Depression years and the Chicago black ghetto, when it was an achievement to survive, and when the Communist Party seemed to offer him an undreamed of freedom, an unqualified social acceptance, and—what indeed it did provide him—the only hope for his existence as a writer.

In sum, and paradoxically, Wright joined the Communist Party for what were, from the Party's point of view, all the wrong reasons. He wished to enlarge his mind through association and discussion with other artists, to cultivate his individuality, and to realize his powers as an artist. In the process of transforming himself he hoped to promote the transformation of society. Such ambitions tend to place Wright in the American transcendentalist tradition, and as he was later to remark in his essay "I Tried to Be a Communist," he was "fantastically naive" to believe that he could fit into the Communist program. But where Wright up through the thirties differed fundamentally from the transcendentalists was in his refusal to trust his intuitive sense of things. In fact he ruthlessly insisted upon denying those intuitive promptings which might have led him to respond to the deep cultural roots to which he was perversely insensitive. Of the period preceding his joining the Communists he wrote, "So far I had managed to keep humanly alive through transfusions from books. In my concrete relations with others I had encountered nothing to encourage me to believe in my feelings. It had been by denying what I saw with my eyes, disputing what I felt with my body, that I had managed to keep my identity intact." This statement formed part of the original *Black Boy* manuscript and is quoted by Constance Webb in her biography, *Richard Wright* (New York, 1968, p. 122).

Like his family and his associates in the South, the Communists grew to fear and distrust Wright because of his irrepressible individuality. Ostensibly he broke with the Party because he would not submit to the Party's manipulation of Negro causes to suit its international policies. But as Wright himself recognized, the true reasons were emotional. Despite his ideological commitments and his long involvement in political action programs for Negroes, he had an overwhelming sense of working in a void. Negroes were the central subject of a series of brilliant books by Wright, books in which he endeavored to force Americans to realize the humanity of the Negro; but his burning sense of the degraded image of the Negro in American life drove him in every book to reproduce an image of the Negro in his most brutalized condition. Finally, in the most effective literary passages of *Native Son*, he produced a scarcely human creature— not an imaginary monster, in Wright's opinion, but a faithful rendering of America's idea of "the American Negro," and thereby a mirror image of American civilization itself.

Early in *Native Son* Bigger Thomas kills a rat in the grim apartment he shares with his mother and sister, and he holds it up to their faces; by the end of the novel the white society is the "Bigger Thomas" holding up its victim in bitter acknowledgment of the sordid world in which it lives. The windy harangues and stilted confrontations of the last third of the novel have little dramatic force; but in the powerful first two-thirds Wright's artistry is driven by the hatred he feels for the total culture, black and white. The philanthropic Daltons, the liberal reformers, the Communists, *and* the degraded blacks are the loathsome generative stuff out of which emerge the murderous Biggers. Borrowing journalese to describe an ape-like Bigger from the Chicago newspapers' actual reports of a Negro's murder trial, and possibly hoping to suggest to the minds of his readers a parallel with Poe's account in "The Murders in the Rue Morgue" of a terrified orangutan stuffing its female victim up the fireplace, Wright piled horror upon horror in the most fully realized parts of the novel as though probing the limits of the public's capacity to accept the monstrosity of "the American Negro."

With Jake Jackson in *Lawd Today* Wright had proceeded with controlled naturalism to present in unrelieved contempt a portrait of a black Chicago worker. The man is created in terms of every popular cliché of Negro homelife, tastes in food and clothing, attitudes toward work and play, his uses of being a Negro, his utter emptiness of value. Other writers have from time to time invoked the Biblical passage of God creating man in His image for ironic effect; Wright uses Lincoln for this purpose, setting the entire novel on Lincoln's birthday, and he repeatedly intrudes the great promise of emancipation into Jake Jackson's day in a counterpoint of contempt. *Lawd Today* the title exclaims; so many decades later and the work of emancipation has not yet begun! If this attack upon the concept of "the American Negro"—a concept, Wright insisted, operative with both black and white men—was drawn in ironic contempt, the conception of the American Negro as a Bigger Thomas was drawn in wrath and despair. It is essential to bear in mind, however, that in both *Lawd Today* and *Native Son* Wright is not presenting a natural human being. With great creative power he is drawing "the American Negro" of popular mythology, breathing life into a vicious caricature in the desperate hope of rooting the myth out of the American mind where for three centuries it has, with variations according to time and place, played its pervasive, corruptive part.

Wright's personal escape from the cultural caul of "the American Negro" had been primarily engineered through literature and through a persistent belief in scarcely dreamed possibilities that were violently contradicted by the facts of his everyday life. He had, at least to his own satisfaction, reached the point where his dream of humanity was sufficiently strong to permit him with radical irony to deny "the American Negro" construct in its own terms—the self-negating "reality" of Jake Jackson and Bigger Thomas. The fact that he could through his artistry create such figures was sufficient proof that America's conception of the American Negro did not exist. But to the American public Richard Wright remained invisible; his artificial "niggers" were visible to all.

In 1941, the year following the publication of *Native Son*, Wright produced a commentary for a group of photographs supposedly recording the folk history of the black American although the book actually had to do not with folk history but with desperate poverty. In 1941 *Twelve Million Black Voices* (New York) went unheard although Wright's text included this observation: "The word 'Negro,' the term by which orally or in print, we black folk in the United States are usually designated, is not really a name at all nor a description, but a psychological island whose objective form is the most unanimous fiat in all American history; a fiat buttressed by popular and national tradition, and written down in many state and city statutes; a fiat which artificially and arbitrarily defines, regulates, and limits in scope of meaning the vital contours of our lives, and the lives of our children and our children's children" (reprinted, New York, 1969, p. 30).

Some criticism of Wright's Bigger Thomas has claimed that the almost subhuman nature of the character detracts from the realism of the work. But Wright's point is in the caricature, not only of Bigger, but of the whole black and white cultural context operative in the novel. The critics were thinking within the very plane of consciousness Wright wished to destroy. They believed in the monster Bigger, because the myth, as critical studies by Ellison and Baldwin have pointed out, was firmly lodged in their minds. The pathos of the situation, Wright suggested in his continuation of *Black Boy* that is reprinted as "The Man Who Went to Chicago" in *Eight Men* (New York, 1969), was in the sordid cultural objectives of white America. The Negro "is doomed to live in isolation, while those who condemn him seek the basest goals of any people on the face of the earth. Perhaps it would be possible for the Negro to become reconciled to his plight if he could be made to believe that his sufferings were for some remote, high sacrificial end; but sharing the culture that condemns him, and seeing that a lust for trash is what blinds the nation to his claims, is what sets storms to rolling in his soul" (p. 181).

Like the great American novelists who tried to break through the vain-

glory of American self-deception and to bring Americans to a self-knowledge on the basis of which something genuinely constructive might grow,
Wright pleaded,

> We black folk, our history and our present being, are a mirror of all the
> manifold experiences of America. What we want, what we represent, what
> we endure is what America *is*. If we black folk perish, America will perish.
> . . .
> The differences between black folk and white folk are not blood or color,
> and the ties that bind us are deeper than those that separate us. . . .
> Look at us and know us and you will know yourselves, for *we* are *you*,
> looking back at you from the dark mirror of our lives! (*Black Voices*, p. 146)

Twelve Million Black Voices and *Black Boy* were efforts to bring to
America's attention the condition and history of its black people, but
while the two works represented successful sociological and artistic
achievement, the writing of them must also have brought to Wright a
private conviction of his personal separateness from the folk whose condition he had set forth. He had become a city man, an intellectual, and
from the time of the John Reed Club was more at ease with mixed racial
groups, or even with white friends, than with black groups. By 1945
Wright was sure of one thing: his loathing for the values of American
culture and its mirror-image, "The American Negro." And he had become
"The Spokesman for His Race," an unofficial office which had as its
function the task of reconciling the American black to the American way
of life.

Wright's books added very little to black folk history, a folk history
that had already been richly documented by both black and white writers.
His eyes had been for so long a time trained to see the horror in the lives
of black Americans that he could see little else. Wright's "colorblindness"
had begun very early in life, not when he went to live in Europe, as
Saunders Redding suggested in "The Alien Land of Richard Wright" (in
Soon, One Morning, ed. Herbert Hill, New York, 1969). When he came to
deal with Negroes in extended works of fiction he was a mature man, well
acquainted with the harsh side of Chicago's life, and an effective political
organizer and propagandist; while he could depict the intimate lives of
poor Negroes with convincing authority, he dealt with them as an outsider
uninterested in their folk history and folk identity.

In a revealing passage in *Black Boy*, Wright offered this speculation:
"Whenever I thought of the essential bleakness of black life in America,
I knew that Negroes had never been allowed to catch the full spirit of
Western civilization, that they lived somehow in it but not of it. And when
I brooded upon the cultural barrenness of black life, I wondered if clean,
positive tenderness, love, honor, loyalty, and the capacity to remember
were native with man. I asked myself if these human qualities were not

fostered, won, struggled and suffered for, preserved in ritual from one generation to another" (p. 33). Wright's remarks, as Ralph Ellison has noted, recall Henry James's complaint of the absence of ritual and tradition in American life as compared with European life. What James wished to emphasize, of course, was that the novelist who would lay hold of the forms and rituals of American life had to exercise a positively "grasping imagination." The unfortunate fact is that far from using his imagination to grasp at such forms and traditions as *did* exist in American black culture, particularly that of Southern Negroes, and thereby growing aware of their possibilities for his life and his art, Wright had allowed his limited recollection of his childhood years to fill the need of his large, immediate concern with political and social justice.

Joining the Communist Party, as was noted above, paradoxically satisfied primarily a *human* need with Wright, and when he left the Party it was with a sense of being drained of human warmth. In his essay, "I Tried to Be a Communist" (reprinted in *The God That Failed*, ed. Richard Crossman, New York, 1949), Wright spoke of how, after he had separated from the Party, he tried to rejoin his former comrades during their May Day parade and had been physically cast aside. It seemed to him that in all the mighty continent "the least known factor of living was the human heart, the least-sought goal of being was a way to live a human life." He wanted "to create a sense of the hunger for life that gnaws in us all, to keep alive in our hearts a sense of the inexpressibly human" (p. 162). Yet despite this need to be accepted in terms of the essentially human, Wright strove continually to be accepted in terms of the image which he had created and apart from the historical reality which had its great share in his making.

Images of burial, of living underground, crept into his writing of the early 1940's. In "The Man Who Went to Chicago" he described how he and three other Negroes worked as obscure creatures, scarcely tolerated in the basement corridors of a great hospital; "we occupied an underground position remembering that we must restrict ourselves . . . so that we would not mingle with white nurses, doctors, or visitors" (*Eight Men*, pp. 192–193). Wright's efforts to understand something of the experiments being carried out on the caged animals they tended were brusquely cut short. In their empty, degraded isolation the men turned violently on one another, upset the cages, and recaged the animals haphazardly, thereby destroying the validity of the records. The episode is a miniature allegory. It seemed to Wright that if the State were to guard itself from the men who truly threaten it, it would not club workers and union men, but would "ferret out those who no longer respond to the system under which they live." It would "fear those who do not dream of the prizes that the nation holds forth, for it is in them, though they may not know it, that a revolution has taken place and is biding its time to translate itself into a new and strange way of life" (*Eight Men*, pp. 191–192). In his story "The Man Who Lived Underground," first published in 1942 (*Accent*, II, Spring), the fugitive Negro rejoices in his perspective of life from the public sewer. In the version of the story published two years later, the sewer-dweller is murdered while trying to communicate his gospel of joy and love to the white police. The policeman who killed the underground man explains, "'You've got to shoot his kind. They'd wreck things.'" (Enlarged version in *Cross-section* 1944, ed. Edwin Seaver, reprinted in *Eight Men*.)

Although he attributes the noblest motives to his underground man, Wright was aware of other motives possible to the ignored and alienated. He drew attention to a remark by William James as to how fiendish a punishment it would be to live in society and yet remain absolutely unnoticed by all. If every person "acted as if we were non-existent things, a kind of rage and impotent despair would ere long well up in us" (Horace Cayton and St. Clair Drake, *Black Metropolis*, New York, 1945). This was more in tune with his personal reaction to being unseen and excluded as an individual person, apart from his race or politics, the reaction which he expressed in metaphors of alienation that were to be extensively developed by later black writers.

II

In her biography, *Richard Wright*, Constance Webb relates how the French Government plucked Wright up from his underground. In response to an unexpected invitation from the French Government (and after overcoming passport obstacles erected by the U.S. State Department), Wright found himself in May of 1946 in the very heart of expatriatedom, Gertrude Stein's apartment in Paris. He responded to his hostess's declaration of her debt to William James by quoting from memory James's words, "a man has as many social selves as there are individuals who recognize him and carry an image of him in their minds," and showing her his quotation from James about the hideousness of treating men as "non-existent things" in the copy of *Black Metropolis* which he presented to her. In Paris the literary vogue of existentialism was at its height, and, utterly miscomprehending Wright's intention in *Native Son*, French critics had seized upon Bigger Thomas as an existentialist hero and upon the author of *Black Boy* as an existentialist man. Thus Wright found a new visibility, and his friendships with Sartre, Simone de Beauvoir, and Camus must certainly have helped determine the direction of his next novel, *The Outsider*. He had not intended to settle permanently in Paris; but a return to New York and the depressing experience of being turned away from restaurants and hotels, of encountering hostility because of his marriage to a white woman, of having to conceal the fact that he, a Negro, owned his Greenwich Village home, of having to consider what his child would soon encounter when she entered school—all this must have seemed to him too grim an echo of the occasion in 1940 when he had revisited Natchez and had had to submit once more to the humiliating Jim Crow treatment. Having always fought against an "American Negro" identity in America, he found it easy to lay that particular burden down on what he described as the "free soil" of France. In an article, "I Choose Exile," which, according to Constance Webb, was written for *Ebony* magazine but rejected as too severe an attack against the United States, Wright pointed out that something was basically wrong with a nation that in its denial of rights to the Negro "could so cynically violate its own Constitution and democratic pretensions." Once more he insisted that the treatment of the Negro produced a dislocation of values which was essentially a destructive war waged by the nation against itself (Webb, p. 290).

Henry James and Mark Twain, writing out of their nineteenth-century expatriate experience, tried to persuade Americans of the errors of their ways—although the ending of *A Connecticut Yankee in King Arthur's Court* suggests that Twain despaired of ever effecting improvements in the damned human race. Hemingway and Henry Miller, instead of persuasion, tried to hold before the eyes of Western culture images of its violence and sterility and to communicate their personal transcendence of cultural problems. There is something of Miller's apocalyptic attitude in Wright's first novel written in Europe, *The Outsider* (New York, 1953). Like Miller, Wright had a sense of rebirth in his new life; and, like Miller again, Wright seemed to have come to the transcendentalist conclusion that one must remake one's self before undertaking to remake the lives of others. But Wright could never go the whole mystical way; he could never quite abandon, even while he looked back in anger, some hope for a rational solution to America's problems.

Although *The Outsider* has been frequently regarded as an existentialist novel and interesting parallels can be drawn between elements in it and in "existentialist" novels by writers from Dostoievski to Camus whose works were quite possibly in Wright's mind as he composed his novel, *The Outsider* bears at its deepest level the hallmark of Wright's compulsion to shape society in accordance with some ideal conception of social justice; there is no consideration of ontological solutions. Other "outsiders" would appear, a "tragic elite" as Wright was elsewhere describing them, to revolutionize the ways men thought, felt, and lived together. As with *Native Son*, *The Outsider* ends with wishful philosophizing and the author's *persona* shifts from the black Damon to the white D.A. Other shifts in the novel are interesting for the light they shed on widening divisions in Wright's mind. Early in the novel Cross Damon expresses his strong dislike for all men of religion because "they could take for granted an interpretation of the world that his sense of life made impossible" (p. 123).

Unlike the priest who is "a kind of dressed-up savage intimidated by totems and taboos," Cross Damon, as existentialist, had to make his own way alone and bear the brunt of the consequences without hope of grace or mercy. By the end of the novel, however, Cross has reached a position that has strongly Emersonian overtones:

> Religion was once an affair of the church; it is now in the streets in each man's heart. Once there were priests; now every man's a priest. Religion's a compulsion, and a compulsion seems to spring from something total in us, catching up in its mighty grip all the other forces of life—sex, intellect, will, physical strength, and carrying them forward toward—what goals? We wish we knew. (pp. 359–360)

Early in the novel civilization "is simply man's frantic effort to hide himself from himself" (p. 135). Towards the end of the novel "civilization" has been limited to the creation of the industrial-capitalist leaders who "preach to their rats that their nation is the best of any of the nations, and that as rats they are the best of all possible rats" (p. 361). But the day will come when "outsiders," "who seek to change the consciousness of the rats who are being controlled," will prove to be the real enemy of the system by altering the public consciousness (p. 362). Dialectically, Wright was the same outsider he had always been, only now he was much farther removed from the humanity he proposed to save and his aesthetic imagination had lost its grasp upon American life. Depending on newspaper clippings, Freudian, Marxist, and existentialist "theories," and old memories, Wright's fictional treatment of the American scene spluttered out in *Savage Holiday* and *The Long Dream*. He had turned in fascination to Europe, Africa, and Asia, and it was in recording the illuminations which his visits to these foreign lands brought him that his imagination finally fastened upon America.

III

In June, 1953, Wright began his visit to the Gold Coast, a visit that was to take him to its ports, villages, and high rain forests, and was to result in hundreds of interviews with natives of all degree. Typically, he had fortified himself with political theory about the emergent nations, with anticolonial statistics, and with "black power" concepts to explain the "tragic elite" who were to lead the new nations on a new course. Typically, he deliberately examined his reactions for evidence of any personal sense of racial identity with the African natives and, like a good Marxist, found none. As his visit progressed, Wright kept a record which became *Black Power, A Record of Reactions in a Land of Pathos* (New York, 1954). In this work, more than ever before, Wright displayed a split which had been present in his work from the beginning—the divergence between the intellectual theories he felt compelled to state and the truth of his acute perception of human experience. *Black Power* from time to time records Wright's political theories and concludes with a fiery letter to Kwame Nkrumah, Wright's Gold Coast host, exhorting him to sweep away tribal cobwebs, to assume dictatorial powers, and through stern social discipline forge the new industrial state. "African life must be militarized," not for war, but against its own tribal heritage and the possible return of colonial powers (p. 347). Contradicting this fierce call to arms at the opening and at the closing of the book, are the mystical utterances of Walt Whitman breathing peace and acceptance: "Not till the sun excludes you do I exclude you," and "Turn back unto this day, and make yourself afresh." It is the spirit of Whitman which informs the essential theme of the book, for *Black Power* records Wright's gradual discovery and absorption in the role which the spirit plays in African life and—since Africa comes to operate for Wright as a metaphor—in all life.

The subtitle of the book, *"A Record of Reactions,"* describes accurately how the book was composed. When he submitted the manuscript to prospective publishers, Wright encountered various objections from them in regard to the content of the book—to the effect that he was too harsh on the British and on the Dutch, that he was not making sufficiently clear his separation from Communism, that the book was too long. In his letter to his agent explaining why he could not cut portions out of the book, Wright made this significant disclosure:

> The trouble with writing a book like this is that the reality of a given phase of the life does not come upon one all at once; for instance, the religion of the people came to me in bits, each bit extending my comprehension of the reality a little more . . . by going from spot to spot, talking to this person and that one, I had to gather this reality as it seeped into me through the personalities of others. (Webb, p. 337)

Even as on one level of his consciousness Wright was comprehending the spiritual reality of African life, on another level he was still thinking in terms of his political rhetoric. His early impressions led him to believe that Nkrumah had "fused tribalism with modern politics," since the natives swore an oath to Nkrumah (p. 59). The British, he decided early on, had slowly destroyed the African's faith in his own religion and customs (like American slaveholders?), "Thereby creating millions of psychologically detribalized Africans living uneasily and frustratedly in two worlds and really believing in neither of them" (p. 65). Religious meetings were "a mixture of tribal ancestor worship, Protestantism, Catholicism—all blended together and directed toward modern political aims" (p. 89). Since Wright had decided on new political goals for the Africans, he "saw" that their old patterns of life were being transmuted to the new. "Mass nationalist movements were, indeed, a new kind of religion. They were politics *plus!*" (p. 56).

As his visit progressed, however, he sensed that the changes were only apparent. The Westerners (i.e. European and Americans whites) and the Africans, he began to see, lived in worlds that are based on assumptions that seem fantastic to one another. Each comes to accept, from necessity, the "false" assumptions of the other and thereby creates a new reality. "Men create the world in which they live by the methods they use to interpret it." (p. 118). As for the African, "the African's whole life was a kind of religious dream" (p. 124). Wright described the African's life as rational, but only in terms of his assumptions—such assumptions as the control of the living by the dead. Compared to a pagan funeral, it seemed to Wright that a Christian funeral was a mockery of religious conviction. Like Twain observing the work of the missionaries in the Sandwich Islands and later in the Holy Land, Wright reported himself as "stunned" at their perverse folly. "They had, prodded by their own neurotic drives, waded in and wrecked an entire philosophy of existence of a people" (p. 152). Unquestionably Wright had in mind what had happened to the Africans who had been torn out of this culture centuries earlier and shipped to America—a thought which becomes explicit when he visits Cape Coast Castle where slaves had been held prior to shipment to the West. Bit by bit, as he said in his letter to his agent, he grew aware of the spiritual dimension of African life; bit by bit, and against all his intellectual conditioning, he saw that he could respect this African consciousness and feel honored to claim it as his heritage.

But this link between African culture and that of the American Negroes comes in the final chapter of the book when Wright's record of reactions had finally overcome his a priori assumptions—and even then the record was not strong enough to prevent his resurgence as tactician in the letter to Nkrumah saved for a conclusion with its manifesto: "Our people must be made to walk, forced draft, into the twentieth century!" (p. 345). On the level of his felt perceptions, the more Wright talked with Africans the more he came to admit that the Africans would indeed have lost if they sacrificed their tribal gods and their magic world to achieve a Chicago or a Detroit. Capturing superbly the essence of the matter, Wright asked, "Would an African, a hundred years from now, after he has been trapped in the labyrinths of industrialization, be able to say when he is dying, when he is on the verge of going to meet his long dead ancestors, those traditional, mysterious words:

> *I'm dying*
> *I'm dying*
> *Something big is happening to me . . . ?*" (p. 227)

It is Wright, the fervid exponent of industrialization, who declares that the gold can be replaced, the timber grown again, but that the mental habits and the vision cannot be restored to a people. "Nothing can give back to them that pride in themselves, that capacity to make decisions, that organic view of existence that made them want to live on this earth and derive from that living a sweet even if sad meaning" (p. 153). Like the writers in America's transcendentalist tradition, Wright saw, as a result of his African reactions, that religion was not an affair of institutions but of life lived. "Africa must and will become a religion, not a religion contained within the four walls of a church, but a religion lived and fought out beneath the glare of a pitiless tropic sun" (p. 159).

In a statement that splendidly amplifies the quotation from Whitman which he used as one of the epigraphs to *Black Power*, Wright expressed a conception of human oneness through the metaphor of Africa. Africa is one's self, one's life, "one's ultimate sense of things" (p. 158). A Western man might be repelled by what he saw in Africa and wish to destroy or to exploit it as something alien to his nature, but in truth it is himself he sees. If he sees it as horrible, it is still the "image of himself which his own soul projected out upon this Africa" (p. 158). Unlike the corrupted cultures of Europe and America—corrupted by the very rationalism and industrialism which Wright is supposed to champion—Africa, Wright found, held an attitude toward life that sprang from "a natural and poetic grasp of existence and all the emotional implications that such an attitude carries" (p. 226). He took exception to the inverted cultural values which disparaged African rites as regrettable "survivals," maintaining that such survivals are a retention of basic and primal attitudes toward life. Obliquely including himself in this African life, Wright pointed out that the social scientist would discover that the same primal attitudes exist among other people. "After all, what are the basic promptings of artists, poets, and actors but primal attitudes consciously held?" (p. 267).

Primal attitudes extended yet further. The man who came to Africa to study and preach a rational modernism insisted that "there is no reason why an African or a person of African descent—in America, England, or France—should abandon his primal outlook upon life if he finds that no other way of life is available, or if he is intimidated in his attempt to grasp the new way" (p. 266). This was a striking concession for Wright to make, and it measures how far he had gone towards accepting his own nature, the racial aspect of his identity, and the role of irrational factors in determining the forms of human culture. Transvaluing his values as he went along, Wright embraced the poetry and mystery of African life and its superb acceptance of its human nature, as distinct from Western life which sought so strenuously to deny primal qualities, to destroy those who could not adjust to its frantic patterns, and, in particular, sought to

rob black Americans of their history by depicting Africa as a dark continent peopled by savages. Africans had not known race consciousness,
Wright pointed out. It was brought "into our lives. It came from without"
(p. 199). Wright's profound discovery, as it emerged in his book, was the
nature of black power: its acceptance of the world as spirit.

The Color Curtain (Cleveland, 1956), based on Wright's visit to the
conference of African and Asian nations held at Bandung, Indonesia, in
1955, carried further Wright's understanding of the emotional factor in
national politics. Logic, he noted, could not solve problems "whose solutions come not by thinking but by living" (p. 55). The ex-Communist
Richard Wright, who still considered himself a Marxist dedicated to
rational plans for organizing society without regard for such outmoded
concepts as race and religion, had to accommodate himself to the Richard
Wright who had to admit that the theoretical political factors which pre-
vailed in Western government were not at all what held the minds of the
Asians and Africans meeting at Bandung. The nonfiction books *Black
Power, The Color Curtain,* and *Pagan Spain* demonstrate clearly that despite
the uninspired novels he was turning out in the 1950's Wright was still
possessed of a gifted imagination and talent. Settings are often given with
great effectiveness, but above all Wright repeatedly gives his information
and insights through skillfully arranged dialogues or through some dramatic encounter. Wright conveys his sense of revelation, as, for example,
on the occasion of Sukarno's address at the opening of the conference. It
came as a revelation to Wright that Sukarno was appealing to race and
religion. These factors, so disdained in the intellectual politics Wright had
absorbed in America and so cried down by the existentialist *monde* of Paris
were the only realities understood by the representatives at Bandung.
"And, as I sat listening," Wright records, "I began to sense a deep and
organic relation here in Bandung between race and religion, *two of the most
powerful and irrational forces in human nature*" (p. 140). The fundamental
reversal of perspective which was taking place in Wright's understanding
of human consciousness made the old concepts by which he had controlled
his fiction obsolete.

The final proof of his new way of perceiving and responding to experience came with his study of Spain. Early in *Pagan Spain* (New York, 1957),
Wright contrives a scene with a Spanish girl wherein he produces a *non
serviam* worthy of Stephen Daedalus: "'I have no religion in the formal
sense of the word. . . . I have no race except that which is forced upon
me. I have no country except that to which I'm obliged to belong. I have
no traditions. I'm free. I have only the future'" (p. 17). It is appropriate
that a young man's book should end with such a declaration; it is equally
appropriate that a mature man's book should begin with it, and the rest
of *Pagan Spain* will demonstrate Wright's responsiveness to the deep degree
to which his perceptions are affected by his religious nature, his sense of

race, his being an American, and the tensions or harmonies he feels as a man conditioned by the traditions of Western culture.

Using a technique similar to that he had employed in his novel *Lawd Today*, Wright inserted throughout *Pagan Spain* selections from the Falangist political catechism in order to dramatize the ridiculous discrepancy between the Falangist concept of the world and the actual concepts upon which life was lived in Spain. Perhaps there was an unintended irony in that much of the Falangist catechism was premised upon the kind of logic and authoritarianism which had characterized Wright's advice to Nkrumah, and his method of catechizing and theorizing in parts of *White Man, Listen!* (New York, 1957). The profound difference that Wright saw between Spain and the rest of the Western world forced him to turn again to the examination of what being Western meant. He finally decided that the difference was "the area of the *secular* that Western man, through the centuries and at tragic cost, had won and wrung from his own religious and irrational consciousness" (p. 192). This would seem to be a positive achievement; but the fact is that man's "religious and irrational" drives continue to force their way through whatever rational structures are grafted upon them. Day by day as the three months of his first visit to Spain passed, Wright observed how the organs of official life, the Falange, the State, the Army, the Church, all "were drawing their vitality from some deep irrational core that made up the heart of Spanish reality" (p. 192). As Wright progresses through Spain, the implications gather that what is true of Spain is true of the "Western" world, and especially of America.

As the title of his book indicates, Wright found Spain to be a pagan country, its primitive nature thinly concealed by modern dress. The statue of the Virgin at Monserrat was, to Wright, as much a fetish as any he had seen in the Gold Coast. Reliquaries in the cathedrals appalled him; it was the sacred ancestral bones of the Ashanti dead all over again. Aristocratic Spaniards and peasants both communicated to Wright their sense of Spain as a mystical entity which transcended distinctions of province, or wealth, or class. Like Hemingway, Wright saw primitive religious forces emerging in strange guises. The bull-fight moved him as a religious ceremony, as a kind of primitive ritual with the matador as priest: "*Death must serve as a secular baptism of emotion to wash the heart clean of its illegal dirt.* . . . And the matador in his bright suit of lights was a kind of lay priest offering up the mass for thirty thousand guilty penitents" (p. 99). The hooded penitents in the Seville Easter procession radiated the *juju* of Africa. With the persecuted Protestant minority, he felt an immediate identification.

As with *Black Power*, bit by bit the meaning of his experiences seeped into his record, and Wright betrayed how far he was from having escaped the nets of his American culture. A bull-fight that he witnessed in a small town outside Madrid brought an image of an American lynching searingly to his mind. After the bull had been killed, the crowd rushed into the bullring and tore pieces from the slain animal, seizing first its testicles. "They went straight to the real object on that dead bull's body that the bull had symbolized for them and poured out the hate and frustration and bewilderment of their troubled and confused consciousness" (p. 135). It must have been the image in Wright's mind of his childhood friend, Bob Robinson, who had been sexually mutilated and lynched (Webb, p. 64). A photograph of a lynched Negro in *Black Voices* showed bits of the body torn away; the image had appeared several times in Wright's fiction and was to appear again in *The Long Dream*. The hooded penitents in Seville brought an image of the Ku Kluxers horribly before his eyes. "Those hooded penitents had been protecting the Virgin, and in the Old American South hooded Ku Kluxers had been protecting 'the purity of white womanhood'" (p. 237). The persecution of the Protestants led Wright to reflect that he had been born a Protestant, and that he had felt toward the Protestants as the Protestants in Spain felt towards the Catholics. "What I felt most keenly in Spain was the needless, unnatural, and utterly barbarous nature of the psychological suffering that the Spanish Protestant was doomed to undergo at the hands of the Church and State officials and his Catholic neighbors. For that exquisite suffering and emotional torture, I have a spontaneous and profound sympathy." Then Wright brought forth his deepest response:

> I am an American Negro with a background of psychological suffering stemming from my previous position as a member of a persecuted racial minority. What drew my attention to the emotional plight of the Protestants in Spain was the undeniable and uncanny psychological affinities that they held in common with American Negroes, Jews, and other oppressed minorities. It is another proof, if any is needed today, that the main and decisive aspects of human reactions are conditioned and are not inborn.
>
> Indeed the quickest and simplest way to introduce this subject to the reader would be to tell him that I shall describe some of the facets of psychological problems and the emotional sufferings of a group of *white Negroes* whom I met in Spain, the assumption being that Negroes are Negroes because they are *treated* as Negroes (p. 138).

This was the very passion and idea which had created *Black Boy* and *Native Son*. The perspective alone was different in that Wright's vision had been enlarged to include all oppressed minorities in the category "Negro," and "America's Metaphor" had become the metaphor of humanity itself.

Plato, in designing his ideal republic, decided that he had to exclude the poets, for these men would bring their myths and their myth-making power with them and set men to dreaming of how the republic might be changed. Such a decision must have been difficult for Plato, the poet and myth-maker. Wright had always had a similar difficulty. His intelligence demanded societies designed on rational lines and a modern, industrial state. But when his felt perceptions of life took over, he became the spokesman of the oppressed minority of dreamers—as when Sarah, in his early story, "Long Black Song," while awaiting the arrival of the white men who are to destroy her husband, muses—"Somehow, men, black men and white men, land and houses, green cornfields and grey skies, gladness and dreams, were all a part of that which made life good. Yes, somehow, they were linked, like the spokes in a spinning wheel."

Native Son: The Personal, Social, and Political Background

by Keneth Kinnamon

In the fiction of social protest, of which Richard Wright's *Native Son* (1940) is surely an outstanding example, the *donnée* has an interest almost equal to that of the artistic treatment. If the concern is with the relation of literature to society, one must not be content merely to grant the novelist his materials and concentrate on his fictional technique; one must examine carefully the factual substance on which the novelist's imagination operates. If this task is preliminary to literary criticism in the strict sense, it is necessary if that criticism is not to be impressionistic or narrowly aesthetic. An examination of Wright's fiction reveals that customarily he drew from personal experience and observation, the condition of the society about him, and his theoretic concerns. In *Native Son,* these elements may be identified respectively as certain episodes in Wright's life in Mississippi and Chicago, the social circumstances of urban Negroes and the Nixon trial, and Communist ideology.

Charles I. Glicksberg is speaking hyperbolically when he asserts that "Richard Wright is Bigger Thomas—one part of him anyway. Bigger Thomas is what Richard Wright, had circumstances worked out differently, might have become."[1] Nevertheless, there is some truth in the assertion, and not merely in the general sense, according to the formulation of James Baldwin, that "no American Negro exists who does not have his private Bigger Thomas living in the skull."[2] The general similarities between Wright at the age of twenty and the fictional protagonist of *Native Son* are obvious enough: both are Mississippi-born Negroes who migrated to Chicago; both live with their mother in the worst slums of the Black Belt of that city; both are motivated by fear and hatred; both are rebellious by temperament; both could explode into violence.

"*Native Son:* The Personal, Social, and Political Background" by Keneth Kinnamon. From *Phylon: The Atlanta University Review of Race and Culture,* 30 (Spring 1969) 66–72. Copyright © 1969 by *Phylon.* Reprinted by permission of *Phylon.*

[1]"The Furies in Negro Fiction," *The Western Review,* XIII (Winter, 1949), 110.

[2]"Many Thousands Gone," *Partisan Review,* XVIII (November-December, 1951), 678. This essay is reprinted in James Baldwin, *Notes of a Native Son* (Boston, 1955), pp. 24–45.

More specific likenesses were recovered from Wright's subconscious by Dr. Frederic Wertham, the eminent psychiatrist. When Wright, as a boy of fifteen, worked for a white family named Bibbs in Jackson, Mississippi, his duties included chopping wood, carrying coal, and tending the fire. The pretty young daughter of the family generally was kind to him within the limits of Southern custom, but when, on one occasion, he chanced upon her in her bedroom while she was dressing, "she reprimanded him and told him to knock before entering a room." The diffident and fearful young Negro handyman, the amiable white girl, the sexually significant situation—these elements, transmuted, found their way into *Native Son*. The name of the wealthy white family for whom Bigger works in the novel, *Dalton,* may itself bear an unconscious symbolic import. In the Chicago hospital where he worked as an orderly in 1931, Wright learned of Daltonism.[3] In their fashion, the Daltons in the novel strive toward color blindness, though they fall tragically short of achieving it.

Essentially, Bigger Thomas is a conscious composite portrait of a number of individual Negroes Wright had observed over the years. In that remarkable exercise in self-examination, *How "Bigger" Was Born*, Wright sketched five such Bigger prototypes he had known in the South. All of them were rebellious defiers of the jim crow order, and all of them suffered for their insurgency: "They were shot, hanged, maimed, lynched, and generally hounded until they were either dead or their spirits broken." In Chicago, especially when Wright worked at the South Side Boys' Club in the middle thirties, he observed other examples of the Bigger Thomas type—fearful, restless, moody, frustrated, alienated, violent youths struggling for survival in the urban jungle.[4]

The slum conditions of the South Side so vividly portrayed in *Native Son* had been the daily reality of a decade in Wright's life (1927–1937). He had lived in a cramped and dirty flat with his aunt, mother, and brother. He had visited hundreds of similar dwellings while working as an insurance agent.[5] The details of the Chicago environment in the novel

[3]Waldemar Kaempffert, "Science in Review: An Author's Mind Plumbed for the Unconscious Factor in the Creation of a Novel," *The New York Times*, September 24, 1944, Sec. 4, p. 11. This article asserts that the Bibbs girl loaned Wright money for his junior high school graduation suit, but Wright's autobiographical *Black Boy: A Record of Childhood and Youth* (New York, 1945) says that her mother did so (p. 156). Dr. Wertham comments briefly on his experiment with Wright in "The Dreams That Heal," his introduction to *The World Within: Fiction Illuminating Neuroses of Our Time*, ed. by Mary Louise Aswell (New York, 1947), xxi.

[4]*How "Bigger" Was Born* (New York, 1940), pp. 6, 28–29. See also Wright's pamphlet *The Negro and Parkway Community House* (Chicago, 1941).

[5]The main source for this period of the novelist's life is Richard Wright, "Early Days in Chicago," *Cross-Section 1945,* ed. by Edwin Seaver (New York, 1945), pp. 306–42. This essay is reprinted, with minor changes, as "The Man Who Went to Chicago" in Wright's *Eight Men* (Cleveland and New York, 1961), pp. 210–50.

have a verisimilitude that is almost photographic. The "Ernie's Kitchen Shack" of the novel, located at Forty-Seventh Street and Indiana Avenue, for example, is a slight disguise for an actual restaurant called "The Chicken Shack," 4647 Indiana Avenue, of which one Ernie Henderson was owner.[6] Similar documentary accuracy is observed throughout the book.

Aside from wide personal experience, moreover, Wright was becoming increasingly more interested in sociology at the time he was writing *Native Son*. The caseworker for the Wright family in Chicago was Mary Wirth, the wife of Louis Wirth of the University of Chicago, who was in the process of conducting an enormous research project on the urban ecology of the city. In Wirth's office Wright examined the files of the project and met Horace R. Cayton, a Negro research associate who was himself to become a distinguished sociologist and a warm friend of the novelist.[7] Sociological concepts, quite as much as Marxist theories, are apparent in the novel, especially in the final part.

In New York, too, where he moved in May, 1937, Wright became intimately acquainted with the conditions of Negro ghettos. Not only did he live for almost a year in Harlem, but as a participant in the Federal Writer's project of New York City, he wrote the Harlem sections of *New York Panorama* (1938) and *New York City Guide* (1939), two volumes in the American Guide Series. He also served during the last five months of 1937 as chief Harlem correspondent for the *Daily Worker*, contributing forty signed articles as well as numerous brief, unsigned dispatches. A fourth of the signed articles deal with hardship of life in Harlem. In one of these Wright reported on a hearing conducted by the New York State Temporary Commission on Conditions Among Urban Negroes. The questioning of Henry Dalton about his real estate policies by Boris Max in the last part of *Native Son* draws directly from this article.[8]

As if to confirm Wright's notions about the Bigger type and society's attitude toward him, when the writer "was halfway through the first draft of *Native Son* a case paralleling Bigger's flared forth in the newspapers of Chicago."[9] This case involved Robert Nixon and Earl Hicks, two young

---

[6]Advertisement, *The Chicago Defender*, January 3, 1933, p. 3.

[7]Horace R. Cayton, *Long Old Road* (New York, 1965), pp. 247–48. Cayton gives further details in a symposium on Wright included in *Anger and Beyond: The Negro Writer in the United States*, ed. by Herbert Hill (New York, 1966), pp. 196–97. Having written the finest fictional portrayal of the South Side, Wright was the inevitable choice of Cayton and St. Clair Drake to write the introduction to their classic sociological treatise on the area, *Black Metropolis* (1945).

[8]"Gouging, Landlord Discrimination Against Negroes Bared at *Hearing*," *Daily Worker*, December 15, 1937, p. 6. Cf. *Native Son* (New York, 1940), pp. 276–79. Parenthetical page references in the text are to this edition.

[9]*How "Bigger" Was Born*, pp. 30–31.

Negroes with backgrounds similar to that of Bigger. According to the first
of a long series of highly sensationalistic articles in the *Chicago Tribune*, on
May 27, 1938, Mrs. Florence Johnson "was beaten to death with a brick
by a colored sex criminal . . . in her apartment."[10] Nixon and Hicks were
arrested soon after and charged with the crime. Though no evidence of
rape was adduced, the *Tribune* from the beginning called the murder a sex
crime and exploited fully this apparently quite false accusation.[11] Nixon
was chosen for special attack, perhaps because he was darker and ostensibly less remorseful than Hicks. He was referred to repeatedly as the
"brick moron," "rapist slayer," "jungle beast," "sex moron," and the like.
His race was constantly emphasized. The casual reader of *Native Son* might
consider the newspaper article which Bigger reads in his cell early in Book
Three greatly exaggerated in its racism;[12] in point of fact, it is an adaptation of an actual piece in the *Tribune*. Although Nixon came from "a pretty
little town in the old south—Tallulah, La.," the *Tribune* reporter wrote,
"there is nothing pretty about Robert Nixon. He has none of the charm
of speech or manner that is characteristic of so many southern darkies."
The reporter proceeded to explain:

> That charm is a mark of civilization, and so far as manner and appear-
> ance go, civilization has left Nixon practically untouched. His hunched
> shoulders and long, sinewy arms that dangle almost to his knees; his out-
> thrust head and catlike tread all suggest the animal.
>
> He is very black—almost pure Negro. His physical characteristics sug-
> gest an earlier link in the species.
>
> Mississippi river steamboat mates, who hire and fire roustabouts by the
> hundreds, would classify Nixon as a jungle Negro. They would hire him
> only if they were sorely in need of rousters. And they would keep close
> watch on him. This type is known to be ferocious and relentless in a fight.
> Though docile enough under ordinary circumstances, they are easily
> aroused. And when this happens the veneer of civilization disappears. . . .
> . . . .
> As he talked yesterday Nixon's dull eyes lighted only when he spoke of
> food. They feed him well at the detective bureau, he said. He liked coconut
> pie and strawberry pop. It was after a generous meal of these refreshments

[10]"Sift Mass of Clews for Sex Killer," *Chicago Daily Tribune*, May 28, 1938, p. 1.

[11]David H. Orro, a Negro reporter, wrote that police stated that Nixon and Hicks were
"bent upon committing a sex crime," but that "authorities were unable to state whether the
woman had been sexually attacked." "'Somebody Did It,' So 2 Youths Who 'Might Have
Done It' Are Arrested." *The Chicago Defender*, May 28, 1938, p. 24. The date as printed is
an error; this is actually the issue of June 4, 1938.

[12]Hubert Creekmore, the white novelist from Mississippi, charged that "the press is shown
as chiefly concerned with unsubtle inspiration of hatred and intolerance. The manner and
content of these newspapers exceed belief. Again Mr. Wright makes them present incidents
and ideas which reflect his own mind rather than an editor's mind or the public mind."
"Social Factors in *Native Son*," *The University of Kansas City Review*, VIII (Winter, 1941), 140.

that he confessed two of his most shocking murders. . . . These killings were accomplished with a ferocity suggestive of Poe's "Murders in the Rue Morgue"—the work of a giant ape.

Again the comparison was drawn between Nixon and the jungle man. Last week when he was taken . . . to demonstrate how he had slain Mrs. Florence Johnson, mother of two small children, a crowd gathered and there were cries of: "Lynch him! Kill him!"

Nixon backed against a wall and bared his teeth. He showed no fear, just as he has shown no remorse.[13]

The article concludes by quoting from a letter from the Louisiana sheriff of Nixon's home parish: "It has been demonstrated here that nothing can be done with Robert Nixon. Only death can cure him."[14]

This remedy was applied almost exactly a year after the murder of Mrs. Johnson. During this year the case became something of a local *cause célèbre*. The Chicago police quickly accused Nixon of a number of other murders, and the Los Angeles police did the same.[15] Early in the case the International Labor Defense became interested, providing Attorney Joseph Roth, white, to aid Negro lawyers in representing Nixon and Hicks.[16] Public emotion ran very high, stimulated by the lurid treatment given the case by the *Tribune*. A week after the crime the Illinois House of Representatives "approved a bill sponsored by State's Attorney Thomas J. Courtney of Cook County to curb moronic attacks." In debate on this bill, Nixon was mentioned prominently.[17] A complicated series of confessions and repudiations, charges of police brutality, and dramatic outbursts of violence[18] preceded the trial, which began in late July under Judge John C. Lewe after attorneys for the youths won a change of venue because of the prejudiced atmosphere.[19] The trial itself, despite some apparently con-

---

[13]Charles Leavelle, "Brick Slayer Is Likened to Jungle Beast," *Chicago Sunday Tribune*, June 5, 1938, Sec. 1, p. 6. Cf. *Native Son*, pp. 238–40.

[14]Leavelle, *op. cit.*

[15]"Science Traps Moron in 5 Murders," *Chicago Daily Tribune*, June 3, 1938, p. 1.

[16]"Robert Nixon Attacked By Irate Hubby," *The Chicago Defender*, June 11, 1938, p. 6.

[17]"Pass Courtney Moron Bill In Heated Debate," *Chicago Daily Tribune*, June 8, 1938, p. 1.

[18]When Nixon and Hicks were taken by police to the scene of the crime, a hostile, lynch-minded mob required police control. Then "a dramatic incident occurred just as the police were about to leave with their prisoners. Elmer Johnson, the bereaved husband . . . drove up with his two children, and his brother-in-law, John Whitton. . . . Johnson said nothing, but Whitton clenched his fists and shouted, 'I'd like to get at them.' Police hurried the prisoners away." "2 Accuse Each Other in Brick Killing." *Chicago Daily Tribune*, May 30, 1938, p. 2. Perhaps Elmer Johnson was merely waiting for a better opportunity, for, at the inquest he attacked the handcuffed Nixon savagely before police intervened. Shortly after this attack, Nixon attempted to retaliate. Johnson explained his intention to a reporter: "I hoped to hit him hard enough so his head would fly back and his skull would be cracked against the wall." "Beats Slayer of Wife; Own Life Menaced," *Chicago Daily Tribune*, June 8, 1938, p. 3. See also "Robert Nixon Attacked By Irate Hubby," p. 6. Cf. the incident in *Native Son* in which Bigger is attacked at the inquest (p. 265).

[19]"Brick Slayers' Trial Assigned To Judge Lewe," *Chicago Daily Tribune*, July 19, 1938, p. 6.

tradictory evidence, was very brief, lasting just over a week before the jury reached a verdict of guilty on the first ballot after only one hour of deliberation. The death sentence was imposed on Nixon.[20] By this time, however, leaders of the Chicago Negro community were thoroughly aroused. The National Negro Congress, which had been providing legal representation for the two youths, continued its efforts on their behalf, including the sponsorship of a fund-raising dance.[21] Prominent Chicago Negro clergymen joined the struggle to save Nixon.[22] With the aid of such support, together with some irregularities in the evidence presented by the state, Nixon was able to win several stays of execution, but his struggle ceased in the Cook County electric chair three minutes after midnight, June 16, 1939.[23]

By the time Nixon was finally executed, Wright had completed *Native Son*. He did not need to wait the outcome of legal appeals and maneuvers to know the "Fate" (his title for Book Three of the novel) of Robert Nixon or of his fictional counterpart, Bigger Thomas. In any event, Wright's use of the Nixon case was that of a novelist, not that of an historian or journalist. He adapted whatever seemed useful to his fictional purpose, changing details as he wished. He followed the facts of the case fairly closely in his account of the newspaper treatment of Bigger Thomas. The inquest and trial scenes, also, resemble in certain respects their factual prototypes. Among the more significant distortions of Nixon material are those relating to Wright's polemic intent as a communist writer.

In the Nixon case the role of the International Labor Defense and its representative, Attorney Joseph Roth, was small and initiatory; it was soon replaced by the National Negro Congress. In *Native Son*, however, Wright magnifies the role of this organization (changing its name slightly to "Labor Defenders") and its radical Jewish attorney, Boris Max, who is made Bigger's sole lawyer. Another change illustrates even more vividly Wright's shift of emphasis in transforming fact to fiction. One of the murders for which Chicago police elicited confessions, later repudiated, from Nixon was that of a Mrs. Florence Thompson Castle a year before the murder of Mrs. Johnson. According to a newspaper report, in his account of this crime Nixon "told of picking up a lipstick belonging to Mrs. Castle and scrawling on the dresser mirror these words: 'Black Legion.' "[24] When Bigger in the novel wishes to divert suspicion to an

---

[20]"Guilty of Brick Murder; Gets Death In Chair," *Chicago Daily Tribune*, August 5, 1938, p. 2.

[21]"Dance Profits To Aid Nixon, Hicks," *The Chicago Defender*, August 20, 1938, p. 5.

[22]"Nixon Plea To Be Given To Governor," *The Chicago Defender*, October 15, 1938, p. 6.

[23]"Nixon Dies In Chair," *The Chicago Defender*, June 17, 1939, pp. 1–2.

[24]"Brick Moron Tells of Killing 2 Women," *Chicago Sunday Tribune*, May 29, 1938, p. 5.

extremist group, he selects leftists rather than fascists, signing the kidnap note to the Daltons in such a way as to implicate the Communist Party (p. 151).

As a fervent party member, Wright maintained a thoroughly communistic point of view in *Native Son*. The courtroom arguments of Max in the final section, of course, are patently leftist. He equates racial and class prejudice, both being based on economic exploitation (pp. 326–27). He repeats the basic party concept of the times regarding the collective status of Negroes in America: "Taken collectively, they are not simply twelve million people; in reality they constitute a separate nation, stunted, stripped, and held captive *within* this nation, devoid of political, social, economic, and property rights" (p. 333). He discerns in Bigger a revolutionary potentiality (pp. 337–38). Not all of Max's courtroom speech reflects so directly communist doctrine, but none of it is inconsistent with the party line on racial matters.

Communist material is obvious enough in the final section of the novel, but it is often implicit elsewhere. Early in Book One, for example, while Bigger and his friend Gus are loafing on the street they amuse themselves by "playing white," assuming roles of the white power structure. The youths are themselves nonpolitical, but the white activities Wright has them imitate are precisely those which he and other communists viewed as typical of the American capitalist system: warfare, high finance, and political racism (pp. 15–17). For Bigger's mother, religion is clearly presented as an opiate, as it is generally for the Negro masses. To accept the consolations of Christianity, Bigger comes to recognize, would be to lay "his head upon a pillow of humility and [give] up his hope of living in the world" (p. 215). The first movie that Bigger and a friend see in Book One, *The Gay Woman*, presents a Hollywood stereotype of a communist as a wild-eyed bomb thrower (pp. 27–28). Indeed, prejudice against communists is frequently depicted in the novel. On the other hand, party members Jan Erlone[25] and Boris Max are idealized portraits of selfless, noble, dedicated strivers toward the new social order.

These, then, are the main elements that went into the composition of *Native Son*. Much of the powerful sense of immediacy felt by the reader of the novel derives from the genesis of the work in the author's personal experience and observation. Though one may have reservations about the validity of Wright's communist ideological orientation, it provided him with an intellectual instrument with which to render meaningful the personal and social materials of the novel. The nice balance of subjective and

[25]Wright may have taken the first name from that of Jan Wittenber, a white friend who was active in the Chicago John Reed Club and served as secretary of the Illinois State International Labor Defense.

objective elements in *Native Son* prevents the work from becoming either a purely personal scream of pain, on the one hand, or a mere ideological tract on the other. Whatever verdict one may finally reach about the artistic merits of *Native Son*, one must take into account the personal, social, and political materials out of which it grew.

Wright's Invisible Native Son

by Donald B. Gibson

The difficulty most critics have who write about Richard Wright's *Native Son* is that they do not see Bigger Thomas.[1] They see him with their outer eyes, but not with the inner eyes, "those eyes with which they look through their physical eyes upon reality."[2] Of course there is a certain sense in which everyone is invisible, a certain sense in which the observer creates the observed, attributing to him qualities whose nature depends upon the viewer's own character. When we see a man in muddy work clothes, we are likely to see him only as a laborer and to have aroused in us whatever ideas we have toward laborers. We rarely look at a man so dressed (assuming that he is unknown to us) and see a father, a church-goer, taxpayer or fisherman, though the man underneath the clothing may theoretically be all these things. If we think about him, we automatically assume certain things about his life style—and his values, his economic and social position, and even his occupation. To the extent that the clothes determine what we see, the person beneath them is invisible to us.

The difficulty comes about when we assume that the outer covering is the essential person. Most critics of Wright's novel see only the outer covering of Bigger Thomas, the blackness of his skin and his resulting social role. Few have seen him as a discrete entity, a particular person who struggles with the burden of his humanity. Wright has gone to great lengths in the novel to create Bigger as a person, to invest the social character with particularizing traits, to delineate the features of a face. The final meaning of the book, as a matter of fact, depends upon the

"Wright's Invisible Native Son" by Donald B. Gibson. From *American Quarterly* 21, No. 4 (1969), 728–738. Copyright © 1969 by Trustees of the University of Pennsylvania. Reprinted by permission of the publisher and author.

[1]Limitations of space preclude naming all the critics I have in mind. A few of them are the following: James Baldwin, "Everybody's Protest Novel" and "Many Thousands Gone," *Notes of a Native Son* (Boston, 1955), pp. 13–23, 24–45; Robert Bone, *The Negro Novel in America* (New Haven, 1958), pp. 140–52; Hugh M. Gloster, *Negro Voices in American Fiction* (Chapel Hill, N.C., 1948), pp. 222–34; John Reilly, "Afterword," *Native Son* (New York, 1966). Critics most nearly exceptions are: Edwin Berry Burgum, *The Novel and the World's Dilemma* (New York, 1963), pp. 223–40; Esther Merle Jackson, "The American Negro and the Image of the Absurd," *Phylon*, XXIII (1962), 359–71; Nathan A. Scott, "Search for Beliefs: The Fiction of Richard Wright," *University of Kansas City Review*, XXIII (1956), 19–24.

[2]Ralph Ellison, *Invisible Man* (New York, 1952), p. 3.

awareness on the part of the reader of Bigger's individuality. The lack of such awareness has led most critics to misread the novel, for almost all of them interpret it as though the social person, Bigger Thomas, were the *real* and *essential* person. The following bit of dialogue, however, suggests a different perspective.

> Max: "Well, this thing's bigger than you, son. . . ."
> Bigger: "They going to kill me anyhow."[3]

This exchange between Max and Bigger reveals that each is looking at the problem at hand in an essentially different way. Max is thinking of the social implications of the situation; Bigger's attention is focused on his own impending doom. Which view is the truer, the more significant in the context of the novel? Wright's critics have generally opted for the view of Max, but if Max's view is true, then most of the whole final section does not make sense. For a careful reading of that third section, "Fate," indicates that the focus of the novel is not on the trial nor on Max, but on Bigger and on his finally successful attempt to come to terms with his imminent death. It need be noted that the trial does not take up the entire third section of the novel as has been often said. In the edition cited above, the third section comprises 126 pages; the trial itself consumes 37 pages and Max's address to the jury, 17 pages. The length of Max's speech and its bearing on what has preceded in the novel to that point have led experienced readers to neglect what else happens in that final section. It has led to many conclusions about the novel which are not borne out by the 89 pages of the last section describing what happens before and after the trial. The degree to which the reader focuses upon Max and Max's speech determines the degree to which Bigger is invisible to him.

In order to assess properly the meaning of the final section, it is necessary to understand what happens in the concluding pages of the novel. First of all it is too simple to say as Baldwin does that "he [Bigger] *wants* to die because he glories in his hatred and prefers, like Lucifer, rather than to rule in hell than serve in heaven."[4] The point is that Bigger, through introspection, finally arrives at a definition of self which is his own and different from that assigned to him by everyone else in the novel. The many instances in the last of the three sections of the novel which show him exploring his deepest thoughts, feelings and emotions reveal Baldwin's statement to be patently false. Shortly after Bigger's capture and imprisonment he lies thinking in his cell.

> And, under and above it all, there was the fear of death before which he
> was naked and without defense; he had to go forward and meet his end like

---

[3]*Native Son* (New York, 1940), p. 312. Subsequent quotations from the novel are from this edition.

[4]*Notes of a Native Son*, p. 44.

any other living thing upon the earth. . . . There would have to hover above him, like the stars in a full sky, a vast configuration of images and symbols whose magic and power could lift him up and make him live so intensely that the dread of being black and unequal would be forgotten; that even death would not matter, that it would be a victory. This would have to happen before he could look them in the face again: a new pride and a new humility would have to be born in him, a humility springing from a new identification with some part of the world in which he lived, and this identification forming the basis for a new hope that would function in him as pride and dignity. (pp. 234–35)

This quotation not only refutes Baldwin's statement about Bigger's motivations, but it as well indicates the focus of the novel at this point is on Bigger Thomas the private person. The emphasis is upon a problem that he faces as an isolated, solitary human whose problem is compounded by race though absolutely not defined by racial considerations. There follows from the point in the novel during which the above quotation occurs a pattern of advance and retrogression as Bigger gropes his way, privately and alone, toward that "new identification," that "pride and dignity" referred to in the passage. From this point on Bigger feels by turns guilt, hate, shame, remorse, fear, anger, and through the knowledge of himself engendered through acquaintance with his basic thoughts and feelings moves toward a sense of identity. There is a good deal of emphasis placed upon the solitary nature of his problem. At least twice he advances to the point at which he recognizes that salvation for him can come only from himself, from his own effort and knowledge.

He was balanced on a hair-line now, but there was no one to push him forward or backward, no one to make him feel that he had any value or worth—no one but himself. (p. 305)

He believed that Max knew how he felt, and once more before he died he wanted to talk with him and feel with as much keenness as possible what his living and dying meant. That was all the hope he had now. If there were any sure and firm knowledge for him, it would have come from himself. (p. 350)

If we see the quotation above (from pp. 234–35) as defining Bigger's essential problem, then it is evident that the passage must have relevance to the concluding pages of the novel. When Bigger has achieved the "new humility," the "pride and dignity" referred to there, if he has achieved it, it should be evidenced somewhere later in the novel. And so it is. During the final two pages of the novel it is clear that Bigger no longer suffers, is no longer in terror about his impending death. "Aw, I reckon I believe in myself. . . . I ain't got nothing else. . . . I got to die" (p. 358—Wright's ellipses). He accepts himself as never before, and in realizing his identity is able to evaluate his past actions objectively. "I didn't want to kill! . . . But what I killed for, I *am*! It must have been pretty deep in me to make me kill! I must have felt it awful hard to murder. . . ."

Because he has come to terms with himself, because he no longer hates and despises himself as he has during most of his life, it is no longer necessary for him to feel hatred. For this reason he is able to pass along through Max a reassuring word to his mother: "Just go and tell Ma I was all right and not to worry none, see? Tell her I was all right and wasn't crying none . . ." (p. 358). Had he "died in hatred," as Bone says,[5] he would hardly have called out his final words to Max, "Tell Jan hello . . ." (p. 359). These words indicate that Bigger's contradictory feelings about himself and his situation have been resolved, for they could only be spoken by virtue of Bigger's having accepted the consequences of his actions and hence himself. He has no choice—if he is to achieve the degree of reconciliation to his fate necessary for him to face death and therefore assert his humanity—but to recognize that he *is* what he has *done*.

The two perspectives of Bigger Thomas contained in the novel exist in tension until in the final pages the focus shifts away entirely from the social emphasis. No matter what the social implications of Bigger's situation, the fact is that he, the private, isolated human must face the consequences. It is no wonder that Bigger is almost totally unable to understand Max's speech during the trial. He grasps something of the tone, but the meanings of the words escape him, for Max is not really thinking about Bigger the existential person, the discrete human entity. When Bigger and Max converse privately, they understand each other reasonably well. But during the trial Max is talking about a symbol, a representative figure. Hence the significant problem becomes not whether Max will save Bigger—the answer to that question is a foregone conclusion—but whether Bigger will save himself in the only possible way, by coming to terms with himself. This we see him doing as we observe him during long, solitary hours of minute introspection and self-analysis.

Probably the critic most responsible for the perception of Bigger Thomas as a social entity and that alone is James Baldwin, who conceived some rather convincing arguments about the limitations of the protest novel and especially of *Native Son*.

> All of Bigger's life is controlled, defined by his hatred and his fear. And later, his fear drives him to murder and his hatred to rape; he dies, having come, through this violence, we are told, for the first time, to a kind of life, having for the first time redeemed his manhood.[6]

Baldwin, for all the persuasiveness of his language, has failed to see Bigger the person. For it is clear enough that Bigger's feeling of elation, of having done a creative thing simply in murdering is not the final outcome. It is rather early in the novel when he feels release, free from the forces which

[5] *The Negro Novel*, p. 150.
[6] *Notes of a Native Son*, p. 22.

have all his life constrained him But after his capture he finds he is indeed
not free; he still has himself to cope with. His final feeling is not—as the
concluding pages of the novel explicitly show—exaltation for having "re-
deemed his manhood." Very soon after the first murder, to be sure, he
does feel that it has had some redeeming effect.

> The thought of what he had done, the awful horror of it, the daring associated
> with such actions, formed for him for the first time in his fear-ridden life a
> barrier of protection between him and a world he feared. He had murdered
> and had created a new life for himself. It was something that was all his
> own, and it was the first time in his life he had had anything that others
> could not take from him. (p. 90)

But this response occurs after all about one-fourth of the way through the
novel. These are not the feelings Bigger has at the end. One need only
imagine this passage as among Bigger's thoughts as we last see him in
order to see how inappropriate it would be as a concluding statement. He
is not in the mood of prideful self-assertion which he feels so often from
the time he disposes of Mary's body until his crime is discovered. Instead,
the conclusion finds him feeling a calm assurance and acceptance of self.
There is neither irony nor condescension in his final "Tell Jan hello," nor
does the last scene in the denotative meanings of its words and the tone
project "hatred and fear" on Bigger's part.

Baldwin's eloquent statement at the end of "Everybody's Protest
Novel" describing how the protest novel fails does not describe the content
of Wright's novel.

> The failure of the protest novel lies in its rejection of life, the human being,
> the denial of his beauty, dread, power, in its insistence that it is his categori-
> zation alone which is real and which cannot be transcended.[7]

The statement itself is not to be questioned; its applicability to *Native Son*
is. There is too much in Wright's novel which suggests that Bigger's
response to his situation does not stem from his categorization, his Negroness, but his humanness. What has the following response, occurring after
Bigger has returned from hearing his sentence, to do with his
"categorization"?

> In self-defense he shut out the night and day from his mind, for if he had
> thought of the sun's rising and setting, of the moon or the stars, of clouds
> or rain, he would have died a thousand deaths before they took him to the
> chair. To accustom his mind to death as much as possible, he made all the
> world beyond his cell a vast grey land where neither night nor day was,
> peopled by strange men and women whom he could not understand, but
> with those lives he longed to mingle once before he went. (p. 349)

[7]P. 23. Edward Margolies explores the opposite view of Wright's novel in *Native Sons: A
Critical Study of Twentieth-Century American Authors* (New York, 1968), pp. 85–86.

These are not the thoughts and feelings of a Negro, as such, but of a man who is about to die and who struggles to cope with the fact. Race, social condition, whatever category a reader might have placed him in, have no relevance here. There are many such passages in the third section of the book showing Bigger's individual response to his situation. For example, the following:

> He had lived and acted on the assumption that he was alone, and now he saw that he had not been. What he had done made others suffer. No matter how much he would long for them to forget him, they would not be able to. His family was a part of him, not only in blood, but in spirit. (p. 254)
>
> He would not mind dying now if he could only find out what this meant, what he was in relation to all the others that lived, and the earth upon which he stood. Was there some battle everybody was fighting, and he had missed it? (p. 307)
>
> His face rested against the bars and he felt tears roll down his cheeks. His wet lips tasted salt. He sank to his knees and sobbed: "I don't want to die. . . . I don't want to die. . . ." (p. 308)

His interpretation of the opening scene of the novel is likewise a measure of the degree to which Baldwin does not see Bigger.

> Rats live there too in the Thomas apartment . . . and we first encounter Bigger in the act of killing one. One may consider that the entire book, from that harsh "Brring!" to Bigger's weak "Good-by" as the lawyer, Max, leaves him in the death cell is an extension, with the roles inverted, of this chilling metaphor.[8]

This interpretation would be true if Bigger were *only* the social figure which critics have seen. But the figure on the final pages of the novel, no matter what he is, is not a rat. He does not die as a rat dies; he is neither fearful nor desperate.

An alternative reading is offered by Edwin Burgum in his essay on *Native Son* in which he says of Bigger's killing of the rat and flaunting it in the faces of his mother and sister, "His courage is that overcompensation for fear called bravado. It passes beyond the needs of the situation and defeats its own end here as in later crises in the novel."[9] This interpretation gets beyond the problem of comparing Bigger with a rat. Certainly Wright's sympathies are with Bigger to a greater degree than his being likened to a rat implies.

It must be admitted that Bigger Thomas, the social figure whom Baldwin and others have seen, has a prominent place in the novel and is by no means a figment. He is a representative figure to Buckley, to the policemen investigating the murder of Mary, and to the public at large.

[8]P. 34.
[9]P. 232.

Wright makes it amply evident that the desire on the part of these people to do away with Bigger reflects a primitive desire to perform ritual murder and, thereby, to do away with the potential threat posed by all other Negroes through sacrificing the representative black figure. But readers need to avoid the error of the characters in the novel by distinguishing between Bigger's qualities as a representative figure and his qualities as a particular person (difficult though this may be in our time and in our society) who, exclusive of race, faces death.

> If he were nothing, if this were all, then why could not he die without hesitancy? Who and what was he to feel the agony of a wonder so intensely that it amounted to fear? Why was this strange impulse always throbbing in him when there was nothing outside of him to meet and explain it? Who or what had traced this restless design in him? Why was this eternal reaching for something that was not there? Why this black gulf between him and the world: warm red blood here and cold blue sky there, and never a wholeness, a oneness, a meeting of the two? (pp. 350–51)

Feeling such things as these and about to die in the electric chair, Bigger ceases to be representative of the Negro and becomes every man whose death is imminent—that is, every man.

The view of Bigger as representative (and hence invisible) comes about in part because Wright's novel has been too frequently seen as a "Negro" novel or a protest novel, and all the limitations of these categories have been ascribed to it. It has been extremely difficult for even the most sophisticated readers to see Bigger's humanity because the idea of an ignorant, uneducated, criminal Negro coming to terms with the human condition, as Bigger finally does, is an alien idea. The novel should be compared not only to *Crime and Punishment*, the work with which it is most frequently compared, but with *The Stranger* as well. Wright's and Camus' novels were published two years apart (1940 and 1942 respectively) and there are many striking parallels between them. The most fruitful result of such a comparison may be to lift Wright's novel out of the context of the racial problem in America and to place it in larger perspective, or at least to reveal the extent to which *Native Son* is not so limited as it has appeared to be.

The limited view has also been responsible for the interpretation of the novel as a propaganda piece for the Communist Party.[10] On the contrary the novel points up the limitations of a system of ideas which by its very nature is incapable of dealing with certain basic human problems. Bigger is saved in the end, but not through the efforts of the Party, which constantly asserts that the individual cannot achieve meaningful salvation. This further implies that the thought processes leading to Wright's break

---

[10]Richard Sullivan, "Afterword" to *Native Son*, Signet, 1961.

with the Party were already in motion as early as 1939, and that his formal public announcement of the break in 1944[11] was a resolution of much earlier distress.

The interpretation of the novel as a propaganda piece for the Communist Party stems from the notion that Max is Wright's spokesman. As a result, a good deal of weight is placed upon Max's address to the jury. Though there is enough evidence to suggest that Max's personal view of Bigger allows for his existence as a discrete individual, the strategy he chooses to defend Bigger requires that he deal with him largely on an abstract level with the intention of convincing his hearers that the abstraction is embodied within the particular individual before them. Thus he says:

> "This boy represents but a tiny aspect of a problem whose reality sprawls over a third of this nation." (p. 330)
> "Multiply Bigger Thomas twelve million times, allowing for environmental and temperamental variations, and for those Negroes who are completely under the influence of the church, and you have the psychology of the Negro people." (p. 333)

The effect of his words on many is simply to enhance Bigger's invisibility.

Rather than being Wright's spokesman, in truth, Max presents one side of a dialogue whose totality is expressed through the dual perspective contained in the novel.[12] Max is indeed a sympathetic character, but for all his good intentions, he has limitations. He never, for example, entirely understands what Bigger is getting at during their conversations. Only in the end, during their final meeting, does he come to have some notion of the fact that he is not superior to Bigger, that he knows no more than Bigger about the kinds of questions the condemned man is asking and consequently is not in a position to explain anything. When Bigger tells Max that he *is* what he has *done* ("What I killed for, I *am*!"), Max's response is to recoil in horror, for even he ultimately is unable to accept any definition of man outside his own preconceived idea. Max cannot accept the implications of Bigger's conclusions nor, indeed, can he fully understand the position that Bigger has finally arrived at. Wright makes this point doubly clear with the line, "Max groped for his hat like a blind man." Now given the nearly explicit meanings which sight and blindness have had in the novel prior to this, it can hardly be a fortuitous simile. Not even Max is completely capable of recognizing and accepting the truth of Bigger's humanity.

Though Max's motivations are good, founded as they are upon his

---

[11]"I Tried to Be a Communist," *Atlantic Monthly*, CLXV (Aug. 1944), 61–70; (Sept. 1944), 48–56.

[12]Margolies believes that the duality of perspective referred to here is unresolved. Pp. 79–80.

basic good character and good feeling, he is unable to finally save Bigger, for Bigger's salvation comes about through his own efforts, through his eventual ability to find freedom from the constraints of his past. All the characters in Wright's major works after *Native Son* achieve the same kind of freedom, or at least the promise of such freedom, in one way or another. This is true of the central character of *Black Boy* (which is more fictional in technique and intention than commonly recognized), *The Long Dream*, *The Outsider* and of "The Man Who Lived Underground." *Native Son* resolves the tension between the two alternatives, the one seeing the salvation of individuals through social change, the other seeing the salvation of individuals through their own efforts. After *Native Son* Wright was never again to suggest the possibility of any individual's achieving meaningful social salvation. The inescapable conclusion is that Wright lost faith entirely in social solutions to human problems and came to believe that ultimately the individual alone can save himself. During that final meeting between Max and Bigger it is made abundantly clear that Bigger has through the course of the third section of the novel come to terms with his most pressing problem, his impending doom. In so doing he achieves the only meaningful salvation possible. (Max speaks first.)

> "But on both sides men want to live; men are fighting for life. Who will win? Well, the side . . . with the most humanity and the most men. That's why . . . y-you've got to b-believe in yourself, Bigger. . . ."
> Max's head jerked up in surprise when Bigger laughed.
> "Aw, I reckon I believe in myself. . . . I ain't got nothing else. . . . I got to die" (p. 358)

Now if the conclusions I have come to here are valid, then two highly significant corollaries follow: (1) Wright did not *simply* emerge from the naturalistic school of Dreiser, Dos Passos and Farrell; he did not simply adapt the techniques and thoughts of the naturalists to the situation of the black man.[13] (2) The existentialist thinking of his later work did not derive from the influence on him of Camus, Sartre and other French existentialists, but grew out of his own experience in America.[14]

I do not want to argue that Wright was not strongly influenced by American literary naturalism; certainly he was. But he was not as confined by the tradition as has been generally believed. If my thesis about *Native Son* is correct, then Wright is not an author whose major novel reflects the final phases of a dying tradition, but he is instead one who out of the thought, techniques and general orientation of the naturalistic writers developed beyond their scope. *Native Son*, as I have described it in this

---

[13]Wright's relation to the naturalistic tradition was first articulated by Alfred Kazin, *On Native Grounds* (New York, 1942), p. 372, and later by Bone in *The Negro Novel*, pp. 142–43.

[14]Margolies concurs with this conclusion. P. 68.

essay, looks forward rather than backward. It is a prototype of the modern existentialist novel and a link between the fiction of the 1930s and a good deal of more modern fiction.

A kind of condescension and a preconception about the potential of a self-educated black man from the very depths of the South have combined to obscure the sources of Wright's proclivity toward existentialism. The following comments made by two writers and critics who were friends of Wright make the point.

REDDING: Dick was a small-town boy—a small-town Mississippi boy— all of his days. The hog maw and the collard greens. He was fascinated by the existentialist group for a while, but he didn't really understand them.

BONTEMPS: Essentially, of course, Wright was and has remained not only an American but a Southerner. Negroes have a special fondness for that old saw, "You can take the boy out of the country, but you can't take the country out of the boy."[15]

In order to understand the sources of the existentialist concern in Wright's work and thought, one need only quote the quality and character of the life described by Wright in *Black Boy* and realize as well that "existentialism" may be described as a mood arising out of the exigencies of certain life situations rather than as a fully developed and articulated systematic philosophy which one chooses to hold or rejects. Though we cannot say that existentialism resulted directly from the experience of Europeans under Nazi occupation, we can certainly say that the occupation, the war itself, created circumstances conducive to the nurturing and development of the existential response. Europeans during the war, especially those engaged in underground activities, daily faced the imminent possibility of death, and the constant awareness of impending death was largely responsible for the emergence of a way of interpreting the meaning of life consonant with that awareness. *Black Boy* of course does not describe a wartime situation, but one cannot help but feel the constant pressure on the person described there, a pressure from a world which threatens unceasingly to destroy him. The earliest of Wright's memories is of an episode which results in his being beaten unconscious, and this at a very young age. Thereafter we see described in the book the progress of an inward, alienated individual, distrustful of all external authority, who learns that his survival depends upon the repudiation of the values of others and a strong reliance upon his own private and personal sense of values. The existential precept, "existence precedes essence," stems as a

---

[15]Saunders Redding and Arna Bontemps in *"Reflections on Richard Wright: A Symposium,"* *Anger and Beyond,* ed., Herbert Hill (New York, 1966), p. 207. Further comments on Wright and existentialism occur on pages 203, 205, 208, 209.

mood from Wright's experience as described in *Black Boy*, but as a condition of his life and not as a consciously held philosophical principle. Herein lie the sources of Bigger Thomas' response to the condition brought about by his crime, capture and condemnation.

A comment made by Wright in response to an unfriendly review of *Native Son* is relevant as a final observation.

> If there had been one person in the Dalton household who viewed Bigger Thomas as a human being, the crime would have been solved in half an hour. Did not Bigger himself know that it was the denial of his personality that enabled him to escape detection so long? The one piece of incriminating evidence which would have solved the "murder mystery" was Bigger's humanity under their very eyes.[16]

We need only make the proper substitutions to see the relevance of Wright's comment to the views of most critics of his novel. "The denial of his personality," and the failure on their part to see "Bigger's humanity under their very eyes" have caused him to be invisible, to be Wright's own invisible native son.

---

[16]"I Bite the Hand That Feeds Me," *Atlantic Monthly*, CLXV (June 1940), 826.

The Conclusion of Richard Wright's
Native Son

by Paul N. Siegel

The conclusion of *Native Son* has perhaps caused more critics, distinguished and obscure, to go astray, reading into it their own preconceptions instead of perceiving the author's purpose, than any other significant portion of a major work of modern American literature. Both Max's lengthy speech in the courtroom and his final scene with Bigger have been grievously misunderstood.

Let us turn to Irving Howe as our prime example:

> The long speech by Bigger's radical lawyer Max . . . is ill-related to the book itself: Wright has not achieved Dreiser's capacity for absorbing everything, even the most recalcitrant philosophical passages, into a unified vision of things. . . . Yet it should be said that the endlessly-repeated criticism that Wright caps his melodrama with a party-line oration tends to oversimplify the novel, for Wright is too honest simply to allow the propagandistic message to constitute the last word. Indeed, the last word is given not to Max but to Bigger. For at the end Bigger remains at the mercy of his hatred and fear, the lawyer retreats helplessly, the projected union between political consciousness and raw revolt has not been achieved—as if Wright were persuaded that, all ideology apart, there is for each Negro an ultimate trial that he can bear only by himself.[1]

Howe, therefore, finds that the "endlessly-repeated criticism" that Max's speech is a "party-line oration"[2] "tends to oversimplify the novel"

[1]"Black Boys and Native Sons," *A World More Attractive* (New York: Horizon, 1963), p. 104.

[2]So, too, Dan McCall sums up "the usual objection voiced against the third part of Wright's novel": "The Party had interrupted Wright's project and falsified the message of 'the bad nigger'" (*The Example of Richard Wright*, New York: Harcourt, 1969, p. 90). McCall, who has written the best criticism on *Native Son*, himself speaks of Max (pp. 90, 101) as "the ideological spokesman" who "can only filter Bigger through the Party's vision." Robert A. Bone, who likewise has written well on *Native Son*, says similarly: "In Book III Wright has allowed his statement as a Communist to overwhelm his statement as an artist. . . . Bigger's lawyer . . . is at once a mouthpiece for the author and a spokesman for the party line"

not because this criticism is incorrect but because it does not go beyond the speech to perceive that the union of Bigger's "raw revolt" and Max's "political consciousness" has not been effected. So, too, Alfred Kazin declares that Wright's method is "to astonish the reader by torrential scenes of cruelty, hunger, rape, murder and flight, and then enlighten him by crude Stalinist homilies."[3] By "crude Stalinist homilies" Kazin undoubtedly means Max's speech and his conversations with Bigger.

Howe, Kazin, Bone, McCall, Margolies, and Brignano and the numerous other critics referred to by Howe and McCall have responded to the courtroom speech with a conditioned reflex: Richard Wright was a Communist; Boris Max is called a Communist (only, to be sure, by the red-baiting prosecuting attorney and newspapers, but that is overlooked); therefore, the speech must be a "party-line oration," a "crude Stalinist" homily. Before we examine the speech, let us see what Ben Davis, Jr., a leading black official of the Communist party at the time, had to say about it in reviewing the book in the *Sunday Worker*, the official organ of the party.

Although Davis concedes that "certain passages in Max's speech show an understanding of the responsibility of capitalism for Bigger's plight," he checks off the following points against Max: "he accepts the idea that Negroes have a criminal psychology"; "he does not challenge the false charge of rape against Bigger"; "he does not deal with the heinous murder of Bessie, tending to accept the bourbon policy that crimes of Negroes against each other don't matter"; "he argues that Bigger, and by implication the whole Negro mass, should be held in jail to protect 'white daughters'"; he "should have argued for Bigger's acquittal in the case, and should have helped stir the political pressure of the Negro and white masses to get that acquittal." "His speech," Davis concludes, ". . . expresses the point of view held . . . by . . . reformist betrayers. . . . The first business of the Communist Party or of the I.L.D. would have been to chuck him out of the case."[4]

Whatever the distortions in the pronouncement of this party bureaucrat turned literary critic,[5] he is, it must be acknowledged, a more authoritative

---

(*Richard Wright*, Minneapolis: Univ. of Minnesota Press, 1969, p. 23). For similar views, see Edward Margolies, *The Art of Richard Wright* (Carbondale: Southern Illinois Univ. Press, 1969), pp. 114–15, and Russell Carl Brignano, *Richard Wright: An Introduction to the Man and His Works* (Pittsburgh: Univ. of Pittsburgh Press, 1969), p. 81.

[3] *On Native Grounds* (New York: Harcourt, 1942), p. 387.

[4] *Sunday Worker*, New York, 14 April 1940, Sec. 2, p. 4. col. 6.

[5] Max's statement that Bigger's existence is "a crime against the state" (Richard Wright, *Native Son*, New York: Harper, 1940, p. 367) is, insofar as it is an indictment at all, far more of an indictment of the state than it is of Bigger. Max does deal with the murder of Bessie (pp. 336–37), making the point that Bigger knew that the white world would be concerned with the murder only of Mary, not of Bessie. He nowhere argues that Bigger, let alone "the whole Negro mass," should be held in jail to protect white daughters.

interpreter of the party line of the time than either Howe or Kazin. Davis obviously wants the simplified propaganda that *Native Son* does not give: a hero who is a completely innocent victim and a lawyer who thunders his client's innocence, who brilliantly exposes a frame-up rooted in a corrupt society, and who calls for giant demonstrations against this frame-up. The fact that Max is not a party-line expounder is one of the points that made the party leaders uneasy about *Native Son,* an uneasiness indicated by the review itself and by the fact that Davis' review appeared a month after the novel's publication.

The novel itself indicates that Max is not a Communist party member. Jan tells Mary (p. 66) that Max is "one of the best lawyers we've got." He does not refer to him as a "comrade," a member of the Communist party, but as one of the lawyers employed by the International Labor Defense, the legal defense organization controlled by the party. Although Max is obviously sympathetic to the causes espoused by the Communists, the fact that he is employed by the International Labor Defense does not indicate that he is a Communist any more than the employment of the noted criminal lawyer, Samuel S. Leibowitz, in the Scottsboro case meant that Leibowitz was a Communist. When he tells Bigger that others besides blacks are hated, he says (p. 295), "They hate trade unions. They hate folks who try to organize.They hate Jan." "They hate Jan"—not "Communists like me and Jan." Later he says, "I'm a Jew and they hate me" (p. 304)—not "I'm a Communist and a Jew and they hate me."

If, then, Max is not the novel's Communist spokesman who delivers a "party-line oration," what are his politics and what does he say in his speech? An old, wise, weary Jew, deeply aware of the radical defects of the society of which he is a member, Max, as we shall see in his courtroom speech, envisions a cataclysmic end to this society and seeks desperately to avert it by striving to have wrongs redressed. He is neither a revolutionist nor a Stalinist.[6]

His speech is not an address to a jury, as Edwin Berry Burgum, James Baldwin, Dan McCall, and Edward Margolies affirm.[7] Max clearly states that, not daring to put Bigger's fate in the hands of a white jury whose minds have been inflamed by the press, he has entered a plea of guilty, which by the laws of Illinois permits him to reject a trial by jury and to have the sentence rendered by the presiding judge. "Dare I," he asks the judge, "... put his fate in the hands of a jury ... whose minds are already

---

[6]James G. Kennedy, in an article ("The Content and Form of *Native Son,*" *College English,* 34, 1972, 269–86) published after I submitted this article to *PMLA,* assumed that Max is to be taken as a Communist party member but asserted (282) that Max reveals himself to be really "an idealist and no Marxist" because "he supposes there can be understanding above classes."

[7]Edwin Berry Burgum, *The Novel and the World's Dilemma* (1947; rpt. New York: Russell, 1963), p. 238; James Baldwin, "Many Thousands Gone," *Notes of a Native Son* (New York: Dial Press, 1963), p. 42; McCall, p. 93; Margolies, p. 112.

conditioned by the press of the nation. . . ? No! I could not! So today I come to face this Court, rejecting a trial by jury, willingly entering a plea of guilty, asking in the light of the laws of this state that this boy's life be spared."[8]

It is to this judge that Max is speaking. Beyond the judge he is speaking to "men of wealth and property," who, if they misread "the consciousness of the submerged millions today" (p.338), will bring about a civil war in the future. It is amazing that James Baldwin can say that Max's speech "is addressed to those among us of good will and it seems to say that, though there are whites and blacks among us who hate each other, we will not; there are those who are betrayed by greed, by guilt, by blood, by blood lust, but not we; we will set our faces against them and join hands and walk together into that dazzling future when there will be no white or black" (p. 47). Baldwin is here carried away by his own rhetoric. There is not a sentence in the speech stating or implying a dazzling future to which black and white will walk hand in hand!

Nor is the speech a savage attack on capitalism or a statement of a "guilt-of-the-nation thesis,"[9] a plea for sympathy for one whose guilt we must all share. "Allow me, Your Honor," says Max (pp. 327–28), ". . . to state emphatically that I do *not* claim that this boy is a victim of injustice, nor do I ask that this Court be sympathetic with him. . . . If I should say that he is a victim of injustice, then I would be asking by implication for sympathy; and if one insists upon looking at this boy in the light of sympathy, he will be swamped by a feeling of guilt so strong as to be indistinguishable from hate."

The mob of would-be lynchers, he says, knowing in its heart of the oppression of Negroes, is as possessed of guilt, fear, and hate as Bigger is. In order to understand the full significance of Bigger's case, he urges the judge, one must rise above such emotion. To do so, he summons him to look upon it from a historical height. The "first wrong," the enslavement of the Negroes, was "understandable and inevitable" (p. 327), for in sub-duing this "harsh and wild country" (p. 328) men had to use other men as tools and weapons. "Men do what they must do" (p. 329). From that first wrong came a sense of guilt, in the attempted stifling of which came hate and fear, a hate and fear that matched that of the Negroes. Injustice practiced on this scale and over that length of time "is injustice no longer; it is an accomplished fact of life" (p. 330). This fact of life is a system of oppression squeezing down upon millions of people. These millions can be stunted, but they cannot be stamped out. And as oppression grows tighter, guilt, fear, and hatred grow stronger on both sides. Killing Bigger will only "swell the tide of pent-up lava that will some day break loose,

---

[8]P. 325. See also pp. 304 and 317. Clarence Darrow similarly pleaded guilty and rejected a trial by jury in the Loeb-Leopold case, to which the novel refers.

[9]Robert Bone, *The Negro Novel in America* (New Haven: Yale Univ. Press, 1966), p. 151.

not in a single, blundering, accidental, individual crime, but in a wild
cataract of emotion that will brook no control" (p. 330). Sentencing him
to life imprisonment, on the other hand, will give him an opportunity to
"build a meaning for his life" (p. 338).

Max's speech is, in short, an agonized plea to the judge to understand
the significance of Bigger and, understanding, to break through the pattern
of hatred and repression that "makes our future seem a looming image of
violence" (p. 337). It has been frequently pointed out that in Book III,
which is entitled "Fate," we see realized the doom of Bigger that has been
foreshadowed from the beginning. This is entirely true, of course, but
"Fate" also refers to the doom of the United States, toward which Max
sees us, "like sleepwalkers" (p. 324), proceeding. "If we can understand
how subtly and yet strongly his life and fate are linked to ours,—if we
can do this, perhaps we shall find the key to our future" (p. 324). Bigger
killed "accidentally"—that is, he was not aware of killing as he killed, but
this does not matter. What matters is that "every thought he thinks is
potential murder" (p. 335). "Who knows when another 'accident' involv-
ing millions of men will happen, an 'accident' that will be the dreadful
day of our doom?" (pp. 337–38).

Max's speech, far from being, as Howe says, "ill-related to the book,"
not a part of "a unified vision of things," grows out of the rest of the novel.
It has, to be sure, a number of weaknesses. It and the prosecuting attorney's speech are not seen and heard from Bigger's point of view, which
is otherwise rigidly adhered to in the novel, the vivid presentation of
Bigger's visceral reactions, as events are registered on his consciousness,
contributing to the novel's force and drive. Max's speech, which takes
sixteen pages, is not, however, summarized and presented through Bigger's consciousness, and at its end we are told that Bigger "had not
understood the speech, but he had felt the meaning of some of it from the
tone of Max's voice" (p. 370). Moreover, the speech, far from being
superimposed on what had gone on before and at variance with it, repeats
too obviously what has already been said. Wright's awareness of this
repetition and his desire to achieve a heightened effect in the final sum-
ming up may explain a rhetoric that is occasionally too highly wrought
and too highly pitched.

That the speech, however, is not an obtrusion is indicated by the
number of recurring themes and images in the novel that the speech
brings together. The first theme that we might consider is that of blindness. Bigger, eating his breakfast the morning after he has killed Mary
and looking upon his family and the world with new eyes, realizes that
his mother, sister, and brother exclude from their vision of the world that
which they do not wish to see. He also realizes that Mrs. Dalton is blind
figuratively as well as literally, that Mr. Dalton and Jan are blind, and
that Mary had been blind in not recognizing that which was in him, the

propensity to kill. When he joins Bessie, he feels the same about her being blind as he does about his family. She knows nothing but hard work in white folks' kitchens and the liquor she drinks to make up for her starved life. In flight, despite the danger of death, Bigger feels a "queer sense of power" at having set the chase in motion, at being engaged in purposeful activity for the first time in his life, and thinks, "He was living, truly and deeply, no matter what others might think, looking at him with their blind eyes" (p. 203). When Jan visits him in prison, he tells Bigger, "I was kind of blind. . . . I didn't know we were so far apart until that night" (p. 244). Bigger, understanding that Jan is expressing his belief in him, for the first time looks upon a white man as a human being. "He saw Jan as though someone had performed an operation upon his eyes" (p. 246).

Max, in his image of the American people proceeding to their doom like sleepwalkers, catches up these images of darkness present on all sides. It is this blindness that he emphasizes throughout his speech. If the judge reacts only to what he has to say about the sufferings of Negroes, he states, he will be "blinded" by a feeling that will prevent him from perceiving reality and acting accordingly. "Rather, I plead with you to see . . . an existence of men growing out of the soil prepared by the collective but blind will of a hundred million people" (p. 328). "Your Honor," he exclaims, "in our blindness we have so contrived and ordered the lives of men" (p. 336) that their every human aspiration constitutes a threat to the state.

Max, then, sees the American people as going unseeingly to their doom because they—except, presumably, for a possibly saving remnant of them such as Max himself and his co-workers—either actively support or passively and unthinkingly accept the institutions of a repressive society. Bigger for his part sees whites as constituting an overwhelming natural force, a part of the structure of the universe. "To Bigger and his kind," says Wright early in the novel, "white people were not really people; they were a sort of great natural force, like a stormy sky looming overhead, or like a deep swirling river stretching suddenly at one's feet in the dark" (p. 97). The snowstorm that covers Chicago after Bigger's murder is symbolic of the hostile white world. When Bigger slips in running, "the white world was tilted at a sharp angle and the icy wind shot past his face" (p. 205). The snow separates Jan and Bigger from each other, as Jan accosts Bigger in the street after Mary's disappearance and tries to speak to him, only to be driven away by Bigger's gun: "In the pale yellow sheen of the street lamp they faced each other; huge wet flakes of snow floated down slowly, forming a delicate screen between them" (p. 146). When Jan gets through to Bigger in prison, an image of the white world as a great natural force is used again, this time a force subject to erosion: "Jan has spoken a declaration of friendship that would make other white men hate him: a particle of white rock had detached itself from that looming mountain of white hate and had rolled down the slope, stopping still at his feet" (p. 246; see also p. 253).

With his fine sensitivity, Max understands Bigger's feelings about whites, which Bigger had conveyed to him in the prison interview, and tries to make the judge understand it, using the same image of the white world as a natural force, not made up of human beings: "When situations like this arise, instead of men feeling that they are facing other men, they feel that they are facing mountains, floods, seas" (p. 327). But the judge blindly does not understand.

Another recurring image is that of the walls or curtain or veil behind which Bigger withdraws and hides rather than face reality. "He knew that the moment he allowed himself to feel to its fullness how [his family] lived, the shame and misery of their lives, he would be swept out of himself with fear and despair. So he held toward them an attitude of iron reserve; he lived with them, but behind a wall, a curtain. And toward himself he was even more exacting. He knew that the moment he allowed what his life meant to enter fully into his consciousness, he would either kill himself or someone else."[10] So, Max says, the killing of Mary was "a sudden and violent rent in the veil behind which he lived" (pp. 330–31), tearing aside his alienated friendliness and enabling him for the first time really to live.

The theme that Bigger's killing has given him a freedom he never before had is sounded frequently. "He had murdered and created a new life for himself. It was something that was all his own, and it was the first time in his life he had had anything that others could not take from him" (p. 90). And again: "He felt that he had his destiny in his grasp. He was more alive than he could ever remember having been; his mind and attention were pointed, focussed toward a goal" (p. 127). And still again: "There remained to him a queer sense of power. *He* had done this. *He* had brought all this about. In all of his life these two murders were the most meaningful things that had ever happened to him" (p. 203).

This is what Max tells the judge. In order to seek to reach him, he dares to speak of the killing as "an act of *creation*" (p. 325). He is not only concerned with conveying to the judge the bondage in which Bigger had lived so that it took this killing to give him "the possibility of choice, of action, the opportunity to act and to feel that his actions carried weight" (p. 333). He is concerned with conveying to him the sense of an impending awful catastrophe in which millions of others learn to be free through killing: "How soon will someone speak the word that resentful millions will understand: the word to be, to act, to live?"[11]

[10]P. 19. See also pp. 24, 91, 203, 226, 240.
[11]P. 337. The theme of blindness was mentioned in Bone, *The Negro Novel*, p. 147, James A. Emanuel, "Fever and Feeling: Notes on the Imagery in *Native Son*," *Negro Digest*, 18 Dec. 1968, 20–21, and Brignano, p. 117; the theme of the white world as a great natural force in

The sense of freedom that Bigger received was only transitory. Caught and imprisoned, Bigger wonders concerning the meaning of his life. Were the intimations of freedom, of "a possible order and meaning in his relations with the people about him" real (p. 234)? Or would freedom and meaning elude him and would he "have to go to his end just as he was, dumb, driven, with the shadow of emptiness in his eyes" (p. 235)? "Maybe they were right when they said that a black skin was bad. . . . Maybe he was just unlucky, a man born for dark doom, an obscene joke."

The big question of Book III is whether Bigger will find himself. It is not answered until the very end of the novel, the farewell scene with Max. "At the end," says Howe, "Bigger remains at the mercy of his hatred and fear." It is hard to make men hear who will not listen. Seven times in the last page and a half of the novel Bigger cries out to Max, "I'm all right," the last time adding, "For real, I am" (p. 359). The repeated assurance "I'm all right" obviously means that Bigger is not at the mercy of fear, that he is sure that he will not, as he had dreaded, have to be dragged to the electric chair, kicking and screaming, filled with animal terror because he had not been able to find human dignity. He has found what he had sought, an understanding of himself that "could lift him up and make him live so intensely that the dread of being black and unequal would be forgotten; that even death would not matter, that it would be a victory" (p. 234). The meaning for his life, which Max had thought to gain him the opportunity to build during life imprisonment, he had grasped from his recent experience under the duress of death.

What was the understanding of himself that he had acquired? Bone believes that Bigger casts out fear by giving himself completely to hatred, thereby in reality suffering a defeat: "What terrifies Max is that Bigger, repossessed by hate, ends by accepting what life has made him: a killer. Bigger's real tragedy is not that he dies, but that he dies in hatred. A tragic figure, he struggles for love and trust against a hostile environment which defeats him in the end" (*The Negro Novel*, p. 150). Since the conclusion has been so misunderstood, it will be necessary to quote at some length from it in order to examine it closely.

Max does not wish to talk to Bigger about the significance of his life, but he is forced to do so by Bigger's insistence. he tells Bigger: "It's too late now for you to . . . work with . . . others who are t-trying to . . . believe [in life, which is thwarted by capitalism] and make the world live again. . . . But it's not too late to believe what you felt, to understand

---

Bone, p. 147 and Brignano, p. 117; the image of the wall or curtain behind which Bigger withdraws in Emanuel, pp. 22–24; the theme of Bigger's killing as a means of liberation in Bone, p. 146, McCall, pp. 87, 100, Margolies, pp. 116–17, Brignano, p. 147. None of these takes note, however, of how these themes and images are gathered up in Max's speech.

what you felt. . . . The job in getting people to fight and have faith is in making them believe in what life has made them feel, making them feel that their feelings are as good as those of others. . . . That's why . . . y-you've got to b-believe in yourself, Bigger" (pp. 357–58).

These words work upon Bigger. They give him what he wants. Ironically, however, they cause him to go further than Max intended. "Bigger, you killed," says Max. "That was wrong. That was not the way to do it." Bigger, however, accepts himself completely, including his overwhelming impulse to kill: "Sounds funny, Mr. Max, but when I think about what you say I kind of feel what I wanted. It makes me feel I was kind of right. . . . They wouldn't let me live and I killed. Maybe it ain't fair to kill, and I reckon I really didn't want to kill. But when I think of why all the killing was, I began to feel what I wanted, what I am. . . . I didn't want to kill! . . . But what I killed for, I *am*! It must've been pretty deep in me to make me kill! . . . What I killed for must've been good! . . . When a man kills, it's for something."[12]

Max's shock on hearing these words seems excessive for one who had shown such an understanding of Bigger and had said, "We are dealing here with an impulse stemming from deep down" (p. 333). Perhaps this is a flaw in the scene. However, we must remember that this is the third great blow he has received. The first was when the judge, the representative of the establishment, had disregarded his desperate plea. The second was when the governor had refused to exercise clemency. These blows make it all the more difficult for him to sustain the blow inflicted by Bigger, the representative of black millions. The catastrophe he foresees seems to him more than ever inescapable.

Is Bigger's acceptance of his feelings of hate a victory or a defeat? If Bone is, like Max, shocked by Bigger's words, and in his shock can only see that Bigger is defeated by his hostile environment, he should consider how Bigger's killing was presented as a means of liberation and so described by Max himself. Wright, of course, is not advocating murder. Murder gave Bigger a sense of freedom, but it also gave him a sense of guilt, and, not giving him a sense of relatedness to others, it finally left him empty. But hatred of the oppressor is a natural, human emotion; it is only unhealthy when it is kept stifled. Used as the motor power of an idea driving toward a goal, it can transform both the individual and society.

So Max in his courtroom speech said of the American Revolutionary

---

[12]P. 358. This was what Jan had told Bigger when he visited him in prison: "You believed enough to kill. You thought you were settling something, or you wouldn't have killed" (p. 246). Apparently, "all the killing" refers to all the times Bigger felt like killing.

War (p. 366): "Your Honor, remember that men can starve from a lack of self-realization as much as they can from a lack of bread! And they can *murder* for it, too! Did we not build a nation, did we not wage war and conquer in the name of a dream to realize our personalities and to make those realized personalities secure!" So, too, Sartre, in summarizing Fanon, echoes the statement that killing can be a creative act (the French existentialists, we may recall, acclaimed Wright and accepted him as one of their own):

> In the period of their helplessness, their mad impulse to murder is the expression of the [colonial] natives' collective unconscious. If this suppressed fury fails to find an outlet, it turns in a vacuum and devastates the oppressed creatures themselves. In order to free themselves they even massacre each other. . . . This irrepressible violence [in a war of national liberation] is . . . man re-creating himself. . . . The native cures himself of colonial neurosis by thrusting out the settler through force of arms. When his rage boils over, he rediscovers his lost innocence and he comes to know himself in that he creates himself.[13]

Bone, moreover, overlooks completely—as does Howe—Bigger's last words before his final "goodbye": "Tell. . . . Tell Mister. . . . Tell Jan hello. . . ." (p. 359; Wright's ellipses). Bigger does not go to death hating all white men. He accepts the comradeship of Jan, for the first time in his life dropping the "mister" in front of a white man's name. But this comradeship he will extend only to those who have earned it in action, not to superficial sympathizers, patronizing philanthropists, or bureaucratically arrogant radical sectarians. His pride in himself would not permit it otherwise.

Bigger realized in his death cell that "if there were any sure and firm knowledge for him, it would have to come from himself" (p. 350). And so it was. And just so, Wright indicates, the inner liberation of the blacks will have to come from within themselves. "There were rare moments," we were told early in the novel (pp. 97–98), "when a feeling and longing for solidarity with other black people would take hold of [Bigger]. . . . He felt that some day there would be a black man who would whip the black people into a tight band and together they would act and end fear and shame." Bigger in prison and in the face of death acquires the belief in himself and in his people that could propel the ghetto millions toward a goal that would catch "the mind and body in certainty and faith" (p. 98).

[13]Introd. to Frantz Fanon, *The Wretched of the Earth* (New York: Grove, 1966), pp. 16–18. With Sartre's point that the suppressed fury of the natives causes them to turn against each other, compare Bigger's violence in Doc's poolroom, when his fear of the hated white man forces him to attack Gus rather than to rob Blum's delicatessen.

Only between such blacks and such whites as Jan, the conclusion of *Native Son* implies, can there be genuine unity in a common struggle for a different and better form of society. This struggle for the third American revolution promises, in view of the adamant position of the ruling class that had rejected Max's plea and caused him to despair, to become, like the Revolutionary War and the Civil War, a bloody conflict before it is victorious.

Bitches, Whores, and Woman Haters: Archetypes and Typologies in the Art of Richard Wright

by Maria K. Mootry

The epigraph for the third and final part of *Lawd Today* is taken from T. S. Eliot's *Waste Land*: ". . . But at my back in a cold blast I hear/The rattle of the bones, and chuckle spread from ear to ear." This parodic voice, chill and despairing, conjures up a twentieth-century vision of Marvell's disquisition on the tyranny of time. Apocalyptic winds, the death's head and a cosmic sneer emblematize man's fate. And so the way of Jake Jackson, Wright's hapless hero in this narrative of frustration and defeat. In twenty-four hours of Jake's life, we see a quintessential anti-hero bungle his mock-quest, stumbling from one prosaic disaster to another. It is essentially a comedic vision, pitiless in its insistence on the absurd, relentless in its pursuit of our smallness as it is trampled by the stampede of time. Jake Jackson is a *schlemiel*, a black brother to Saul Bellow's luckless hero, Tommy Wilheim of *Seize the Day*. But while Tommy wants one more chance to make it big, Jake merely wants to survive with a modicum of dignity; to be able to entertain his pals and to assuage his burgeoning sexual needs. Jake's quest is the quest of all of Wright's heroes: the pursuit of Manhood. In the final analysis it is a *macho* quest in which the hero, battling the odds of economic determinism, institutional racism, and personal flaws, counts as one of his most serious obstacles that ubiquitous, irritating presence, the black woman.

Set during the Depression years in Chicago, *Lawd Today* is a post-Harlem Renaissance, pre-*Native Son* novel in ambiance and technique. Jake Jackson's very name recalls the vagabond "low-life" hero of Claude McKay's novels of black urban life. In those novels, too, the essential fable was the fable of black male camaraderie. Music, cabaret, and familylessness were the givens. But now it is after the Crash and Jake, blessed with a good job at the Chicago post office, cannot afford to let go.

"Bitches, Whores, and Woman Haters: Archetypes and Typologies in the Art of Richard Wright" by Maria K. Mootry. Printed with permission from the author.

117

Besides, the entire world is in a state of upheaval, as learned by looking over Jake's shoulder when he reads the morning paper: Einstein discovering that space bends, Communists rioting in New York, Hitler calling on the world to smash Jews. There is no escaping to Marseilles; Jake can only read, offer his naive, uninformed commentary, and turn on his whiny wife, Lillian, when she makes another dumb remark. Jake, for all his vanity, is a victim of forces he cannot understand. McKay's men were victims, too, but he transmuted their oppression into a mystique of black exoticism and elasticity. But while McKay's heroes, Jake and his pal, Ray, are allegories of instinct and intellect, acting out McKay's predetermined affirmative stance, in *Lawd Today* the hero's growing sense of powerlessness unmasks a paranoia that anticipates the psychopathology of his successor, Bigger Thomas. The remarkable achievement is Wright's ironic controlling tone which distances us from his hero. We laugh, albeit embarrassedly at Jake; Bigger Thomas will be no joke.

Wright's fictions illustrate the maxim that the great writer has only one story to tell and he tells it over and over again. Wright's heroes, beginning with Jake Jackson, are all of a piece. Narcissistic, they value the company of men above all; they are childless; and they define themselves in opposition to women, either by using them, by perceiving themselves as being used by them, or in extreme situations, by transmuting the impulse to love to the impulse to violence and even death. If this latter fusion of *eros* and *thanatos* sounds familiar, it should, because Wright's artistic vision accords strikingly well with that malady diagnosed by D. H. Lawrence in *Studies in Classical American Literature* and later by Leslie Fiedler in *Love and Death in the American Novel*. As James Baldwin noted in his essay, "Alas, Poor Richard," there is a space in Wright's fiction where love should be, and that space is filled with violence. If there is a difference between Wright's heroes and the other American heroes, it is that Wright's men ostensibly turn to violence out of a sense of having been violated by the racial-economic injustices of America. And the black woman, as we shall see, is perceived as a co-conspirator of the oppressor.

Jake's narcissism is the primary narcissism of the street man, the zoot suiter, the hipster, the superfly. In his autobiography, Malcolm X recreates vividly his stage as a macho pimp, conked hair and bad rags, the glorification of maleness to an almost aesthetic plane. Gwendolyn Brooks, in her finely honed poem, "Sundays of Satin Legs Smith," memorializes the type, evoking the narrow selfishness and survival tactic of pride in satin underwear and the elegant wardrobe; the concentration upon self which renders women merely warm bodies, scarcely bared of limb and leg, to assuage a lonely Sunday afternoon. Accordingly, while poor wife Lillian moans over ill health and doctor bills, Jake grooms himself for his little odyssey into the street. The scene of Jake standing before his closet is skillfully handled; Wright, as Booth has suggested a good author should, correctly renders his hero sympathetic by staying with his point of view, yet achieves complicity with the reader by irony. Jake's taste in clothes is atrocious, but we grant him his culture and smile indulgently when he pivots in front of his mirror and pronounces the final verdict: "Like a Maltese kitten." Only the huge imitation ruby, that "burned like a smear of fresh blood," infuses the ominous note that foreshadows Jake's untidy defeat.

There is some evidence that Wright himself indulged in this primary narcissism, although his self-centeredness reached a more subtle level. In a letter included in a tribute to Wright, Harry Birdoff recalls that Wright was "a Natty dresser."[1] More significant is the way Wright consistently depicts himself as a superior being in the company of barely comprehending women in various autobiographical pieces. In *Black Boy*, for example, Wright recalls his encounter with two women in Memphis, Tennessee where he stops on his way north. In this episode, Wright finds himself "threatened" by the peasant mentality of his landlady, Mrs. Moss and her daugher, Bess.[2] Simple Bess is ready to be had and pounces on poor Richard for a prospective husband. "You like Bess, Richard?" Mrs. Moss asks at their first meeting. Richard is astounded. "What kind of people were these?" he asks incredulously. Wright dismisses poor Bess with this passage:

> Later, after I had grown to understand the peasant mentality of Bess and her mother, I learned the full degree to which my life at home had cut me off, not only from white people but from Negroes as well. To Bess and her mother, money was important, but they did not strive for it too hard. *They had no tensions, unappeasable longings, no desire to do something to redeem themselves.* The main value in their lives was simple, clean, good living and when they thought they had found those same qualities in one of their race, they instinctively embraced him, liked him, and asked no questions. But such simple unaffected trust flabbergasted me. It was impossible. (234) [Emphasis mine.]

Bess and her mother are avatars of the feudal, simplistic Southern peasant, while Wright is the hero, on his quest to the urban industrial North. They are part of the obstacles every hero must overcome in his quest for himself. Tensionless Bess can only offer Richard food ("You can eat with us any time you like"). Food, Sex and Religion are the anodynes with which these women are associated—everything to narcotize an intelligent, questioning spirit. "Would they be angry with me when they learned that my life was a million miles from theirs?" Wright immodestly wonders (p. 234).

Interestingly, it was not only the black woman who precipitated this

---

[1] In Richard Wright: *Impressions and Perspectives,* eds. David Ray and Robert Farnsworth (Ann Arbor, 1973), p. 81.

[2] *Black Boy* (New York, 1966); pp. 228–243, *passim.*

sense of superior separateness in Wright. In his essay, "The Man Who Went to Chicago," Wright contemplates his fellow white women workers in a similar fashion.[3] Once again we find the persona looking down at a preconsciousness that astounds him. This time he attributes the atrophied sensibilities of the female to the seduction of American materialism:

> During my lunch hour, which I spent on a bench in a near-by park, the waitresses would come and sit beside me, talking at random, laughing, joking, smoking cigarettes. I learned about their tawdry dreams, their simple hopes, their home lives, their fear of feeling anything deeply, their sex problems, their husbands. They were an eager, restless, talkative, ignorant bunch, but casually kind, and impersonal for all that. *They knew nothing of hate and fear, and strove instinctively to avoid all passion.* (179) [Emphasis mine]

With somewhat contradictory logic, Wright finds these women workers lacking precisely because they are not "Negro":

> I often wondered what they were trying to get out of life, but I never stumbled upon a clue, and I doubt if they themselves had any notion. They lived on the surface of their days; their smiles were surface smiles, and their tears were surface tears. Negroes lived a truer and deeper life than they, but I wished that Negroes, too, could live as thoughtlessly, serenely, as they. The girls never talked of their feelings; *none of them possessed the insight or the emotional equipment to understand themselves or others.* How far apart in culture we stood! *All my life I had done nothing but feel and cultivate my feelings; all their lives they had done nothing but strive for petty goals,* the trivial material prizes of American life. We shared a common tongue, but my language was a different language from theirs. (179) [Emphasis mine]

Later, Bigger Thomas would find himself besieged by a rich white girl whose vacuous life impels her to seek real experience by demanding that he act as her guide to that mysterious world of the Chicago black ghetto.

Jake and Al and Bob and Slim in *Lawd Today*; Bigger and Gus and Jack in *Native Son*; Fishbelly and his friends in *The Long Dream*—these are the communities of equals Wright constructs in his fiction. Eventually the hero, an isolato and loner, moves beyond even this community, but it is here that he is nourished and formed. Some of the conversations between males in Wright's fiction read like stream-of-consciousness passages. Man-to-man they understand the sexual jokes, the shared information, the cathartic complaints, the swagger of profanity. Language among males is an inclusive ritual for Wright; a language reserved for men only. *Lawd Today* contains this dialogue at its best. Here is an example of how Wright uses dialogue to establish character, provide information and above all, to illustrate the ritualistic function of language among black males:

---

[3]Included in *Eight Men* (New York, 1961), this autobiographical essay is part of the then unpublished manuscript, "American Hunger."

> They were silent. Steam hissed in the radiator. Jake belched and nestled
> his head deep into a corner of the sofa. He was pleasantly vacuous. . . .
>
> "Gawd, I wish Al and Slim would come on."
> "Me too."
> "We could have a game then."
> "Don't time pass slow?"
> "Don't it."
> "Just drags."
> "Makes you nervous."
> " 'Specially when you ain't got nothing to do."
> "I never did like to just *set*."
> "Me neither."
> "Yeah, it gets on your nerves."
> Jake took another drink.
> "Say, ain't that too bad about Slim?"[4]

And so on, for a page or two.

Perhaps more important than the fact that this is an all male conversation is the superior status Wright gives his reader. Through the unspoken rhetoric of his fiction, he creates a community of author and reader: we enter into complicity with the distanced narrator who is telling us that, macho though this group may be, they are ultimately an assemblage of victims in a world hounded by illness, underemployment and the inexorable march of time. In this scene Wright provides the dimension James Baldwin complained was missing from *Native Son*, "this dimension being the relationship that Negroes bear to one another, that depth of involvement and unspoken recognition of shared experience which creates a way of life."[5] But Wright's genius goes beyond the simple celebration of black culture; his is the true ironic mode, the classic "myth of winter" where we see a hero "inferior in power or intelligence to ourselves, so that we have the sense of looking down on a scene of bondage, frustration or absurdity."[6] From Squirrel's Cage to Rat's Alley, Jake's situation, mediated though it is by his capacity for friendship and participation in black rituals, is still one of "unrelieved bondage . . . the nightmare of social tyranny."[7] This is comedy in the ultimate sense. As Louis Kronenberger observed in "Some Prefatory Words on Comedy," it is closer to pessimism than to optimism, associated at any rate "with a belief in the smallness that survives as against the greatness that is scarred or destroyed."[8]

[4]*Lawd Today* (New York, 1963), p. 66. Written between 1935 and 1937, the novel was published posthumously.

[5]See Baldwin's famous criticism of Wright in "Many Thousands Gone," in *Notes of a Native Son*, p. 27.

[6]Northrop Frye, *Anatomy of Criticism* (Princeton, 1957), p. 34.

[7]*Ibid.*, p. 238.

[8]*The Thread of Laughter* (New York: Knopf, 1952), p. 3.

The determinism of *Lawd Today* notwithstanding, Wright's heroes often find themselves in a state of what Heidegger has called "throwness-into-being": they are extra-conscious, full of contingency and potentiality. If the men embody this concept, however, the women are the exact opposite; they exist in a state of prehistory, embedded inchoately in the *condition humaine*. Only to the extent that men define themselves in opposition to women are they validated as recreated, autonomous beings. If one accepts the philosophy of archetypal study, then Erich Neumann's description of the elementary character of the Negative Feminine aptly describes the pattern of male-female relationships in Wright's fiction. Neumann states:

> The phases in the development of consciousness appear then as embryonic containment in the mother, as childlike dependence on the mother, as the relation of the beloved son to the Great Mother, and finally as the heroic struggle of the male hero against the Great Mother. In other words, the dialectical relation of consciousness to the unconscious takes the symbolic mythological form of a struggle between the Maternal-Feminine and the male child, and here the growing strength of the male corresponds to the increasing power of consciousness in human development.[9]

In one sense, Wright creates archetypes in his fiction; his characters are typologies which personify the hero in opposition to his environment, which includes "the feminine." In this sense they project a truth of the black experience, indeed of human experience, Baldwin's attacks on Wright notwithstanding. For Wright's men and women and their conflicts are *real* in the sense that Lukács defines realism. According to Lukács in *Realism in Our Time: Literature and the Class Struggle:*

> The literature of realism, aiming at a truthful reflection of reality, must demonstrate both the concrete and abstract potentialities of human beings. . . .[10]

Typology, for Lukács, is the gift of the great realist writer, more desirable than day-to-day detail. As he explains:

> Typology and perspective are thus related in a special way. The great realist writer is alone able to grasp and portray trends and phenomena truthfully in their historical development—"trends" in that area where human behaviour is moulded and evaluated, where existing types are developed further and new types emerge.[11]

For a man of Wright's time, the basis of his typology, of his "unconscious possession of a perspective independent of, and reaching beyond, his understanding of the contemporary scene," lay in his perception of the de-feudalization of the black experience. Beginning with the turn of

---

[9]Erich Neumann, *The Great Mother: An Analysis of the Archetype* (Princeton, 1972), p. 148.
[10]See the essay, "Critical Realism and Socialist Realism," in *Realism in Our Time* (New York, 1964), pp. 93–135. This citation from p. 56.
[11]*Ibid.*, p. 57.

the century blacks were steadily, in spurts and waves, leaving the agrarian South with its culture in all its parameters: the folk imagination and the religious worldview. And every plot Wright devised was a commentary on this historical development; every character he created a player upon that stage. The conflicts between men and women in his fiction, while meeting Neumann's criteria for archetypal struggle dramatizes a central conflict in the specific black experience. All of Wright's women, as has been observed of Baldwin's fiction, are Mothers or Whores.[12] As mothers, the women are equated with the Christian-Feudal-Folk element of the black experience; as whores they are associated with the abstract, formless, and isolated freedom found in a world grown increasingly technological and industrial.

Nowhere is the schematic positioning of men and women clearer than in *Native Son.* In this shocking tale of a black youth who recreates himself through crime, Wright's naturalism congeals into archetypal typology. Bigger's well-meaning mother, like almost all of Wright's fictional mothers, represents the timidity and refuge of a folk-feudal mentality; Bigger's girlfriend, Bessie Mears, represents the deracinated worker living in the alien industrial world; and Mary Dalton, the wealthy white radical who befriends Bigger, is a nouvelle Desdemona, the bitch goddess of American success, the forbidden fruit of Marxism and white womanhood. Each is a form of consciousness, a kind of threat or conscience at the same time that they are examples of reductive feminineness; and both are threats that Bigger, in his desperate quest for manhood, must "blot out." The schema is multifaceted. Bigger is a black everyman, the hero whose essence is existential, contingent, protean; Mrs. Thomas, his mother, represents the sacred ethos epitomized in the spirituals; Bessie represents the secular culture, particularly the aesthetic and existential stance of the blues; and Mary Dalton represents the integrationist, global ethic of scientific socialism. The three women further represent three types of love: maternal, sexual or erotic, and political (platonic). In a sense, the very plot of the novel involves the encounter with and the ensuing demise of the various forms of love (including the *agape* or fraternal love of Bigger's friends), as Bigger moves toward his final "shock of recognition."

Bigger's conflict with his mother and his final rejection of her maternal love belongs to a "phenomenon truthful in the historical development" of Black Americans. Who can forget Lena Younger in Lorraine Hansberry's *Raisin in the Sun* cowing her twenty-two-year old daughter and thirty-five-year old son into respect for her person and her religious convictions? Too often, and this is not without its positive side, but too often in the black

---

[12]See "The Stink of Reality: Mothers and Whores in James Baldwin's Fiction" by Charlotte Alexander, in *James Baldwin: A Collection of Critical Essays,* ed. Keneth Kinnamon (Englewood Cliffs, N.J., 1974), 77–95.

community, Mama is an awesome blend of maternal love, spiritual
authority and physical support. "We wouldn't have to live in this garbage
dump if you had any manhood in you," she reminds him, at once demanding, critical, bitchy. Her faith is lost on alienated Bigger and completely
ironical given the fate that awaits her son. When she sings:

> Life is like a mountain railroad
> With an engineer that's brave
> We must make the run successful
> From the cradle to the grave. . . (14)

she does not realize how ironic her lyrics are; Bigger will go to an early
grave, but no Christian *caritas* or loving engineer will give him a "successful" run. At other times, Mrs. Thomas functions as a kind of jeremiah
chorus when she warns:

> ". . . mark my word, some of these days you going to set down and *cry*.
> Some of these days you going to wish you had made something out of
> yourself, instead of just a tramp. But it'll be too late then." (13)

Bigger replies impatiently, "Stop prophesying about me." We are
reminded of Grier and Cobbs' analysis in *Black Rage* (1968): according to
them, women like Mrs. Thomas offer a perversion of love; a love warped
by their own suffering. Giving up youth, beauty, and sex, these women
narrow their vision to "the most essential feminine function—mothering,
nurturing, and protecting their children."[13] Their love is essentially an
inhibiting force. Certainly Mrs. Thomas' attitude recalls the portrayal of
Wright's mother in his autobiographical essay, "The Ethics of Living Jim
Crow."[14] There Wright describes how his mother beat him mercilessly
when she discovered he had fought white boys. "How come yuh didn't
hide?" she asked, "How come yuh always fightin'?" As Grier and Cobbs
explained:

> In the black household the man faces greater than usual odds in making
> his way. The care and rearing of children falls even more heavily on the
> wife; she is the culture bearer. She interprets the society to the children and
> takes as her task the shaping of their character to meet the world as she
> knows it. This is every mother's task. But the black mother has a more
> ominous message for her child and feels more urgently the need to get the
> message across. The child must know that the white world is dangerous
> and that if he does not understand its rules it may kill him. (61)

The result is that the black man develops considerable hostility toward
black women because they are, in spite of their professed love, perceived

---

[13]William Grier and Price Cobbs, *Black Rage* (New York, 1968), pp. 53–54.
[14]Included in the collection of short stories by Wright, *Uncle Tom's Children* (New York,
1965), pp. 3–15.

as "inhibiting instruments of an oppressive system," and because their message is essentially contradictory. Even as Mrs. Thomas demands that Bigger act like a man she displays little confidence in him and even wonders aloud why she "birthed" him. Again, as Grier and Cobbs observed:

> She may have been permissive in some areas and punitive and rigid in others. There are remembrances of stimulation and gratification coexisting with memories of deprivation and rejection There is always the feeling that the behaviour of the mother was purposeful and deliberate.
>
> The black man remembers that his mother underwent frequent and rapid shifts of mood. He remembers the cruelty. The mother who sang spirituals gently at church was capable of inflicting senseless pain at home. These themes of gratification and cruelty are consistent enough to suggest that they played a critical role in preparing the boy for adulthood. (61–62)

Little wonder Bigger "escapes" this suffocating maternal "love" for the rough camaraderie of his pals. They can share fantasies while watching typical movies like *The Gay Woman* (Wright himself was fond of the cinema). All too soon, of course, Bigger's intense fears and ambivalence about indulging in street crime will disrupt even this peer-group solidarity.

Mary Dalton, Bigger's American Aphrodite, his nouvelle Desdemona, represents the dual lures of two forbidden fruits: white womanhood and Marxist politics. At first, the "love" she offers him is almost platonic: she is the first white person to respond to Bigger as an equal; and her queries about Bigger's membership in a union imply her acceptance of Bigger as a working man. Her very simplicity "confounds" Bigger. He is not used to such uncritical attitudes, from whites or blacks. Yet there are early overtones that the Bigger-Mary attraction is "perverted": her excessive drinking and her curiosity about "black life" suggests that she associates Bigger with the sensual, the taboo. Bigger, already goaded by the blonde heroine in his afternoon film, refuses to see Mary as a person: she is the rich white girl, the real counterpart of the Ginger Rogers, Jean Harlow, and Janet Gaynor posters that decorate his room in the Dalton home. She is the American bitch goddess of success, a "whore," yet everything he has been brainwashed to believe the ultimate of femininity to be: she is beautiful, slender, and soft, much softer than Bessie. And so, in the dark and feeling warmed by too much rum, he rapes her (psychologically if not physically; there is some evidence that the rape actually occurs in an earlier version of the novel). He steals the white man's pride, he desecrates the shrine, the pristine vessel of white womanhood, he asserts his black manhood through the one force allowed him in a nay-saying society; his sexual organ.

Of course, not quite. In the South, the archetypal pattern of black-white love had led to death or literal dissolution. Wright, in a "nightmare of remembrance," recalled an episode on the job:

> One of the bell-boys was caught in bed with a white prostitute. He was castrated and run out of town. Immediately after this all the bell-boys and hall-boys were called together and warned. We were given to understand that the boy who had been castrated was a "mighty, mighty lucky bastard." We were impressed with the fact that next time the management of the hotel would not be responsible for the lives of "trouble-makin' niggers." (12)

And so we find Bigger acting out his self-imposed role in a ritualistic American drama. When a long slow sigh goes up from the bed into the air of the darkened room, it is the final, irrevocable sigh of death, of death in love, of the death of love between black and white. In a sense, Mary Dalton becomes a kind of sacrifice: she offers herself in "love," making her death a necessity; she causes the birth of a new Bigger. In a reversal of the classical lynching pattern, she becomes the whore-as-*pharmakos*, taking on herself the sins of her society, dying that black manhood may be born.

The theme of love-and-death is equally germane to the Bigger/Bessie relationship. This relationship shows a new trend in the black experience. Lukács called for " 'trends' not so much in the social and political field, as in that area where human behaviour is moulded and evaluated, where existing types are developed further and new types emerge." Bessie Mears, a maid in a white neighborhood whose only recreation is alcohol and sex, is a new type. She is the secularized blues individual; her love for Bigger is a bluesy kind of love; undemanding, with no expectations, laced with pain and an acute sense of *temporariness*. The Bessies of black life, from Ma Rainey to Bessie Smith, are the products of the increasing alienation of an urban, proletarianized culture. Bessie represents "the suffering woman caught up in the web of uncontrollable destructive forces."[15] Love, for her, becomes another form of self-immolation; already oppressed, she seeks in Bigger another oppressor—anything to assuage her sense of *anomie*. The moments when she rises above her femaleness, her vulnerability, and begins to act as a reality principle for him, are rejected by Bigger; he prefers to relate to her as an embodiment of need, of suffering, of willlessness, of mindless whoredom.[16] He wants only erotic love from Bessie. As they walk in the snow Bigger longs to "suddenly be back in bed with her, feeling her body warm and pliant to his" (133). But the look on her face threatens him: it is hard and distant; it asks questions. "He wished he could clench his fist and swing his arm and blot out, kill, sweep

---

[15]Watson, p. 169.

[16]Saundra Towns in "The Black Woman as Whore: Genesis of the Myth" explains, "When a man calls his woman 'whore,' he says several things: that she is lower than the prostitute, who is, after all, earning a living; that she is virtueless, unprincipled as well as promiscuous; that her base sexual instincts take precedence over deeper feelings; that she is untrustworthy, her love worthless and defiled" (p. 39).

away the Bessie on Bessie's face and leave the other helpless and yielding before him" (133).

Like Mary Dalton, in death Bessie is more meaningful to Bigger than in life. Bigger's triumph over his oppression and his transformation to a conscious hero is catalyzed by contemplating what Bessie's life *meant*. During the trial which will end in Bigger's own death sentence, he sees the totality of Bessie's life from a heightened perspective, from the perspective Lukács required of the realist writer himself "independent of, and reaching beyond, his understanding of the contemporary scene":

> .. he felt a deeper sympathy for Bessie than at any time when she was alive. . . . Anger quickened in him; an old feeling that Bessie had often described to him when she had come from long hours of hot toil in the white folks' kitchens, a feeling of being forever commanded by others so much that thinking and feeling for one's self was impossible. . . . (307)

In *Love and Death in the American Novel,* Leslie Fiedler theorizes that "our great novelists though experts on indignity and assault, on loneliness and terror, tend to avoid treating the passionate encounter of a man and woman, which we expect at the center of a novel. Indeed, they rather shy away from permitting in their fictions the presence of any full-fledged mature women giving us instead monsters of virtue or bitchery, symbols of the rejection or fear of sexuality" (45). At first glance, Wright does not seem to belong to this "tradition." Yet, in a curious way, his fictions do lack *passion*. Bigger Thomas is no innocent Huck, but the encounters of this hero with females are essentially passionless. Love, in much of Wright's fiction, and certainly in *Native Son,* is primarily love of self—it is narcissism as a survival tactic seeking the shock of experience. It is indissolubly linked with death, the deaths of old selves, making way for recreated selves. However brutal and unfair to women (and to our idea of love) Wright seems to be, we must accept his treatment of the relations between men and women for what it is: a metaphor for the struggle of an oppressed people to deal with history with dignity and meaning, a vision that for all of its rigid compartmentalization into bitches, whores, and woman-haters offers a painful and powerful truth of our history which should never be "blotted out."

The Existential Quest:
Freedom and Enclosure

The American Negro and the Image of the Absurd

by Esther Merle Jackson

One of the factors affecting the changing status of the American Negro today is the rise of certain new perspectives which have altered our perception of the condition of man. The modern arts, in particular the art of literature, have dramatized the fact that an ever larger segment of humanity seems to share the kind of existence which has been the lot of the Negro for some three centuries or more. The shape of human suffering, defined by Dostoevsky, Proust, Gide, Malraux, Mann, Sartre, and others, mirrors the actual condition of the Negro: his alienation from the larger community, his isolation within abstract walls, his loss of freedom, and his legacy of despair. Although many modern writers trace their vision of the human dilemma to developments in European intellectual history, it is quite clear that one of the perceptions profoundly affecting the modern mind has been the image of the Negro. Indeed, it may be said that he has served as a prototype of that contemporary philosophic species, "the absurd."[1]

But the image of man as the absurd is not new. For the absurd sensibility is an acute consciousness of human crisis: it celebrates man's desperate struggle to order the moral universe, without recourse to powers outside of himself. Like all symbols, the image of man as the absurd has had an extended aesthetic and philosophic history. Characteristic aspects of this perception may be seen throughout Western literature: in the work of Aeschylus, Euripides, Shakespeare, Cervantes, Milton, Molière, and Goethe, among others. Albert Camus, in his catalogue of heroes, cites Quixote, Hamlet, and Don Juan, along with Sisyphus, Prometheus, and Jesus Christ. While certain components of this radical perception appear in earlier forms of literature, philosophy, and theology, the actual elevation of man to the plane of ultimate power and responsibility in and for the world is, in the main, the contribution of the contemporaries. The modern

"The American Negro and the Image of the Absurd" by Esther Merle Jackson. From *Phylon: The Atlanta Review of Race and Culture,* 23 (Winter 1962), 359–60, 364–68. Copyright © 1962 by *Phylon.* Reprinted by permission of *Phylon* and the author.

[1] Albert Camus, *The Myth of Sisyphus,* trans. Justin O'Brien (New York, 1955).

perspective begins, writes Camus, at the moment when Dostoevsky's Raskolnikov declares that "everything is possible." It is this universe of infinite human possibility that Camus and others have named "the absurd."

It is, perhaps, fitting that the American Negro should stand as a symbol, a sign, of the total condition of man in the twentieth century. For in many ways, the Negro is the very ground of the human conflict in our time. Like America itself, he may be described as a *synthesis,* as an attempt to reconcile certain antithetical ideas embodied in the terms: Europe and Africa, black and white, master and slave. But the fundamental absurdity of his condition—like that of modern man in general—may be traced to an even more critical ideological encounter: to the tension arising from the collision between the ethic of power and the idea of moral law. It is this moral crisis—the culmination of a long historical struggle—which engages the mind of our epoch; its implications extend far beyond the projected solution of the Negro's immediate problem to the question of human survival on this planet.

American literature has always reflected an interest in the idea of a responsible humanity. European writers of the twentieth century are heavily indebted to the American Classicists, Hawthorne, Emerson, Whitman, Melville, and O'Neill, as well as to more contemporary minded artists such as Poe, James, Faulkner, Wright, Steinbeck, Hemingway, and others. While no one of these, with the possible exception of O'Neill, has been consciously concerned with the idea of the Negro as the absurd, there have been suggestions of this theme in the work of many less popular artists, particularly in that of Negro writers such as Langston Hughes. In the main, however, the image of the Negro as hero in American literature is fragmentary. We may, however, piece together a vision of his role in the moral universe, from partialities. Three such component visions are William Faulkner's *Light in August,* Richard Wright's *Native Son,* and Ralph Ellison's *Invisible Man.* While these works have, formerly, been interpreted in light of other critical perspectives, they may now be read as studies in phases of the absurd sensibility. Together, they compose an anti-traditional image of the Negro. For they may be read as a composite chronicle of his journey toward understanding, knowledge, and responsibility, in the climate of the absurd.

[In a section of this essay entitled "Absurd Walls," the author traces Faulkner's depiction of Joe Christmas in *Light in August* as an "outsider" like Camus' Sisyphus, a "cosmic fugitive," a tragic figure isolated between the privileged world of the white characters and the "dehumanized" black world of Yoknapatawpha County. He is at once an actual fugitive and a "metaphysical traveller." "The odyssey of Joe Christmas thus includes two simultaneous movements. . . . One, a ritual progression toward capture and defeat, moves in time; the other, a gesture toward self-knowledge, triumph, and salvation, exists outside of time. . . ." "Although Christmas progresses in his absurd odyssey, in the critical phase of his journey toward freedom, his nerve fails. He is unable to complete the cycle of revolt; rather, he allows himself, finally, to be crucified."]

Absurd Revolt

If William Faulkner's *Light in August* provides an effective image of a Negro as an absurd sufferer, Richard Wright's *Native Son* is, perhaps, to this time, the most moving and passion-filled portrait of a Negro as man in revolt against Fate.[2] Interpreted in the forties primarily as a sociopolitical tract, *Native Son* may in the light of recent history—political and intellectual—be seen for its greater merit: as a record of a man's dramatic encounter with Fate in the climate of the absurd. To be understood clearly, *Native Son* should be viewed in the light of other works in the contemporary genre. Like *Crime and Punishment*, or *The Stranger*, it is a study in the second phase of the absurd cycle—revolt. It is the chronicle of a terror-filled and terrifying search for a way to escape the absurd walls.[3]

Although Bigger Thomas is like Joe Christmas in the essentials of the dilemma he endures, he differs from Faulkner's protagonist in ways which are, perhaps, to be expected. For Wright seems to understand the internal life of his character more clearly, and is thus able to give him richer motivation. Bigger's complexity connotes his advance in consciousness over that of the earlier protagonist. Like Hamlet, he not only feels his dilemma, he understands it. He perceives his role, his alienation from the two worlds which compose the absurd universe. Wright describes him as living in a kind of "No Man's Land."

> But they made him feel his black skin by just standing there looking at him, one holding his hand and the other smiling. He felt he had no physical existence at all right then; he was something he hated, the badge of shame which he knew was attached to a black skin. It was a shadowy region, a No Man's Land, the ground that separated the white world from the black that he stood upon. He felt naked, transparent. . . .[4]

Wright takes his point of departure from the story of a man in desperate circumstance, a South-side Chicago Negro named Bigger Thomas. Bigger, like Christmas, lives in a schizoid universe, a world articulated into conflicting and seemingly unreconcilable modes of reality. Like Christmas, Bigger is an alien from both of these worlds. But Bigger's consciousness

---

[2]Revolt is one theme of the discussion of *Native Son* in Morris Weitz, *A Philosophy of the Arts* (Cambridge, Massachusetts, 1950), pp. 137–41.

[3]See Robert A. Bone, *The Negro Novel in America* (New Haven, 1958), p. 144.

[4]Richard Wright, *Native Son* (New York, 1940), p. 58.

is more complex than that of the Southern Negro Christmas, for he sees his situation as the face of profound universal disorder. Bigger views the conflict between black and white not simply as the face of individual crises or of political and social upheaval, but rather as a sign of cosmic tension between force and submission, love and hate, life and death. In the early moments of the novel, he sees himself as a victim of this struggle, as a man caught in the lines of force between that power represented by the "white" world and that servility embodied in the "black." Like Christmas, Bigger sees himself as a creature deprived of being:

> To Bigger and his kind white people were not really people; they were a sort of great natural force, like a stormy sky looming overhead; or like a deep swirling river stretching suddenly at one's feet in the dark. As long as he and his black folks did not go beyond certain limits, there was no need to fear that white force. But whether they feared it or not, each and every day of their lives they lived with it; even when words did not sound its name, they acknowledged its reality.[5]

Bigger, like Hamlet, broods upon his dilemma. Similarly, he seeks to amend his fate by choosing to identify himself with that idea which he believes to have been the genesis of his suffering. He elects power as the sign of his being. It is important at this point to remember that *Native Son* was written in the thirties, at a time when the question which confronted Bigger Thomas absorbed the world consciousness. Bigger Thomas, child of his age, chooses to join the cult of the Nietzschean "superman." He elects violence, crime, and vengeance as the signs of life. *Native Son* has, then, certain significant elements of the more conventional tragic vision, especially of Aeschylean form. For Bigger, like his modern European counterpart, echoes the Promethean, the metaphysical criminal, in revolt against established law. *Native Son* is the chronicle of a man's collision with Fate, in the climate of the absurd.

Many of the difficulties which have arisen in connection with the interpretation of this novel have grown out of a critical tendency to view Wright's work purely in terms of certain deterministically oriented nineteenth century perspectives. Such perspectives define man as a creature dominated by biological, sociological, political, and psychological drives rather than as a free being, capable of exercising individual will. The absurd view attempts to recover for man the principle of freedom, a freedom which is the goal of Bigger's revolt. In *Native Son* this motive is often obscured by the novelist's use of emotion-charged symbolic structures. Like Faulkner, Wright employs the explosive myth of color as a significant element of his language. But there is a second factor which has been even more distracting to American critics. For, as Professor Robert

Bone points out, Wright, like other writers of the Depression Era, has integrated elements of Marxist theory into the fabric of his linguistic structure. In 1962, it is clear that *Native Son* transcends these elements of language. Whatever Wright's intention, *Native Son* is not now primarily a story of racial, political, or social injustice in America of the thirties and forties. As in Sophocles' *Antigone*, the particulars only serve as a way in to the larger question. Wright's novel is a study of the question which threatened the world of the thirties and forties and which remains, essentially, unanswered: What is man's responsibility in a universe where everything is possible? The story of Bigger Thomas, like that of Hamlet, is an attempt to probe this moral problem.

Now if Faulkner is often thought to be unaware of many of the latent contents of *Light in August*, Wright was not at all naïve about the meaning of his work. In an article, "How 'Bigger' Was Born," he wrote that he attempted to create an image of man consistent with the moral confusion of the forties:

> More than anything else, as a writer, I was fascinated by the similarity of the emotional tensions of Bigger in America and Bigger in Nazi Germany and Bigger in old Russia. All Bigger Thomases, white and black, felt tense, afraid, nervous, hysterical and restless.[6]

He describes the world of Bigger in these terms:

> A world whose fundamental assumptions could no longer be taken for granted; a world ridden with national and class strife; a world whose metaphysical meanings had vanished; ... a world in which men could no longer retain their faith in an ultimate hereafter.[7]

The adoption of the absurd view as a critical perspective raises, in this case especially, several important questions: Is Bigger a hero or a victim? Can he be described, with justification, as a man seeking to engage Fate? Can we accept a criminal as hero? In each case, the question of Bigger's guilt is critical, for on it hangs the main argument of the novel. It is impossible, from the point of view of this essay, to claim that Bigger moves toward revolt by accident. For the murder of Mary Dalton, like Hamlet's murder of Polonius, Meursault's murder of the Arab, or Christmas' murder of Joanna Burden, is merely an external gesture which gives shape to the motives and ideas which have been seething in his consciousness. Fate simply provides Bigger Thomas with the circumstances; he is, in the contemporary sense, guilty. It is true, certainly, that Wright confuses his plot by introducing long discussions of society's involvement in Bigger's crime. The guilt of society, however, is another matter which is related

---

[6]Richard Wright, "How 'Bigger' Was Born," *Saturday Review of Literature*, XXII (June 1, 1940), 3–4, 17–20.

[7]*Ibid.*

to, but not responsible for, Bigger's action. Insofar as this essay is concerned, the pivot of the plot is the consciousness of guilt—both actual and metaphysical—which grows in the mind of the protagonist. For out of this knowledge, he gains an understanding of his own meaning in the universe.

> The shame and fear and hate which Mary and Jan and Mr. Dalton and that huge rich house had made rise so hard and hot in him had now cooled and softened. Had he not done what they thought he never could? His being black and at the bottom of the world was something which he could take with a new-born strength. What his knife and gun had once meant to him, his knowledge of having secretly murdered Mary now meant. No matter how they laughed at him for his being black and clownlike, he could look them in the eye and not feel angry. The feeling of always being enclosed in the stifling embrace of an invisible force had gone from him.[8]

It is for Bigger, then, as it has always been for the hero, this consciousness of guilt which is the access to knowledge. Through his cycle of suffering and revolt, he comes at last to a passion for life itself, to the threshold of meaning:

> "I ain't trying to forgive nobody and I ain't asking for nobody to forgive me. I ain't going to cry. They wouldn't let me live and I killed. Maybe it ain't fair to kill, and I reckon I didn't really want to kill. But when I think of what all the killing was, I begin to feel what I wanted, what I am. . . ."
> . . . .
> "I didn't want to kill!" Bigger shouted. "But what I killed for, I am! It must have been pretty deep in me to make me kill! I must have felt it awful hard to murder. . . ."
> . . . .
> "What I killed for must've been good!" Bigger's voice was full of frenzied anguish. "It must have been good! When a man kills, it's for something. . . . I didn't know I was really alive in this world until I felt things hard enough to kill for 'em. . . . It's the truth, Mr. Max. I can say it now, 'cause I'm going to die. . . ."[9]

Absurd Freedom

Wright poses, but does not clearly answer, the critical question as it affects his protagonist in the climate of the absurd: What are the conditions of heroism in the modern world? What is the actual nature of the freedom which modern man seeks? It is to this question that the last, and in many senses most important, of these works is directed. Indeed, perhaps the only novel which seems to be consciously concerned with discovering an

[8]There are many moments when Bigger admits this. See page 127.
[9]Wright, *Native Son*, p. 358.

answer to this question as it affects the American Negro is Ralph Ellison's distinguished work, *Invisible Man*. This novel shows, of course, many correspondences to the contemporary European form of Malraux, Sartre, Camus, and others. The novel, like the work of the Europeans cited, is the imitation of a search for intellectual clarity and order. *Invisible Man* recapitulates the odyssey of the philosophic "I," the journey of the fragmentary self through experience to knowledge and, ultimately, to being.

Invisible Man may be described as a philosophical novel; that is to say, its major interest lies in the illumination of, if not the answer to, the question of the human freedom. Ellison's work differs in certain significant ways from that of both Wright and Faulkner. To begin with, the novelist endows his protagonist with a higher level of consciousness than that of Christmas or of Bigger. For Ellison's protagonist is not only the "I" of experience; he is also the reasoning "I," the thinking self in search of a mode of reconciliation in which all of the conflicts present in existence may be unified. Ellison describes such reconciliation as "visibility."[10]

Like other modern novelists, Ellison constructs his image of reality after the example of *Hamlet*, as a play within a play. The novel is both the "mirror of experience" and the "face of conscience." At the portals of the interior "theatre" stands the searcher, the philosophic "I," through whose vision the images of experience flow. The novel is thus related on simultaneous planes of narration, on the Dionysian level of felt experience, as well as on the Apollonian level of reflection—the systematic presentation of ideas. In order to examine his experience at the reflective level, Ellison constructs a kind of schematic arrangement, what Ortega y Gasset has described as "scaffold," which identifies human experience in terms of philosophical alternatives.[11]

At the first level of narration, Ellison's "I" examines much the same world as do the protagonists of Faulkner and Wright, a world divided into modes of reality called "black" and "white." But for Ellison there are shadings in this pattern; that is to say, his protagonist finds grey areas, a limited access between worlds. Indeed, some of the finest writing in this novel is given to the expression of the protagonist's emotions about his anguished movement between these modes of being. Perhaps the most dramatic point in the expressive document is that at which the protagonist's confusion about these realities reaches proportions of insanity:

WHAT IS YOUR NAME?

A tremor shook me; it was as though he had suddenly given a name to, had organized the vagueness that drifted through my head, and I was overcome

---

[10]Ralph Ellison, *Invisible Man* (New York, 1947).

[11]See Ortega y Gasset's discussion of the contemporary search for a mode of objectification of experience in *The Dehumanization of Art and other Writings on Art and Culture* (Garden City, New York, 1956).

with swift shame. I realized that I no longer knew my own name. I shut my eyes and shook my head with sorrow. Here was the first warm attempt to communicate with me and I was failing. I tried again, plunging into the blackness of my mind. It was no use; I found nothing but pain. . . .[12]

But Ellison's novel is more than an account of critical insanity. His protagonist is engaged in an urgent mission, for he seeks to discover in the chaotic universe in which he has his partial existence, an ethic. Ellison's protagonist may be described as Hegelian man, a symbol of humanity in search of a viable moral principle. The protagonist, the "I," searches for this principle externally, in the communities to which his odyssey takes him: (1) the Southern town of his birth; (2) a Negro college; (3) a segregated community in the North; (4) the Northern world of industry; (5) a revolutionary political group; (6) a Negro ghetto in a Northern city.[13] The protagonist discovers, as the absurd hero is always to discover, that there can not exist such a community; that the creation of an ethic must be, in fact, the responsibility of the individual. Thereupon, the hero takes an action described by the critic René-Marill Albérès as the "descent into the self." M. Albérès has described the work of Sartre, Camus, Anouilh, and others in language appropriate to this discussion:

> Each of their heroes has for his mission to work out his destiny in solitude without the help of social patterns of divine grace, and each of these heroes also invents for his life an ethic for which the price is the refusal of all attitudes already achieved and modeled on social dishonesty and pretext.[14]

The symbol of this self-imposed alienation is for Ellison a hole in the ground, a complex image representing many things, among them what professor Bone describes as solitude, despair, death, and the whole "underground" life of the nation.[15]

It is at this point in consciousness that a third journey takes place; indeed, has, at the beginning of the book, already taken place. For the *raison d'être* of the novel is actually this account of the third odyssey, the journey within the self. It is here that the problem left essentially unanswered by Faulkner and Wright is confronted: How can the hero find freedom in the absurd world of "black" and "white?"

Ellison's "I" examines the possibilities which commend themselves:

> I am an invisible man. . . . I am invisible, understand, simply because people refuse to see me. Like the bodiless heads you see sometimes in circus sideshows, it is as though I have been surrounded by mirrors of hard,

[12]Ellison, *op. cit.*, p. 182.
[13]See Robert Bone's discussion of Ellison, *The Contemporary Negro Novel*, pp. 196–212.
[14]René-Marill Albérès, *La Révolte des écrivains d'aujourd'hui* (Paris: Correa, 1949), p. 15.
[15]Bone, *op. cit.*, pp. 201–03.

distorting glass. When they approach me they see only my surroundings, themselves, or figments of their imagination—indeed, everything and anything except me.
. . . .
That invisibility to which I refer occurs because of a peculiar disposition of the eyes of those with whom I come in contact. A matter of the construction of their *inner* eyes, those eyes with which they look through their physical eyes upon reality. . . . Or again, you often doubt if you really exist. You wonder whether you aren't simply a phantom in other people's minds. Say, a figure in a nightmare which the sleeper tries with all his strength to destroy. . . . You ache with the need to convince yourself that you do exist in a real world, that you're a part of all the sound and anguish and you strike out with your fists, you curse and you swear to make them recognize you. And, alas, it's seldom successful.[16]

Like Bigger, Ralph Ellison's protagonist comes to reject the vision of himself as a victim, and wills instead to assume responsibility for his own destiny:

You go along for years knowing something is wrong, then suddenly you discover that you're as transparent as air. At first you tell yourself that it's all a dirty joke, or that it's due to the "political situation." But deep down you come to suspect that you're yourself to blame, and you stand naked and shivering before the millions of eyes who look through you unseeingly.[17]

The protagonist, seeking to discern the nature of his own ethical alternatives, considers four possibilities: (1) formal segregation; (2) voluntary segregation; (3) integration; (4) revolt. Like Christmas and Bigger, Ellison's "I" chooses revolt. But the nature of his revolt is different from that of other figures whom we have considered, for it is not primarily physical. It is, rather, the revolt of consciousness—a renunciation which leads the protagonist finally into solitude. Like Dante's poet, the philosophic "I" descends into the depths of his own soul to begin the unraveling of the mystery of the self, to work out the details of his ethic. Ellison's "I" moves in paradoxical motion: backward to the beginning—the point of rebellion, the origin of his descent into despair—and, by the same token, forward in ascent to the beginning of knowledge, freedom, and visibility.

Absurd freedom for Ellison is the classic triumph of knowledge, the illumination of suffering:

Since you never recognize me even when in closest contact with me, and since, no doubt, you'll hardly believe that I exist, it won't matter if you know that I tapped a power line leading into the building and ran it into my hole in the ground. Before that I lived in the darkness into which I was

[16]Ellison, p. 3.
[17]*Ibid.*, p. 434.

chased, but now I see. I've illuminated the blackness of my invisibility—and vice versa. And so I play the invisible music of my isolation.[18]

Ellison's philosophic "I" discovers that the light which crowns torture with triumph is truth. Freedom is not escape from Hell through death or violence, but mastery of it. Like Camus' Sisyphus, Ellison's hero makes of his damnation his art. It is this qualitative heroism which gives meaning and sense to the life of the protagonist and which grants him that freedom which the absurd seeks. Ellison's final comment is a significant comment on the absurd journey: "And it is that which frightens me: Who knows but that, on the lower frequencies, I speak for you?"[19]

[18]*Ibid.*, p. 11.
[19]*Ibid.*, p. 439.

The Ordeal of Richard Wright

by Nick Aaron Ford

In their book *The Theory of Literature*, Wellek and Warren say that a work of art may embody the *dream* of an author rather than his actual life, or it may be the mask, the antiself, behind which his real self is hiding, or it may be a picture of the life from which the author wants to escape. In the writings of Richard Wright, there are glimpses at different times of all three of these purposes. But his dreams are often nightmares, and his masks are designed to reveal more than they hide. Perhaps to a greater extent than any other contemporary American novelist, Wright's authorship is a creature of environment and tortured memories.

Born on a plantation near Natchez, Mississippi, his early life consisted of a series of moves from one unsatisfactory place to another, of gnawing hunger, of parental neglect and misunderstanding, and of incredible humiliation inflicted by white employers. The earliest experience he remembers is one of horror and fear. At the age of four he set fire to his parents' home and barely escaped being burned to death under it. For that act, despite his tender years, his mother beat him into unconsciousness. The effect is summarized in *Black Boy,* his autobiography, in the following manner: "I was beaten out of my senses and later I found myself in bed screaming, determined to run away, tussling with my mother and father who were trying to keep me still. . . . But for a long time I was chastened whenever I remembered that my mother had come close to killing me."

At six he was a drunkard, spending his waking hours begging drinks from patrons of a near-by tavern, while his mother worked in domestic service to support him and his younger brother. At twelve he fought bitterly with his aunt, threatening to cut her throat with a butcher knife which he angrily clutched in his fist. At sixteen he burglarized a neighbor's house and a college storeroom and sold the stolen goods.

Then came the turning point. He stumbled upon *A Book of Prefaces* by H. L. Mencken. Of this experience he says:

"The Ordeal of Richard Wright" by Nick Aaron Ford. From *College English*, 15 (October 1953), 87–94. Copyright © by the National Council of Teachers of English. Reprinted by permission of the publisher and the author.

That night in my rented room, while letting the hot water run over my can of pork and beans in the sink, I opened *A Book of Prefaces* and began to read. I was jarred and shocked by the style, the clear, clean, sweeping sentences.... This man was fighting, fighting with words. He was using words as a weapon, using them as one would use a club. Could words be weapons? Well, yes, for there they were. Then, maybe, perhaps, I could use them as weapons?

The next year Richard left the South for Chicago and a new life. The past was dead; only its roots would persist as a memory of the days that had gone. But the memory was bitter. And out of it has flowed the bitter experiences of *Uncle Tom's Children,* of *Native Son,* of *Black Boy,* and of *The Outsider.*

Wright first gained national attention in 1938, when he won the $500 prize, awarded by *Story Magazine,* for his book of short stories entitled *Uncle Tom's Children.* The following year Edward O'Brien, the distinguished anthologist, selected Wright's "Bright and Morning Star" as one of the two best short stories published in 1939 and one of the fifty best stories published in America since 1915.

Although our chief concern is with his novels, *Native Son* (1940) and *The Outsider* (1953), a bare statement of the plots of his prize-winning stories will assist in creating additional background for a better understanding of the major works.

Each of the four stories in *Uncle Tom's Children* portrays the Negro in violent revolt against some phase of his environment. In "Big Boy Leaves Home" the revolt against white suppression and brutality ends in the murder of a white man by two Negro boys, whose companion had been killed without provocation by the white man. In "Down by the Riverside" a long-suffering Negro revolts against conditions that deny his wife an equal chance at medical care and hospitalization; he is lynched after killing a white man who symbolizes that repression. In "Long Black Song" the Negro husband revolts against the idea of a white man's using his wife for sexual purposes and returning the next morning to collect money for a phonograph which he had persuaded the victim to accept. The husband slays the seducer and waits with loaded gun for the lynching mob he knows will come. In "Fire and Cloud" the revolt is against crooked white politicians who try to frighten Negroes into political inactivity by mob violence against their leaders. In these stories Wright is perfecting a technique which reaches its fullest development in *Native Son.*

The main character in *Native Son* is Bigger Thomas, a twenty-year-old Chicago Negro who accidentally kills his wealthy employer's daughter. After he discovers the victim's death, fear drives him to burn her body in the furnace and later kill his frightened Negro girl friend who he thinks might, under police torture, betray his secret.

The murder of the white girl is purely accidental, accomplished by the pressure of a pillow over her mouth to keep her from telling her blind mother that he, the chauffeur, had brought her upstairs in his arms when he discovered she was too intoxicated to walk up under her own power. Although Bigger felt responsible for returning his employer's daughter safely to her room, he was afraid his employers might dismiss him if they should know that he, a Negro, had found it necessary to fulfil this responsibility by carrying the incapacitated girl in his arms.

One of the ironic facts of the story is that although the murder was an accident, it need not have been. For Bigger hated all white folks. He hated them enough to murder without provocation. He felt that he had been cheated out of everything good in life that he had wanted and that white people—all white people—were responsible for his unhappy predicament.

The action of the story is sensational, containing such a ghastly spectacle as the furnace scene, in which Bigger, who has thrust the dead girl's body into the red-hot furnace feet-foremost, discovers that the dangling head cannot be forced in. He takes the long, razor-sharp knife from his pocket and attempts to cut off the head, but the bones are too hard for his small instrument. Then he glances around the room until he sees a hatchet, which he uses to finish the job.

In one of the most pathetic scenes imaginable, the fleeing murderer, completely crazed by the fear of being captured, takes up a brick and beats out the brains of his innocent, trusting sleeping girl friend who has obediently agreed to stay with him until the end.

But the power of this book does not reside in the action or in the portrayal of character. It resides rather in the ethical and sociological implications of the action. The truth of this observation was recently impressed upon me when I saw the motion-picture version of the story, adapted for the screen by Wright himself and produced in Argentina. Without the doctrinal overtones of the novel, it turns out to be just another murder mystery of the kind that bombards the air waves every night from seven to eleven.

Wright's major purpose in this novel was to show that social and economic barriers against race lead to grave injustices toward racial minorities and that those injustices so distort character and personality growth that criminal monstrosities, such as Bigger, are produced. Wright attempted to support his theory by means of testimony presented in the murder trial of Bigger, which comprises approximately one-third of the novel. It is revealed that Mr. Dalton, father of the girl that Bigger killed, has donated large sums of money to Negro charity and that he owns the South Side Real Estate Company in Chicago from which Bigger's family rents the one-room, rat-infested apartment in which the mother, daughter, and two sons live. When the defense attorney asks Mr. Dalton why he does not charge Negro tenants less rent for such uninhabitable accommodations, the philanthropist replies that it would be unethical to undersell his competitors. When he is asked why rent for Negroes is higher than that for whites, he replies that a housing shortage exists in the Negro community. Although he admits that he owns houses in other sections of the city where no shortage exists, he says he will not rent them to Negroes because he thinks Negroes are happier living together in one section. He further admits that, of all the Negroes his philanthropy has helped to educate, he has never employed one in the operation of his vast business enterprises.

The attorney for the defense, therefore, charged Mr. Dalton with the murder of his own daughter, for it was he who helped to prepare the soil in which a Bigger Thomas could grow. It was he who closed his eyes to the deeper longings of Negroes for justice and equality, attempting to salve his conscience by giving huge sums to racial charities. It was he who had shielded his daughter from all Negro contact, thus leaving her at the crucial moment incapable of wisely dealing with a rebel such as Bigger. If he had provided clean and decent apartments for Negroes as he had for whites; if he had established playgrounds for Negro children as he had for whites; if he had used his influence to open employment opportunities equally to Negroes and whites, a monster like Bigger might not have arisen to take his daughter's life.

It is plain to see that, in so far as this doctrine is philosophy at all, it is a philosophy of social and environmental responsibility. Bigger became what he was, not because he was free to choose his course of action, but because circumstances over which he had no control had driven him to his doom. This is the philosophy of Karl Marx, of whom Wright at that time was a devoted disciple.

According to his own admission in *The God That Failed,* Wright was a member of the American Communist party from 1934 to 1944. When he wrote *Native Son* he believed that there was "no agency in the world so capable of making men feel the earth and the people on it as the Communist Party."

It is always hazardous to attempt to guess at the motivation for human action. One cannot know with certainty why Wright became a willing dupe for the Communists. His minority status and long history of unemployment, segregation, and physical deprivations undoubtedly contributed to his decision. But, above all, Wright believed then, as now, that the greatest tragedy of mankind lies in the inability of the individual to find satisfactory fellowship in the group. This theme is apparent in *Native Son,* takes on added significance in *Black Boy,* and becomes the underlying assumption of *The Outsider.* It is a theme, however, which Wright was not the first to discover or explore. Hawthorne was gravely concerned with it more than a century ago, and in our own day James Joyce and Thomas Wolfe gave it life. Joyce epitomized it in *Ulysses* when he presented the perplexities and sorrows of Dedalus in search of his father (the symbol of a kindred spirit rather than a blood relationship). Wolfe made it the burden of all his books. In *Of Time and the River* he exclaimed: "We are so lost, so naked and so lonely in America . . . for America has a thousand lights and weathers and we walk the streets, we walk the streets forever, we walk the streets of life alone."

But Hawthorne and Joyce and Wolfe were not Negroes. They knew that that eternal loneliness of the individual is universal, not racial. They knew it could not be remedied by political party or social organization. But perhaps Wright thought the identification of the comrade with the Communist cell, which recognizes no racial distinctions, could be the solution to the problem. Ten years were required to convince him that he was mistaken. And the mental agony which accompanied his awakening was almost unbearable.

Thirteen years after *Native Son*, Wright's second novel, *The Outsider*, was issued by his original publishers. It is more violent than *Native Son*, but it is also more imaginative, more challenging, and more philosophical. Cross Damon, the protagonist, kills four men and drives the woman he loves to commit suicide. But Cross is not motivated by physical fear as was Bigger. He is caught in the cross-currents of an ideological warfare going on within himself. Except in the first case, he commits his murders to avenge an injured sense of justice, which, he believes, except for his intervention would continue unchecked and unpunished.

In this novel Wright repudiates with vehemence many of the ideological and philosophical tenets he had espoused in *Native Son*. No longer does he believe that environment and the social milieu creates the man. To him now, man is the product of his own free choice, and his destiny cannot be charged to any force or forces outside himself. He illustrates this theory by permitting Cross to become suddenly freed of all previous commitments which may have been entered into by some type of compulsion or by pure chance. He accomplishes this by allowing his hero to emerge from a subway wreck incognito. The newspapers announce that Cross Damon is dead, his body so mutilated in the wreck that it could be identified only by the coat he had been wearing. Cross accepts his freedom and makes plans to leave Chicago for New York and a new life.

From the moment Cross decides to accept the news of his "death" as a reality, he begins deliberately to choose every act which he performs thereafter. His first significant act is the murder of a friend who recognizes him in Chicago. There is no outside compulsion that drives him to this murder. It is purely an act of freedom, performed in the interest of continued freedom. The other three murders are also the result of passionless deliberation, an exercise of the godlike freedom to which man is continually aspiring.

In 1946 Wright moved to Paris, where he has been living with his family ever since. Among his new-found friends is Jean-Paul Sartre, chief promulgator of the philosophy of existentialism. A warm friendship has developed between the two men, and it appears that Wright has been converted to his friend's philosophy. The American admits that he has found it urgently necessary "to search for a new attitude to replace the set of Marxist assumptions which had in the past more or less guided the direction of my writings." Although he asserts that "*The Outsider* is the first literary effort of mine projected out of a heart preoccupied with no ideological burden save that of rendering an account of reality as it strikes my sensibilities and imagination," the critical reader cannot escape the conclusion that this book is not only strongly anti-Communist but also markedly existentialist.

Let us examine the first charge. In *Native Son* Jan and Mac, the Communist leaders, were presented as unselfish men who were willing to sacrifice themselves to the cause of racial justice and equality at a time when racial tolerance was much more unpopular than it is today. But in this book he has presented Blount, Hilton, and Blimen as jealous, hypocritical, perverted, unscrupulous, power-crazed puppets dancing to the satanic music of an all-consuming party. He describes the party leaders as follows:

> Their Aims? Direct and naked power! They know as few others that there is no valid, functioning religion to take the place of the values and creeds of yesterday; and they know that political power, if it is to perform in the minds and emotions of men the role that the idea of God once performed, must be total and absolute.
> . . . They will commit any crime, but never in passion. . . . And whatever natural terrors of life there are in the hearts of man, whatever stupid prejudices they harbor in their damp souls, they know how to rouse and sustain those terrors and prejudices and mobilize them for *their* ends.

But in his relentless delineation of the brutality, stupidity, and revolting inhumanity of Communist methods, Wright does not forget to warn his readers that the opponents of these methods are in grave danger of succumbing to the very evils they are attempting to destroy. It seems to be a law of life, Cross discovers, that to fight an enemy means fighting him on his own ground, and that in itself is a defeat. Perhaps he was staring right now at the focal point of history: "If you fought men who tried to conquer you in terms of total power you too had to use total power and in the end you became what you tried to defeat."

Although communism and existentialism have one thing in common—the denial of the existence of God—they are deadly enemies on many other counts. What, then, are the basic principles of existentialism in this novel? I shall limit myself to the discussion of three.

First, the assumption that there is no God is necessary to the development of modern man, who must be self-reliant and self-sufficient and, above all, free.

Sartre explains in his brief treatise on existentialism[1] that if God did exist, man could never be free. He would be forever hemmed in by a priori values already determined before his creation. He could always find excuses for his actions and seek to escape the consequences of them. But if God does not exist, there is no explaining things away by reference to fixed a priori values. Such a position condemns man to complete freedom. Once he enters the world, he *alone* is entirely responsible for everything he does.

When the dying Cross, who had killed four men during the few weeks of his new life and had in turn been shot by his Communist enemies, is asked by the district attorney why he had chosen to live as he had, replies: "I wanted to be free . . . to feel what I was worth . . . what living meant to me."

On an earlier occasion when Cross is discussing with his Communist acquaintances the backgrounds of modern thought, he says:

> All of this brings us to one central, decisive fact: the consequences of the atheistic position of modern man, for most men today are atheists, even though they don't know it or won't admit it.
> . . . Now what does this mean—that I don't believe in God? It means that I, and you too, can do what we damn well please on this earth. Many men have been doing just that, of course, for a long time, but they didn't have the courage to admit it.[2]

Second, there is no reality beyond subjectivity. Man can be no more nor less than what he conceives himself to be.

Sartre says: "Subjectivism means, on the one hand, that an individual chooses and makes himself; and on the other, that it is impossible for man to transcend human subjectivity. The second of these is the essential meaning of existentialism."

Wright makes Cross reach the following conclusion as he reasons with himself concerning his predicament: "Every man interprets the world in the light of his habits and desires."

In a more extended discussion with the district attorney, Cross, who speaks for Wright, declares:

> God, the millions of prisons in this world! Men simply copied the realities of their hearts when they built prisons. They simply extended into objective reality what was already a subjective reality. Only jailers really believe in jails. Only men full of criminal feelings can create a criminal code.

---

[1] *Existentialism* (New York: Philosophical Library, 1947).

[2] "Dostoievsky said, 'If God didn't exist everything would be possible.' That is the very starting point of existentialism. Indeed everything is permissible if God does not exist" (Sartre, *op. cit.* p. 27).

Third, there is no human nature. Each age develops according to dialectical laws, and what men are depends upon the age and not on a human nature.

The existentialists argue that human nature could be the product only of a godlike Creator, who would conceive and create man according to a common specification. Since they deny God, they deny the possibility of the individual man being the product of a general concept in the mind of a Creator. Hence there can be no such thing as human nature.[3]

Wright puts in the mouth of his protagonist the following speech:

> We twentieth century Westerners have outlived the faith of our fathers; our minds have grown so skeptical that we cannot accept the old scheme of moral precepts which once guided man's life. In our modern industrial society we try to steer our hearts by improvised, pragmatic rules which are, in the end, no rules at all. If there are people who tell you they live by traditional values and precepts—as the English sometimes pretend—then they are either lying to you or to themselves.

To move from a Marxist position, such as *Native Son* represents, to the nearly opposite philosophy of existentialism in less than eight years is a difficult feat, even for the agile-minded Richard Wright. Consequently, one should not be surprised to find here and there in *The Outsider* undigested and contradictory bits of the new philosophy. For instance, how can an existentialist reconcile the following quotation from *The Outsider* with the atheistic doctrine of his philosophy: "Man is a promise that he must never break"? *A promise to whom?*

In his treatment of race relations Wright has also moved away from the methods of *Native Son*. Although the main character in *The Outsider* is a Negro, the novel cannot be classified as racial literature. It is primarily the presentation of the experiences of a man (race is incidental) who seeks to repudiate his common humanity, a man who, as Wright phrases it, has "wantonly violated every commitment that civilized men owe, in terms of common honesty and sacred honor, to those with whom they live."

Despite the nonracial design, however, Wright does not hesitate to condemn attitudes of racial intolerance and prejudice wherever they appear. But unlike the deadly seriousness of *Native Son,* these attacks are made by light irony and ridicule. For instance, Cross, who is somewhat scholarly, having spent two years studying philosophy at the University of Chicago, sets out to obtain a false birth certificate by pretending to be the kind of Negro stereotype that the white clerks appreciate. When his turn comes to present his case, he says to the clerk in a plaintive querulous tone:

> "He told me to come up here and get the paper."
> The clerk blinked and looked annoyed. "What?"

[3]Sartre, *op. cit.,* pp. 16–18.

"The paper, Mister. My boss told me to come and get it."

"What kind of paper are you talking about, boy?"

"The one that say I was born. . . ."

The clerk smiled, then laughed: "Maybe you weren't born, boy. Are you *sure* you were?"

Cross batted his eyes stupidly. He saw that he was making the poorly paid clerk happy; his pretense of dumbness made the clerk feel superior, white.

"Well, they *say* I was born. If I wasn't born I can't keep my job. That's why my boss told me to come here and get the paper."

Two hours later Cross had the duplicate birth certificate . . . and had left in the minds of the clerks a picture of a Negro whom the nation loved and of whom the clerks would speak in the future with contemptuous affection. Maybe someday I could rule the nation with means like this, Cross mused as he rode back to New York.

In the main, Wright appears to have concluded that the problems of racial justice and brotherhood are a part of the larger problems of human relations and that the most successful methods of attack are those directed on the wider front.

Although Wright's philosophical and racial horizons have expanded considerably since *Native Son,* his literary craftsmanship has shown no noticeable improvement. In fact, *The Outsider* is inferior to its predecessor in plot construction, organization, and emotional depth.

In *Native Son* coincidence plays no part in plot construction. Whatever happens is the result of causal relationships generated by the natural consequences of place, time, and environment. But in *The Outsider* the crucial incident (the subway wreck) which enables the protagonist to achieve a new identity is attended by a far-fetched coincidence which alone is responsible for the possibility of all later developments. *It just happened that one other Negro who resembled Cross "in color and build" was in the subway car and that this Negro, who was sitting across the aisle, was thrown against him by the force of the collision in such a manner that he (Cross) had to beat the lifeless head into an unrecognizable pulp in order to free himself from the wreckage. It was a coincidence, too, that Cross unconsciously left his overcoat so entangled with the lifeless body of the Negro victim that it became the mark of identification that proved to the world that Cross was "dead." Later in New York it just happened that Cross was near by when a typical Fascist and a typical Communist (both of whom Cross hated) became engaged in a violent physical battle and that, because of the peculiar situation, Cross was able to slip into the "locked" room unnoticed and administer death blows to each without himself being immediately suspected.*

The motivation in *Native Son* is natural and compelling. Bigger's first act of murder is accidental, and the second is the result of overpowering fear. But the motivation for the four murders committed by Cross is neither natural nor compelling. It lies outside the normal pattern of human psychology.

There are some long speeches in *Native Son*, speeches delivered by the attorneys at Bigger's trial. The courtroom is a natural setting in which long-winded, one-sided oratory is customary. The eloquence is appropriate, for a verdict of life or death hangs upon the delicately balanced arguments. But in *The Outsider* the long, learned discussions on the origin, development, and functions of religions, governments, political parties, and economic systems carried on by Cross and District Attorney Houston and by Cross and his Communist antagonists have no natural setting. They seem forced and stagy. They appear to be part of an obvious scheme to drag in irrelevant lectures on special doctrines, whose outcome can have no possible effect on the lives of any of the characters.

The other stylistic qualities which have made all of Wright's books worthy literary experiences have suffered no diminution. The vivid diction, the effective sentence structure, and the pleasing rhythms are still predominant. His emotional control is more apparent than it was in the earlier novel. He declared after the publication of *Uncle Tom's Children* that he was through with sentimentality. He has kept that promise. There is an emotional toughness in *The Outsider* which exceeds the hardness of *Native Son*. One may curse and fume over the harrowing experiences of this book, but never weep.

In conclusion, it is only fair to emphasize that Wright has come a long way in the art of philosophic thought since *Native Son*. It may be that another thirteen years between novels will reduce the groping tension that now beclouds the mind of this talented writer. It may be that his next novel will be a fulfilment of the promise of *Uncle Tom's Children*, of *Native Son*, and of *Black Boy*.

The Dark and Haunted Tower
of Richard Wright

by Nathan A. Scott, Jr.

The existentialist overtones and the explicit allusions to Nietzsche and Heidegger in *The Outsider* led some of the reviewers of his book of 1953 to conclude that Richard Wright was misguidedly experimenting with intellectual traditions outside his actual experience and that he had taken a wrong turning. This was a judgment, however, which surely had to require as its basic premise something like the rather incomprehensible mystique about the Negro intellectual which is occasionally invoked by fools and professional obscurantists, that he is somehow ancestrally fated to exclusion from the general Atlantic community of cultural exchange simply because his racial identity does itself, in some ineffable way, consign him to a permanent ghetto of the mind. But, if this mystique is abandoned as the nonsense that it really is, there should have been no occasion for surprise at the expression which *The Outsider* provided of the extent to which Mr. Wright, after several years of residence in France, had been influenced by the secular modes of European existentialism. For here is a philosophical movement which has found its basic subject matter not so much in the history of philosophy as in the crises and distempers of human existence in the twentieth century. The fundamental reality about which it has very often wanted to speak is that of "the extreme situation"—the situation, that is, in which man's essential dignity is radically challenged by an unconscionable subversion of justice and an intolerable distance between master and slave. And this is precisely the reality that stirred Mr. Wright's imagination into life—from the time of his first forays into the literary life, under the sponsorship of the Communist Party, while still a Chicago postal employee in the 'thirties, up to the time of his sudden death in Paris in November of 1960.

So there was nothing at all unnatural in this American Negro writer having responded affirmatively to the *Angst*-ridden accents and idioms of Jean-Paul Sartre and Georges Bataille and Maurice Blanchot. For, among

"The Dark and Haunted Tower of Richard Wright" by Nathan A. Scott, Jr. Originally published in *Graduate Comment* (Wayne State University), VII (1964), 93–99; reprinted from revised version published in *Five Black Writers,* ed. Donald B. Gibson (New York: New York University Press, 1970), 12–25; reprinted by permission of the author.

those Negro intellectuals of his time whose gift of expression enabled them to have a "voice," it may well be that there was none for whom the reality of their "extreme situation" constituted so great a burden. The social statisticians today are busy, of course, in their notations of the steadily increasing improvement in what they call "race relations," and it is probably the case that the moral quality of our life is, in this dimension, something less of an embarrassment than it was a decade or so ago. But the tokens of acceptance that the Negro has won here and there are not yet so great as to make it impossible for others to imagine that he, when he is sensitive and discerning, still feels his status to be precarious and undecided. He has only to contemplate the bitter intransigence of the South and the subtle but firmly maintained exclusions of the North to be reminded of how meager and insubstantial is the new ground that he has recently gained. Though it is only in the occasional pockets of Southern depravity that he is still exposed to the nakeder forms of violence and intimidation, he knows that the actuality of the American experience continues to involve for him that most unhinging kind of frustration which is a result of the glitter and promise of life in a great country being near enough for the mind to be dazzled by the sense of their availability, and yet far enough away to exact a sense of defeat more exacerbating than anything a slave could possibly feel. When this bitter irony is explored by a radical imagination, the nature of the human material is surely such as will permit its being seized by way of the image of Tantalus: for all of the bland notations of achieved progress that may be offered by the social scientist, there is still an *agonia* here whose gall partakes of the "extreme situation"—and this was the perspective by which Richard Wright was consistently guided in all his efforts to shape the story of the American Negro into something whose tragic sorrow might quicken the conscience of our time.

Though he had numerous minor predecessors, Mr. Wright was the first American Negro writer of large ambitions to win a major reputation in our literary life. *Uncle Tom's Children,* his first collection of stories, achieved a limited currency in the late 'thirties among readers of leftist social sympathies, but it was not until *Native Son* burst upon the scene in 1940 that he won access to the kind of forum that Sunday Supplement reviewers and a national book club could give. Within a month after its publication tens of thousands of copies were moving across book dealers' counters all over the land; it frequently was being said that nothing so comparable to the great tragic fictions of Dostoevski had yet appeared in our literature; and hordes of Mr. Wright's readers were enjoying that great thrilling shiver of delight that the intellectual middle class in this country during the 'thirties had come to find in what Eric Bentley has called "the fun-world of proletarian legend," particularly when the fun involved the tabooed exoticism of the Negro. The very simplicity and violence of the novel's didacticism did, in a way, permit many people to envisage themselves as in league with Mr. Wright and with Christ in the harrowing of a Hell full of all the forces of reaction and illiberality; and, in this way perhaps, the illusion grew that *Native Son,* by itself and quite suddenly, had very greatly enlarged and deepened our imaginative understanding of a whole dimension of American experience.

This was, however, an illusion, and when one reads today the story of Bigger Thomas, one cannot but be struck by how little the novel gives us of the bite and flavor either of social actuality or of the particular kind of human individual of whom Bigger is offered as an exemplum. To read such a book, for example, as Ralph Ellison's brilliant novel of 1953, *Invisible Man,* is to find, among one's richest satisfactions, the sense of immersion in all the concrete materialities of Negro life. One hears the very buzz and hum of Harlem in the racy, pungent speech of his West Indians and his native hipsters, and all the grotesquerie in his opening account of the dreary little backwater of a remote Southern Negro college has in it a certain kind of empirically absolute rightness. Indeed, the book is packed full of the acutest observations of the manners and idioms and human styles that constitute the ethos of Negro life in the American metropolis; and it gives us such a sense of social fact as can be come by nowhere in the stiffly pedantic manuals of academic sociology.

But, at its center, *Native Son* exhibits nothing other than a socially discarnate and demoniac wraith. In the moments before her "little death," the Negrophile Joanna Burden in *Light in August* cries out to her Negro lover Joe Christmas, "Negro, Negro," as if, in the instant of sexual transport, his human particularity were of no account; and, in the same novel, a lynch mob, Faulkner tells us, "believed aloud that it was an anonymous Negro crime committed not by a Negro but by Negro. . . ." And this is the character whom we find to be the protagonist of Richard Wright's novel of 1940—called, yes, for the sake of the novelistic convention, Bigger Thomas, but really Negro, *Negro.* Thus it is that, for all of the anger the novel directs at the moral imagination that has been poisoned by racism, its own pathos is, finally, a consequence of the degree to which it is overwhelmed by the cancer it wants to cauterize. From the moment, on its first page, when Bigger is awakened by the *Brrriiiinnng!* of his alarm clock, until his "faint, wry, bitter smile" of farewell at Mr. Max on the final page, the novel is controlled by precisely those hopeless assumptions about Negro life which elicited its rage, and its protagonist's sense of his own identity is formed by just that image of himself which, as it lives in the larger culture, has caused his despair. So, in its entirety, the novel moves wholly within the envenomed abstractions of racial myth.

In one of the stories in *Uncle Tom's Children,* "Long Black Song," the husband of a Negro woman who has been seduced by a white salesman says: "The white folks ain never gimme a chance! They ain never give no black man a chance! There ain nothing in yo whole life yuh kin keep from em! . . . Ahm gonna be hard like they is! So hep me Gawd, Ahm gonna be *hard!* When they come fer me Ahm gonna *be here!*" Not only is this the posture of all but one of his protagonists in the stories that make up his first collection, it is also the posture of the young Chicago Negro whose story Mr. Wright tells in *Native Son.* He, too, is one who intends to "be hard"; indeed, as he says, "Every time I think about it I feel like somebody's poking a red-hot iron down my throat." So it is with a sullen suspiciousness that he faces the Chicago philanthropist who takes him off the relief rolls by hiring him as a chauffeur. And it is with an even greater skepticism that he views his employer's daughter and her communist sweetheart who makes gestures of fraternity toward him by inviting him to join them in a café as an equal. But this is a relation that never becomes genuinely complicated, for, at the end of their first evening together, the girl is so intoxicated that Bigger, having been entrusted with seeing her home, has to carry her bodily from the family automobile to her bedroom—into which her blind mother comes suddenly, just in the moment when he is contemplating taking Mary sexually. And, in order to prevent the mother's knowing that he and Mary are in the room, he smothers the girl and then, in his panic, stuffs her body into the furnace. This, in turn, leads eventually to his second crime, against his mistress Bessie, to whom he confesses the first deed and whom he must finally remove to prevent her betraying him to the police. But he cannot ultimately avoid his nemesis and is at last captured on a South Side tenement rooftop, as a raging mob clamors for his life in the street below.

Now the engine that Mr. Wright desperately relied upon to whip his lurid fairy tale into some semblance of probability was the courtroom defense of Bigger by his Jewish lawyer, Mr. Max. And here is what we are told, that Bigger

> . . . murdered Mary Dalton accidentally, without thinking, without plan, without conscious motive. But, after he murdered, he accepted the crime. And that's the important thing. It was the first full act of his life; it was the most meaningful, exciting and stirring thing that had ever happened to him. He accepted it because it made him free, gave him the possibility of choice, of action, the opportunity to act and to feel that his actions carried weight. . . .
>
> Let me tell you more. Before this trial the newspapers and the prosecution said that this boy had committed other crimes. It is true. He is guilty of numerous crimes. But search until the day of judgment, and you will find not one shred of evidence of them. He has murdered many times, but there are no corpses. Let me explain. This Negro boy's entire attitude toward life is a *crime!* The hate and fear which we have inspired in him, woven by our civilization into the very structure of his consciousness, into his blood and bones, into the hourly functioning of his personality, have become the justification of his existence.

> Every time he comes in contact with us, he kills! It is a physiological and psychological reaction, embedded in his being. Every thought he thinks is potential murder. . . . Every desire, every dream, no matter how intimate or personal, is a plot or a conspiracy. Every hope is a plan for insurrection. Every glance of the eye is a threat. *His very existence is a crime.* . . .

And, what is more, we are told that we have only to "multiply Bigger Thomas twelve million times, allowing for environmental and temperamental variations, and for those Negroes who are completely under the influence of the church, and you have the psychology of the Negro people."

Thus it is, I say, that the novel is, paradoxically, controlled by precisely the assumptions about Negro life that elicited its rage, for the astonishing thing that it finally does is to offer a depraved and inhuman beast as the comprehensive archetypal image of the American Negro.

The imagination that we meet here, in other words, is extremist and melodramatic, feeding on the horrific themes of alienation and violence and abysmal fear, and its single occupation is with the racial tragedy. But all the great ones have had what was two hundred years ago called a "ruling passion," and it does indeed seem to be very much a part of the kind of brilliance and assertiveness that we associate with major art. That Mr. Wright should have had his ruling passion is not, therefore, something that we shall hold against him; what was unfortunate in him was his utter defenselessness before it. And here I mean that, despite his cursory tutelage under European existentialism in the late 'forties and 'fifties and despite the attention which he gave to the literature of modern psychology and social science, he never won such a point of purchase in the realm of systematic ideas as might have afforded his mind some protection against the deracinative force of the tragic encounters which it had had with the world. After reading, for example, the heartrendingly poignant story that is told in *Black Boy,* his autobiography of 1945—which is one of the great human testaments in modern American literature—it would surely take an exceedingly sluggish moral imagination for one not to perceive how inevitable it was that this man should bear to his grave the scars of the scalding humiliations that, as a Negro, he was subjected to in his youth in the state of Mississippi. Here, indeed, was a man who knew the insidious day-by-day intimidation, the fear that is in the air, and the atrocious brutality that make up the moral stench of the concentration camp; and, unlike the German Jew under Hitler, he lived this infernal life of the damned and the rejected not just for a few nightmarish years that were known to be absurdly discontinuous with the normal state of things, but he lived it as the historic inheritance of his people; this was all that he knew, from infancy until he was old enough to risk the journey of flight from Memphis to Chicago. So we accept the authenticity of the rage and the anger which were the emotions with which he impulsively faced the world. But, when some such extremity as this constitutes his basic situation, whatever the needs of the existing human being, the artist needs to be equipped with some defense against the intensity of his own experience, for, unless he has some means of supporting or controlling it, the great likelihood is that his work will then express not a coherent ordering of human experience in objective form but only the emotional ties of his own incipient hysteria. And it was just some such vantage point as this that might have enabled him to distance himself from his *agonia* and to be released to the sheer labor of composition itself—it was just this that Mr. Wright never managed. In his famous essay on "Technique as Discovery," Professor Mark Schorer has, of course, proposed that it is in the dynamism of the creative process itself, and through his wrestling with the medium of his language, that the artist comes by those major insights into the meaning of his experience that enable him to take control of it. But the logic whereby *technique* is assigned so decisive a role in the formation of *vision* is something that still escapes me. So mine, therefore, is the older axiom, that an artist needs to know a very great deal *before* he puts pen to paper; and if he does not, he may then, I take it, be expected to provide us with some variety of what the late R. P. Blackmur called "the fallacy of expressive form."

Now this was, I believe, at bottom, Mr. Wright's crucial failure: he simply did not *know* enough about the labyrinthine interiorities of the human soul. His own life-experience conditioned him, of course, to keep a lively awareness that (as W. H. Auden says) "Ubiquitous within the bond / Of one impoverishing sky, / Vast spiritual disorders lie." Yet these were, not really *spiritual* disorders, since he made no allowance for human existence having anything other than a purely social-historical dimension. In the *New Year Letter* Mr. Auden suggests that

> There are two atlases: the one
> The public space where acts are done,
> In theory common to us all. . . .
> The other is the inner space
> Of private ownership, the place
> That each of us is forced to own,
> Like his own life from which it's grown,
> The landscape of his will and need. . . .

But so obsessed was Mr. Wright with the demonic aberrations that disfigure "the public space" that he lost any deep sense of what wretchedness there is within "the inner space," within what Mr. Auden calls "our parish of immediacy." T. S. Eliot once said of Ezra Pound's *Cantos* that they posit a Hell for other people, not for Mr. Pound or his readers. It might also be said of the books of Richard Wright that, though theirs is a Hell for most of Mr. Wright's readers (who are white), it is not a Hell for Mr. Wright himself and his racial kinsmen; both he and they bear upon themselves the stigmata of its fury, but both he and they are exempted from that which is generally problematic in the human soul, and from which the fury proceeds. The complex relations between the "two atlases" are not explored. And, in this way, it was possible for Mr. Wright to envisage the human community as though it were split into two opposed camps, the one black and the other white. But, in this way, it was never possible for him even to approximate the Baudelairean astringency—*"Hypocrite lecteur,—mon semblable,—mon frère!"*

And it is also this exclusive and simplistic concentration upon the one atlas, "the public space," which enabled Mr. Wright so disastrously to insist upon racial humiliation as the ultimate suffering, the ultimate indignity. And I speak of the disastrousness of it, because, however thumpingly tautologous it may be to assert that evil is evil, whatever its aspect, this is, nevertheless, the fact of the matter; and to assert that some special evil is the ultimate evil, simply because this is that by which one has oneself been most hurtfully victimized, is merely to indulge in a desperate kind of sentimentality. This was, however, the unpromising position that consistently controlled Mr. Wright's way of performing the act of self-definition as an artist, and, for all of the ardor, it is this sentimentality which makes so humanly impertinent a body of writing than which there is none in our time that ought to have greater pertinence to those like ourselves, who are drenched in the particular American experience that gave to Mr. Wright his ruling passion.

In his review of *Native Son* in March of 1940, Malcolm Cowley, having in mind the consistency with which Mr. Wright's executive design, both in the stories of *Uncle Tom's Children* and in his novel, had been a design of violence, suggested that his "sense of the indignities heaped on his race" might well go so deep as to make it his unconscious tendency in his fiction to revenge himself "by a whole series of symbolic murders." And though Mr. Cowley may at this point have been somewhat overstating things, the propensity for violence cannot, it is true, be gain-said: Mr. Wright may not have been bent on symbolic murder, but at least it can be asserted that he was eager to sound a hue and a cry and had something of a penchant for "holding a loaded pistol at the head of the white world while he [muttered] between clenched teeth: 'Either you grant us equal rights as human beings or else this is what will happen.'"[1] But, of course, the unfortunate consequence of his taking this kind of position was that, inevitably, it compelled him to practice a terrible brutalization upon his characters: he had, as in the wronged husband of "Long Black Song," to make them "hard," in order to give dramatic substance to the threat he wanted to utter; and, in thus sweeping them into the raging abysses of violent criminality, he forged an image of *la présence noire* that is in no great way

[1]Charles I. Glicksberg, "Negro Fiction in America," *The South Atlantic Quarterly*, XLV (October 1946), 482.

removed from the wild and lickerish nigger who inhabits the demented imagination of the racial paranoiac. For all of the new sophistications that appeared in *The Outsider,* this is as true of his novel of 1953 as it is of his early work of the 'thirties.

Cross Damon is a half-educated intellectual who bears the Negro's ancestral burden of rejection and marginality, but his concern with what is socially problematic in his situation is but one phase of a deeper concern with what is metaphysically problematic in human life. He is a man whose sense of the world has been formed by that tradition of philosophic radicalism that runs from Nietzsche to contemporary existentialists like Heidegger and Sartre, and so he is particularly alert to the religious vacuum which this tradition has asserted to be at the heart of modern experience. He regards the old "myths" as a mischievous and archaistic legacy bequeathed us by the primitive ages of human history in which man,

> naked and afraid, found that only one thing could really quiet his terrors: that is *Untruth.* He . . . was afraid of the clamoring world of storms, volcanoes, and heaving waves, and he wanted to change that world. His myths sought to recast that world, tame it, make it more humanly meaningful and endurable. The more abjectly frightened the nation or race of men, the more their myths and religions projected out upon the world another world in *front* of the real world, or, in another way of speaking, they projected another world *behind* the real world they saw, lived, suffered, and died in. Until today almost all of man's worlds have been either pre-worlds or backworlds, *never* the real world. . . .

But in this "real world" in which modern man must live today the nonexistence of God is not to be argued; it is simply to be taken for granted, and the theistic hypothesis is simply to be understood as "something projected compulsively from men's minds in answer to their chronic need to be rid of fear, something to meet the obscure needs of daily lives lived amidst strange and threatening facts." And this means, in Cross Damon's analysis of the modern predicament, that the dreadful burden which man must bear today is the burden of freedom, the burden, as he says, of being "nothing in particular," except what man chooses through his actions to become. This is why panic sometimes drapes the world which Cross looks out upon, for what he knows himself to confront is "the empty possibility of action," the necessity of actually making something of himself, and the knowledge that he can do what he damn well pleases on this earth, that everything is permitted, and that he must discover

> good or evil through his own actions, which were more exacting than the edicts of any God because it was he alone who had to bear the brunt of their consequences with a sense of absoluteness made intolerable by knowing that this life was all he had and would ever have. For him there was no grace or mercy if he failed.

He has, in other words, undergone the most expensive denudation that a man can suffer, for to Cross Damon God is dead. And, being thus stripped of that which might alone furnish some objective warrant for the human enterprise, there is nothing else to which he owes any loyalty; he is on his own, a pure *isolé*, and he gives his suffrage to neither family nor tradition nor church nor state; nor does he give it to race. "My hero," said Mr. Wright, "could have been of any race."

When we first meet Cross he is a clerk in a Chicago post office, and his personal life, like that of Sartre's Mathieu in the initial phase of his drama, is in a state of messy disorder. As a result of an early and unsuccessful marriage, he is having to support a wife with whom he no longer lives and three children. And then there is little Dot, his mistress, whom he had supposed to be seventeen years of age but whom he discovers, after the onset of her pregnancy, to be not quite sixteen. Gladys refuses to give him a divorce so that he may marry the girl, and Dot, desperately hoping somehow to trap him into a marriage, intends to seek legal counsel. When Gladys learns of this, she begins to be fearful that Cross may be jailed and that she and the children may be robbed of his support: so she demands that he sign over the house and the car to her. She further demands that he borrow eight hundred dollars from the Postal Union on his salary, so that the titles on both the house and the car may be cleared, and she tells him that, if he refuses, she will go to the police with Dot and assist her in filing charges of rape against him. So Cross has no alternative but to accede to her requests.

But then, on that fateful night when he is returning home after having just received from the Postal Union the eight hundred dollars which he is to deliver to Gladys on the following morning, he is involved in a subway accident in which it is supposed that he has lost his life, the smashed body of another man being identified as his. This is, of course, Cross' great chance, and he is quick to seize it, for it means an opportunity to gain release from the inauthenticity of his existence, an opportunity to escape all those pledges and promises to his wife and his mother and his mistress "which he had not intended to make and whose implied obligations had been slowly smothering his spirit." By this "stroke of freakish good luck" he is able to "rip the viscous strands" of that "vast web of pledges and promises . . . and fling them behind him." Now, for the first time, this young man feels that his life is determined by a really valid project—namely, that of making something of himself and of giving some vital definition to his human identity.

So he takes a train out of Chicago for New York City, where he quickly becomes involved in a phantasmagoric drama of the Communist underworld which culminates in his committing murder three times and in the suicide of Eva Blount, the widow of one of his victims, who, after falling in love with him, cannot bear the truth, when she finally learns of the

terrible deeds that he has performed. And Cross at last is destroyed by
the Party's assassins.

Now, when the novel is thus summarized, it may appear to be only a
rather lurid sort of potboiler; and, to be sure, there is no minimizing the
harshness of its violence. Yet, for all of its melodramatic sensationalism,
it is an impressive book. Indeed, it is one of the very few American novels
of our time that, in admitting into itself a large body of systematic ideas,
makes us think that it wants seriously to compete with the major
philosophic intelligence of the contemporary period. And it may well be
that the strange kind of indifference or even outright denigration that the
book elicited at the time of its appearance demands to be understood in
terms of the easy assumption which is habitually made in our literary life,
that the difference in method and intention between poetry and philosophy
ordains the impropriety of a work of fiction being complicated by the
dialectical tensions of systematic thought. But this is a kind of finickiness
notably unsupported by the European tradition exemplified by such books
as Mann's *Doctor Faustus* and Malraux's *La Condition Humaine* and Camus'
La Peste. And it was toward this tradition that Mr. Wright was reaching
in *The Outsider*, which, though it is a very imperfect work, is yet (after
Black Boy) his finest achievement and, as the one emphatically existentialist novel in contemporary American literature, a book that deserves
to have commanded a great deal more attention than it has.

Though Mr. Wright insisted that his hero "could have been of any
race" and that his primary quality was the metaphysical horror he felt
before the yawning emptiness in things created by the demise of the old
"myths," the fact remains, however, that Cross is a Negro. And, as such,
he is dubiously privileged to have what the prosecutor Ely Houston calls
"a dreadful objectivity," the kind of "double vision," that is, which belongs
to one who is "both inside and outside of our culture." But, given the
ardency of his commitment to atheistic premises, the actual content of
this "double vision" proves to be the conviction of Ivan Karamazov, that
therefore "everything is permitted," not even murder being debarred. And
so that night when he walked into the room where the Fascist nigger-hater
Herndon and the Communist Blount were fighting and bludgeoned them
both to death, he was "not taking sides . . . not preferring the lesser evil,"
for, in the world as it was apprehended by Cross, there were no sides to
be taken; he no longer slept in the old myths of the Greeks and the Jews,
and he knew that nothing was to be preferred to anything else. So his act
was simply "a sweeping and supreme gesture of disdain and disgust with
both of them!" The logic, in other words, is this, that to be a Negro is to
be an outsider, not only in a sociological sense but also, and more deci-
sively, in a moral sense as well. And the mission of the outsider, like that
of Camus' Caligula, is to reveal to mankind that the human City is really
a jungle and that all the disciplines and restraints of civilization are "just

screens which men have used" to throw a kind of "veneer of order" over the disorder that still seethes beneath the surface. But since, as it appears, this is a mission that cannot be accomplished apart from terrorism, Mr. Wright's conclusion of 1953 entailed essentially the same mischievousness that had been implicit thirteen years earlier in *Native Son*, the notion that the natural life-movement of the Negro who bears the full burden of his situation is toward a great blasting moment of supreme destruction. Bigger Thomas is an inarticulate proletarian who enacts his role unthinkingly, whereas Cross Damon, having read his Nietzschean primers, accepts his mission with deliberation and in the spirit of a kind of inverted messianism—but this is the only significant difference between them, for both aim, as it were, at getting outside of history altogether, through an act of consummate violence. Like Conrad's Kurtz, Cross does, to be sure, behold at last "the horror," as he gaspingly admits to Houston a moment before his death; but he has, nevertheless, tasted the terrible joy of his murderous orgasm: he has burst the belt and been "hard" and won through at least to the unhistorical realm of the dream—which is of revenge.

Mr. Wright was always too impatient with what Henry James called the "proving disciplines" of art to win the kind of genuine distinction as a writer for which his talents qualified him. And, like George Orwell, for him the greatest uses of art were not those by which we distance ourselves from the world in order to contemplate more strenuously its pattern and meaning. They were, rather, those by which we seek a more direct entry into the world for the sake of redeeming it from the brutality and the indecencies by which it must otherwise be overwhelmed. So it is rather a sad irony that his own art did in point of fact so often drift toward a definition of man, and particularly of the American Negro, that deeply undercut his conscious intention to make it serve a genuinely humane vision. As James Baldwin has said, the real tragedy of Bigger Thomas "is not that he is cold or black or hungry, not even that he is American, black, but that he has accepted a theology that denies him life, that he admits the possibility of his being subhuman and feels constrained, therefore, to battle for his humanity according to those brutal criteria bequeathed him at his birth."[2] And this is precisely what it is that renders so ambiguous many of the other chief protagonists in Mr. Wright's fiction.

His last years, unhappily, were not, it seems, a period of rich fulfillment and harvest. Mr. Baldwin has reported[3] on some of the asperities that increasingly isolated him from friends and acquaintances and young American Negro and African intellectuals who were living in Paris. And I suspect that his crotchetiness was not unconnected with the fortunes of his reputation in the literary life. Though *The Outsider* won a respectful

[2]*Notes of a Native Son* (Boston: The Beacon Press, 1955), p. 23.
[3]*Nobody Knows My Name* (New York: The Dial Press, 1961), pp. 200–215.

reception in some quarters, it by no means achieved any large *succès d'estime* in the critical forum; and the novel of 1958, *The Long Dream,* met little more than polite indifference. So it was the publication in 1945 of *Black Boy* which had brought him to the zenith of his success. Thereafter his fiction and his political criticism, though no different in tone and emphasis from his earlier work, seemed to be nettling in their effect, and the reputation of the early 'forties has today become merely a minor datum of that earlier time. This is of course in part, I suspect, but a particular case of the more general demise of the naturalism of the American nineteen-thirties. At the beginning of the decade Edmund Wilson had suggested in *Axel's Castle* that this was an idiom which could survive only by consenting to be complicated by disciplines of intelligence and imagination that he somewhat clumsily denominated as "Symbolism," but this was a challenge that did not begin to be responded to until the early 'fifties, by the generation of Ralph Ellison and Saul Bellow and William Styron. And, however robust our respect may still be for the Dos Passos of the *U.S.A.* trilogy or the Steinbeck of *The Grapes of Wrath* or the Wright of *Native Son,* we find them today to be writers with whom it is virtually impossible any longer to have a genuinely reciprocal relation, for the simple fact is that the rhetoric of what once used to be called "reportage" proves itself, with the passage of time, to be a language lacking in the kind of amplitude and resonance that *lasts.* This may not be the precise judgment which the cunning of history, in its ultimate justice, will sustain, but it is, at any rate, *ours.*

It may, of course, be that this is a kind of verdict on our fiction of twenty-five or thirty years ago that has sometimes been applied with too alacritous a facility by the high priests of our present dispensation, and I am prepared even now to confess to the irritation that I recently felt when I came again upon the patrician hauteur of a sentence of the late R. P. Blackmur's in which it is asserted that "*Native Son* is one of those books in which everything is undertaken with seriousness except the writing." But whatever may in turn be history's ultimate verdict on our present way of dealing with the American naturalism of the recent past, there is, quite apart from the line that in this respect we want now to take, a more specific and more cogent reason for the revision that we may want to practice on the accolades of the early 'forties for Mr. Wright's work (the enthusiastic equations of the author of *Native Son* with Dostoevski, etc.), and it is a reason which is clarified by the collection of stories entitled *Eight Men* that appeared a few weeks after his death.

At least three of the stories of which this book is composed were written before 1945, but, since the collection was supervised by the author himself, we are justified in assuming that they do all reflect his final sense of life—and what is most remarkable about the book is the summation that it provides of the consistencies which, throughout his career, formed

Richard Wright's personal signature. In each of the eight stories which make up this volume the central figure is a black *isolé* whose crucifixion by a hostile world is offered as type and example of a collective suffering and a collective fate. And all these various statements are marked by an immoderate and melodramatic imagination of the world as "split in two, a white world and a black one, the white one being separated from the black by a million psychological miles." The last of the eight pieces, "The Man Who Went to Chicago"—which is, I take it, autobiographical—ingeniously interweaves narrative and essay, and at one point, in recounting his experience in the early 'thirties "as an orderly to a medical research institute in one of the largest and wealthiest hospitals in Chicago," Mr. Wright says:

> Each Saturday morning I assisted a young Jewish doctor in slitting the vocal cords of a fresh batch of dogs from the city pound. The object was to devocalize the dogs so that their howls would not disturb the patients in the other parts of the hospital. I held each dog as the doctor injected Nembutal into its veins to make it unconscious; then I held the dog's jaws open as the doctor inserted the scalpel and severed the vocal cords. Later, when the dogs came to, they would lift their heads to the ceiling and gape in a soundless wail. The sight became lodged in my imagination as a symbol of silent suffering.

And though the image comes toward the close of this collection, once it is encountered it seems then to resonate backward across the entire book, indeed across the entire *œuvre,* and we feel that the human presence at the center of Mr. Wright's dramatic world has itself somehow been converted into a howling dog whose wails are soundless. In one instance, the long story called "The Man Who Lived Underground," this is an extremism which makes for a wonderfully scarifying and improbable piece of Gothicism which is absolutely self-contained and brilliant. And the piece called "Man of All Work" is a beautifully constructed account of a man who, not being able to find any employment, disguises himself as a woman and, in his wife's clothes, hires himself out as a domestic, being certain that, since Negroes are never really looked at anyway, he'll be able to carry the stunt off—a situation which enables Mr. Wright, with a remarkable deftness and irony, to probe the kind of demasculinization of the male and the kind of resulting rupture of the primitive bonds of the family which have often occurred in Negro life; nor does he also fail, with a savage funniness, to suggest what is outrageous in the sexual panic of American whites. But in every other case, as we move through the stories in *Eight Men,* though we are kept going from page to page and though the writing has the minor virtues of a professionally skillful naturalism, we are dealing with a body of work which totters and collapses under the pressure of a radical imagination unequipped with any defense against its own radicalism; and nowhere else is there a fully achieved work of art.

But, when we have done, it may be that we ought to remember that there are in human experience issues weightier and more exacting than the issues of aesthetics and literary criticism. And it may also be that, in whatever kingdom of the spirit Richard Wright now dwells, as he broods over this uncongenial world of earth, he finds it sufficient merely to say, "I am the man, I suffer'd, I was there." Of this I am reminded, as I glance now at the Dedication of *The Outsider*—"For Rachel, my daughter who was born on alien soil."

The Outsider: Revision of an Idea

by Darwin T. Turner

Richard Wright's *The Outsider* (1953) disappointed many critics who, for more than a decade, had waited for a second novel from the author of *Native Son* (1940). They had honored him with the accolades traditionally showered on only one Negro writer during each decade. White critics had judged *Native Son* the most powerful novel ever written by an American Negro. Whenever they could identify a new novelist as Negro, they compared him with Wright as monotonously as sportswriters today seek a new Willie Mays in every dark-skinned young outfielder. Negro critics had been more ambivalent because some doubted that a Negro novelist should proclaim in public that black Bigger Thomases live and lust. Nevertheless, even these critics had admitted Wright's talents and had warmed their racial pride in the spotlight shining on his book. And young black writers had given the highest praise: They had pilgrimaged to Paris to listen to him speak, and they had imitated his writing.

For a decade, all these had waited. New authors attracted attention— Ann Petry, Chester Himes, Frank Yerby, Willard Motley, William Gardner Smith, Saunders Redding, then James Baldwin and Ralph Ellison. Finally, Wright's second novel appeared. Disappointedly, the critics wrote that Wright had been sipping too much French existentialism *chez* Sartre, or as Arna Bontemps put it, "He has had a roll in the hay with the existentialism of Sartre, and apparently he liked it."[1] The king was dead, and the mourners rushed from the funeral to find a new king.

The critics were partially correct. *The Outsider* fails to evoke the emotional intensity which stunned readers of *Native Son* in 1940 and which continues to affect many readers who discover the book for the first time in 1969. *The Outsider*'s frequent echoes of *Crime and Punishment* and of the now familiar tenets of existentialism—these disclose the conscious craftsmanship of a well-read author. Thus, the book lacks the aura of uniqueness, originality, and artless spontaneity which characterizes

---

"*The Outsider:* Revision of an Idea" by Darwin T. Turner. From *CLA Journal*, 12 (June, 1969), 310–321. Copyright © 1969 by the College Language Association. Reprinted by permission of the College Language Association and the author.

[1]Bontemps, "Three Portraits of the Negro," *Saturday Review*, XXXVI (March 28, 1953), p. 15.

Wright's first novel. *Native Son* seems to be a hoarse cry from the heart of the ghetto; *The Outsider* is an idea shaped by philosophical men who have conquered their emotions.

Nevertheless, *The Outsider* should not be judged merely as a failure by a competent naturalistic novelist who, succumbing to foreign influences, made the mistake of dabbling in existentialism. Actually, Wright leaned toward existentialism long before the philosophy earned its literary reputation in America and perhaps even before he fully realized the philosophical position which he was articulating. Whereas many readers of *Native Son* saw only the implacable forces of environment crushing a helpless black pawn, Bigger Thomas evolves from that pawn into a protagonist who instinctively, not consciously, rejects the standards of a world which is meaningless to him. As Edward Margolies has explained, once Bigger has murdered, he becomes a metaphysical revolutionary challenging an absurd, hostile world and determined to bring that universe into accord with his sense of justice, or "if this fails . . . to match in himself its injustice and chaos."[2]

Considered in this respect, *The Outsider* is not Wright's first venture into existentialism. Instead, it can be viewed as an effort, after he had broken fully with Communism, to redefine the idea which he had failed to clarify in *Native Son.* Simultaneously, he attempted, consciously or unconsciously, to improve his work artistically by answering critics' objections to the characterization of his protagonist and to the development of his thesis. In order to justify this argument that *The Outsider* is a revision and redefinition of *Native Son,* it is necessary to look at the close resemblances between the two works.

Native Son is the ironic title of the story of twenty-year-old Bigger Thomas, an uneducated, Mississippi-born, Negro resident of Chicago. The title is ironic because, even though Bigger has been born in America, he is an outsider. As a Negro, he recognizes his exclusion from American life.

> I know I oughtn't think about it, but I can't help it. . . . We live here and they live there. We black and they white. They got things and we ain't. It's just like living in jail. Half the time I feel like I'm on the outside of the world peeping in through a knothole in the fence (*Native Son,* p. 23).[3]

Because he is shut out from the American dream which he sees in motion pictures, Bigger envies and hates the white people who can realize the dream. He cannot express his hatred directly, forcefully, consciously; for he fears white people too much. As Wright explains,

[2]Margolies, *Native Sons* (Philadelphia, 1968), p. 82.
[3]This quotation and all succeeding references to *Native Son* are taken from the Perennial Classic edition (New York: Harper & Row, 1966).

> To Bigger and his kind white people were not really people; they were
> a sort of great natural force, like a stormy sky looming overhead . . . (*Native
> Son*, p. 109).

Instead, Bigger directs all of his frustration and resentment towards a
more vulnerable target, his fellow Negroes. By bullying other Negroes, he
seeks to affirm his manliness and courage, even though he subconsciously
knows that he cowers from a direct confrontation with white people. For
instance, he fights a Negro companion in order to avoid robbing a white
storekeeper. In short, although Bigger lives and plays with Negroes, he
is not a "soul brother." He rejects them as the visible manifestations of
his inferiority:

> There were rare moments when a feeling and longing for solidarity with
> other black people would take hold of him. He would dream of making a
> stand against that white force, but that dream would fade when he looked
> at the other black people near him. Even though black like them, he felt
> that there was too much difference between him and them to allow for a
> common binding and a common life. . . . Dimly, he felt that there should
> be one direction in which he and all other black people could go whole-
> heartedly. . . . But he felt that such would never happen to him and his
> black people, and he hated them and wanted to wave his hand and blot
> them out (*Native Son*, p. 109).

Bigger is even alienated from his own family. He taunts his sister. He
quarrels with, deceives, and deserts his mother. He must maintain a
distance between himself and them in order to prevent himself from
becoming conscious of his impotence. As Wright says,

> He hated his family because he knew that they were suffering and that he
> was powerless to help them. He knew that the moment he allowed himself
> to feel to its fullness how they lived, the shame and misery of their lives, he
> would be swept out of himself with fear and despair. So he held toward
> them an attitude of iron reserve; he lived with them, but behind a wall, a
> curtain (*Native Son*, pp. 13–14).

Reluctantly, Bigger accepts a position as chauffeur for the Daltons—
wealthy people who derive their income partly from exorbitant rents
charged to Negro ghetto dwellers, but who take pride in their minor acts
of charity for Negroes. The first evening on the job, Bigger is forced to
help the employer's drunken daughter to her bedroom. Surprised there
by the girl's blind mother, fearful that he will be accused of attempted
rape if he is discovered, Bigger accidentally smothers the girl while desperately trying to prevent her from attracting her mother to the bedside
where he cowers.

Ironically, however, the accidental murder gives meaning to Bigger's
life; in a larger sense, the accidental murder gives life to Bigger. Previously,

he has merely reacted viscerally to stimuli thrust upon him in his ghetto prison, just as a caged rat would respond involuntarily to casual, intermittent proddings by the being who has trapped it. After the murder, however, Bigger is no longer trapped by the world which has surrounded him. He is free to act voluntarily, to choose his course.

Now confident of his ability not merely to talk with white people but even to outsmart them, Bigger matches wits with reporters and investigators. When he is discovered and pursued, however, he voluntarily murders a second person—his Negro sweetheart, Bessie. Bigger himself has escaped from the insecurities, the fears, the feelings of inferiority etched into the Negro psyche by centuries of repression in a white-dominated society. In Bessie, he sees a continuation of those mental chains. She is still lazily amoral, timid, compliant—in short, the Sambo personality which threatens the existence of the new Bigger. In order to live, Bigger must destroy her, the last link that reminds him of and binds him to his Negroness. And he does destroy her, in one of the most brutal murders ever described by an author with a predilection for violence. He rapes her; then he smashes her face with a brick; then he drops her body down an airshaft.

It is worth noting that Bigger might have dispatched her more deftly with his gun, but the brutal assault emphasizes the violence of Bigger's rejection of his Negro personality. Bessie dies slowly, neither from the beating nor from the fall, but from pneumonia contracted while lying in the shaft. It is, in fact, as difficult for Bigger to destroy the symbol of his Negro personality as it is later for Ralph Ellison's Invisible Man to rid himself of a comparable symbol—the Sambo dancing doll.

Bigger is totally free only after he has killed Bessie. He has destroyed the white force smothering him, and he has smashed the black chains binding him. The capture and execution of the physical body of Bigger are less important to the theme, for spiritually he has become free to think and to feel and to live.

Critics of the novel raised an objection which may have troubled Wright. Some argued that Bigger seemed too sensitive to be considered typical. That is, insisting that Bigger be evaluated as a naturalistic representative of uneducated, working Negroes, they presumed that such Negroes not only would be incapable of articulating their feelings but would even be unaware of their hatreds and their fears. Furthermore, most critics evaluated the work merely as Wright's protest against the treatment of Negroes in America.

Wright attempted to redirect the thoughts of his critics. In "How Bigger Was Born,"[4] he explained that he had not intended to portray Bigger merely as a naturalistic pawn; he wanted to show an individual capable

---

[4]*Saturday Review*, XXII (June 1, 1940), pp. 3–4, 17–20.

of making conscious choices about his life. Moreover, Wright continued, Bigger's story is not merely the story of an American Negro; it is the story of the oppressed peoples of the world. Whether or not Wright believed that he had persuaded his critics through his essay, in his next novel he retraced the pattern of *Native Son*.

The Outsider is the story of Cross Damon, a twenty-six-year-old postal worker in Chicago. At the beginning of the story, Cross is in an intolerable position emotionally. His fifteen-year-old lover, who is pregnant, hopes to force him to marry her by threatening to charge him with statutory rape if he refuses. His wife, from whom he is separated, refuses to give him a divorce. Instead, she insists that he borrow $800 so that he can complete payments for the house and car, which he must give to her. If he refuses, she will create scandal which will cost him his job at the post office. At every opportunity, his mother reminds him that he is not behaving as she taught him.

When he is presumed to have died in a subway accident, Damon sees opportunity to begin a new life. But, to protect this new identity, he first must kill a former friend who, having recognized him, intends to reveal the secret.

In New York, where he has fled, Cross is introduced to Gil and Eva Blount, Communists, who invite him to live with them while he studies Communism. Shortly after Damon has moved in, Blount fights with the Fascist landlord, who refuses to permit a Negro to continue to live in his house. While the two are fighting, Cross seizes a table leg and bludgeons both to death. Cross and Blount's widow fall in love; but, when Eva Blount realizes that Cross has been responsible for the death of her husband, the landlord, and another Communist, she kills herself by jumping from a window. The District Attorney knows that Cross has murdered the three men but refuses to press charges because he has no proof. Cross, however, is killed by Communists who suspect his guilt.

In general plot idea, *The Outsider* corresponds to *Native Son*. Like *Native Son*, it is located first in Chicago in winter. Structurally also it resembles *Native Son*. It is divided into five sections: Dread, Dream, Descent, Despair, and Decision. Section I—Dread—corresponds to Section I of *Native Son*—Fear. Section I in *The Outsider* begins with a scene of banter among Cross and three friends. Except for the differences in the ages of the characters, the scene closely resembles Chapter Two of *Native Son*, a chapter in which Bigger Thomas talks and jokes with three friends. Interestingly, Wright first proposed to begin *Native Son* with that chapter. In Section I of *The Outsider* as of *Native Son*, accidental death leads to a new life for the protagonist.

The most significant parallels are seen, however, in the background of Cross Damon and his relationship to other people.

For many readers, the resemblances between Cross Damon and Bigger

Thomas are obscured by the differences resulting from Cross's superior educational background and his conscious interest in ideas. A former college student, Cross can find employment as a postal clerk rather than as a chauffeur. Although he is not wealthy, he lives on a standard which Bigger and his family identify with the successful white man. He owns a house and car—or, in the tradition of America, the finance company owns a house and car for which he is paying. Undoubtedly, Bigger would envy Cross's possessions and his opportunities. Considered in this way, Cross represents the middle-class Negro who aspires to the American dream. In contrast, Bigger is the lower-class individual who, glimpsing the dream only in romantic motion pictures, rejects it as an impossibility.

By creating a character on a different economic and social level, Wright emphasized the theme which some critics failed to discern in *Native Son*. He was concerned with the problem of existence itself, a frustrating enigma not merely for the poor and the black but for all who refuse to accept the roles in which they are cast.

Apparent differences between Cross and Bigger, however, are more superficial than actual. Education seems to have relieved Damon of some of the problems which vex Bigger; but, in reality, by creating new aware-ness and new aspirations, it has reproduced the same problems on a different level. For example, Bigger suffers from economic deprivation. He lives in one room with his family; he subsists on welfare. Cross Damon has a job, a house, a car, and an apartment. But these are minimal standards for his class. To pay for them, he must borrow money. Who then is freer economically—Bigger, who must borrow pennies from mother, or Cross, who borrows hundreds from the union?

In character, the two seem identical. Bigger bullies others to conceal his own fears; Cross plays practical jokes. Both rebel against their mothers, who typify an older generation which urged Negro children to live accord-ing to the ethics taught in Christian churches and prescribed for Negroes by a society dominated by white men.

Bigger loves no woman. He experiences sexual satisfaction and com-panionship with Bessie, but they have no enduring relationship. Eventu-ally, he uses her, deserts her, and destroys her. Cross married a woman who befriended him. He had been lonely and sexually frustrated; she had risked her reputation by sleeping with him. Grateful to her, unwilling to assume the guilt of abandoning her, and doubtful of finding any better partner, he proposed. Within a year after the birth of their first child, however, he realized that he had confused compassion for her with love. During the marriage and after the separation, Cross had affairs with women, but these escapades frustrated him emotionally: drunkenly, he approached women in bars, bargained with them, and then retreated in self-disgust. His mistress, Dot, seemed different. She was young and beau-tiful; he was lonely. When she became pregnant and refused to consider an abortion, he proposed to do the "right" thing—to live with her and support her. Damon realizes, however, that he no longer desires her and has never loved her. He meets a prostitute, who hopes that he will help her escape from Chicago. After buying a bus ticket for her, he deserts her. He learns to love only when he meets sensitive, artistic Eva Blount, the first woman who becomes mind as well as body for him. But Eva, an escapist, an idealist, cannot endure the reality of Damon. She pitied him as one being used by the Communists as she had been used; she loved him as one child might turn to another for mutual comfort against a hostile world; but she retreats in horror from the realization that he also is merciless and destructive.

Neither Bigger nor Cross can realize satisfactory companionship with women because both subconsciously regard women essentially as instruments for the temporary relief of physical and emotional needs. However, because he has been taught that a man should protect a woman's honor, Cross feels guilt when he betrays that principle. Therefore, the relationships with women do not merely fail to bring him close to another human being, they also intensify his hatred of himself.

Alienated from others, both Cross Damon and Bigger Thomas hate themselves. Of Bigger, Wright wrote, "He knew that the moment he allowed what his life meant to enter fully into his consciousness, he would either kill himself or someone else" (*Native Son*, p. 14). Damon, however, has not sought to repress his awareness. To the contrary, he has searched for the meaning of life; he has "thought . . . [his] way through the many veils of illusion" (*The Outsider*, p. 29).[5] It is not surprising, therefore, that he considers suicide and, finally, commits murder.

Both Bigger and Damon are reborn through accidental deaths of white people. Bigger finds meaning for his life in his efforts to benefit from his accidental murder as well as to escape its consequences. Damon experiences rebirth in a more obviously symbolic scene. Having plunged underground in a subway train, he finds himself trapped inside the overturned car. His legs are wedged to the wall by a train seat held in place by a white man's head. The only way he can free himself is to smash the dead man's head. Wright describes the action in words which echo the horror and tension of the moment at which Bigger discovered that he needed to hack off Mary Dalton's head in order to conceal her body in a furnace. Having freed himself from the pinned position behind the seat, Cross can escape from the train only by stepping on the body of a dead white woman.

As I have stated, the symbolism is obvious. In revising his idea, Wright took no chances that a reader's imagination must be limited to consideration of a Negro youth's lust for a drunkenly helpless white girl. By

[5]This quotation and all subsequent references to *The Outsider* are taken from the Perennial Classic edition (New York: Harper & Row, 1965).

specifying the race of the individuals blocking Damon's path, Wright emphasized his belief that Negroes can find freedom and new life only after they have first crushed the male and female white forces that trap them in a separate and submerged world.

Once free, Cross, like Bigger, wants to share his new understanding with a woman. Cross confides in Jenny, a white prostitute, as Bigger confides in Bessie. Both protagonists subsequently berate themselves when they realize that the women are incapable of perceiving the emotional and spiritual significance of what has happened. In both works, Wright suggests that the male protagonist cannot discover the needed intellectual and spiritual companionship with women of a particular type. Bessie and Jennie can ease physical and mental tensions; they are opiates which one may use to escape from reality; but they lack the resources to share reality.

In *Native Son,* Wright's meaning is blurred somewhat because he used one figure—Bessie—to represent both the Sambo mentality which Bigger must destroy and the personality of the inadequate female. Consequently, readers may misinterpret Bigger's murder of Bessie as his need to destroy the inadequate female. Wright clarified his meaning in *The Outsider* by representing the concepts through two different individuals. Since Jenny merely represents the sensual companionship in human relationships, Damon does not need to destroy her; instead, he deserts her as previously he has alienated himself from his mother and from Negro women, both as wives and as lovers. He symbolically destroys his Negro personality by murdering Joe, a fellow postal clerk. In an obvious parallel to the murder of Bessie, he hits Joe on the head and drops him from a window to a roof, where his body lies for some time before it is discovered.

Both Cross Damon and Bigger Thomas need more money than they can earn. Bigger steals $125 from Mary Dalton, but he loses it by forgetting to retrieve it from Bessie before he kills her. Damon borrows money from the union, gives part of it to Jenny, but retains most. Consequently, at the end of Section I, he has the money to finance a new life.

From this point, the stories diverge, but continue to parallel each other. To conceal his guilt from the Daltons, the newspaper reporters, and the investigators, Bigger assumes the guise of Sambo, the stereotype of the lovably ignorant, harmless darky. As the pose proves effective, he gains confidence in matching himself intellectually with whites. Damon needs no such support; his experiences in integrated schools have taught him that he can compete intellectually. Hence, he does not hesitate to oppose a white woman who threatens to assault a Negro waiter or to discuss life with a philosophical district attorney. But, in order to obtain a birth certificate verifying his new identity, he too assumes the Sambo guise, which works as effectively for him as it works for Bigger.

Bigger fears Communists but learns from the Communist lawyer Max a way of articulating his new ideas. In 1940 Wright had not clarified his own dilemmas. Although he continued to work with the Communist Party and to respect its philosophy, he was disillusioned by the methods used by the Party. By 1953, however, his break was complete, and his ideas were clear. He had been forced to reject the Communist philosophy as one which could not be attained because of the limitations of the human beings who controlled the Communist Party. Cross Damon reflects Wright's new certainty. Able to judge Communists objectively, Damon rejects or destroys them as mercilessly as he rejects Fascists.

At this stage of *The Outsider,* therefore, Wright reached a philosophical position which he could not have attained through uneducated, inarticulate Bigger Thomas. Cross Damon is an intellectual, a student of philosophy who read voraciously until he learned that books did not include the ideas he sought. Through Damon, Wright could ask, "What happens to an individual who finds no comfort in the traditional human relationships and institutions?"

> When a man had been born and bred with other men, had shared and participated in their traditions, he was not required of himself to conceive the total meaning or direction of his life; broad, basic definitions of his existence were already contained implicitly in the general scope of other men's hopes and fears; and, by living and acting with them—a living and acting he will have commenced long before he could have been able to give his real consent—he will have assumed the responsibility for promises and pledges made for him and in his name by others. Now, depending only upon his lonely will, he saw that to map out his life entirely upon his own assumptions was a task that terrified him just to think of it, for he knew that he first had to know what he thought life was, had to know consciously all the multitude of assumptions which other men took for granted, and he did not know them and he knew that he did not know them. The question summed itself up: What's a man? He had unknowingly set himself a project of no less magnitude than contained in that awful question (*The Outsider,* pp. 90–91).

Perhaps the problem is more critical for a black man, but it seems to pose an irresolvable dilemma for any man. Family, marriage, church—all have failed him. His passion is ideas, but he finds no solution in the dominant ideas—democracy, capitalism, fascism, communism. What is the future for such a man?

Wright had no satisfactory answer. Bigger Thomas is executed by a capitalistic democracy. In *The Outsider,* the district attorney, a legal representative of the capitalistic democracy, admits that he cannot destroy Cross Damon, but Damon is murdered by Communists. In the revision, as in the original, Wright suggested that the sensitive, questioning individual, the existentialist, will be destroyed by the organized institutions which fear him because they do not understand him and fear his questions because they cannot answer them.

These parallels, I believe, suggest that Wright either consciously or unconsciously was trying to develop more effectively the theme which he explored in *Native Son*. Intellectually, he succeeded: the thought of *The Outsider* is more persuasive. But artistically he failed.

The fault lies partly in his conception of the protagonist. When he created Bigger Thomas, he planned an individual who would provoke shock rather than pity. Bigger does. Nevertheless, readers experience an indefinable feeling of compassion, emerging perhaps from the pathos of the realization that Bigger is not an absolutely self-determining individual but has been grotesquely distorted by a society in which he is inarticulate.

Compassion cannot be felt as easily for Cross Damon. Because he possesses the conventional attributes of the middle-class, his problem does not evoke the sentimentality which can be showered on those judged to be socially and economically inferior. His more intellectual, more abstract problem lacks an emotional analogue. That is, even if one cannot identify emotionally with Bigger's frustration as a Negro, he can relate emotionally to Bigger's efforts to elude the investigators and the police. There is no such emotional analogue in *The Outsider*. Strangely, however, Damon's problem might elicit more sympathetic response in 1969 than it did in 1953, for it suggests the current rebellion of affluent youth against a society which offers material comfort but no spiritual satisfaction.

After *The Outsider*, Wright never again explored the theme as deeply. His last major study of the problem of existence in America is restricted to the Southern Negro, and the answer is a different one: Destruction can be avoided only if one flees from America.

Black Existentialism: Richard Wright

by Kingsley Widmer

In Richard Wright's most successful fiction, the novella *The Man Who Lived Underground* (first complete version 1944; collected posthumously in *Eight Men,* 1961), his isolated black man hiding out in the sewers and contemplating crimes thinks to himself, "Maybe *any*thing's right. . . . Yes, if the world as man has made it was right, then anything else was right, any act a man took to satisfy himself. . . ." Yet the man who says it, bitter author as well as desperate underground character, ends tormented with isolation, overpowered by obscure guilts, and urged towards self-destruction.

This is the preoccupying, indeed obsessive, moral drama focusing almost all of Wright's writings. Traditionally, we and Wright recognize it as Ivan Karamazov's brain-fevered perplexity, his just conclusion that in a cruel and purposeless world "Everything is permitted." But father and God and all values dead, only guilty anguish remains, the demon of destruction and self-destruction. Wright repeatedly and overwhelmingly felt that perplexity, not only individually but as a black in white America, though one who came to recognize much of that "blackness" as the universal human condition. With the old myths gone, he discovers that black revenge *is* permitted—violation, crime, hatred, killing—but results in ultimate revenge against the self. Just as the final obedience the authoritarian parent exacts from the son is self-hatred, and the major work the master exacts from the slave is self-abasement, so American racist injustice exacts guilty black self-destruction. Domination, exploitation, and other human viciousness, succeed all too well, and most horribly in the victim's vengeance against himself for being a victim.

The Man Who Lived Underground seems paradigmatic. Fred Daniels, a simple black falsely accused of murdering a white woman, hides out underground but feels terribly guilty of some unnameable crime. In the lonely and foul depths, each black man finds "the secret of his existence, the guilt that he could never get rid of," the "dreadful offense" of his very

This is the author's extensive revision (1971) of "The Existential Darkness: Richard Wright's *The Outsider,*" *Wisconsin Studies in Contemporary Literature,* I, no. 3 (1960), 13–21. Copyright © 1960 by the Regents of the University of Wisconsin. Reprinted by permission of the author and the original publisher.

being in the world of white contempt and hatred. Living for days in a cave off the city sewers, the outcast collects and plays with the "serious toys" of the overground world—money, jewels, machines, clocks, a meat cleaver. But, in his dreadful freedom and anxious isolation, those things can have no meaning. Nor can the lives of that other world. From his subterranean access to stores and offices, to a church and a movie theatre and a funeral parlor, he looks in on the phantasmagoric pathos and obscenity and guilt of the ordinary social order. In his separation, he crouches free of such mis-reality, so free that his very identity (even his sense of his name) begins to dissolve in the lonely and placeless and timeless depths. So he comes above ground to admit to the police that though he did not kill the woman, "I'm guilty!" All men are. To be, he must in this society be guilty of something. But the police have found a different criminal to blame for that particular woman's death. Reluctantly following the crazedly submissive guilty outcast back toward his secret sewer cache, the white cops kill him: "You've got to shoot his kind. They'd wreck things." Though naturalistic in much of its detail, this fervid guilt fantasy is a nightmare which can only end with the black man's death in the sewer with a "mouth full of thick, bitter" understanding.

This harshly seminal fable, indebted to Dostoyevsky's *Notes from Underground* and providing the basic tropes for Ellison's *Invisible Man,* is what Wright could best do, and perhaps only do. From the pathetically fumbling murders and self-hatred of Bigger Thomas in Chicago in Wright's first, and quasi-Marxian determinist, novel, *Native Son* (1940), through the slyer crimes and self-disgusted flight imposed by the white South on black Fishbelly in his last work of rhetorical naturalism, *The Long Dream* (1958), Wright mostly played variations on the black outsider as guilty underground victim. The isolated and despised black compulsively strikes out for his freedom in violations which demand self-destruction in a world of whited sepulchers.

The personal dimensions of Wright's existential paradigm may be followed out in his most poignant book, the autobiographical *Black Boy* (1945). Raised fatherless in Mississippi by a fanatical puritan mother, his later isolated heroes usually guiltily punish an uncomprehending "good woman." White Southerners gave Wright every reason for the sense of degradation, self-disgust and embittered flight which compels all of his protagonists. And the sensitivity and intelligence of the black boy brutally victimized by white Americans demand Wright's intense commitment to rage, accusation and exacerbated black insight.

The intellectual dimensions of this outcast being receive fullest development in his "novel of ideas," *The Outsider* (1953). Though faltering in style and characterization—Wright's rage drove him into rhetorical abstraction in all of his books—it was his most thoughtful novel. Written with a partial detachment provided by some years of deracinated escape from America in exile in Paris, it is often condemned by other black writers and those identifying with them. For though the central figure is a black man in ghettoized America, and such experiences inform the scenes and themes, the issues, as Wright pointed out in the novel, do not confine themselves to "racial consciousness" and its "self-loathing." Blackness but provides special emphases of the more universal outsider state. Similar perplexities of "freedom and dread" apply to all men, all of us guilty. The race issue is the broadly human, not merely ethnic, one. All sensitive men must recognize their "black existence."

The Outsider is an explicitly philosophical novel framed with epigraphs from Kierkegaard and Nietzsche and developed on Sartrean dialectics. One of the few American self-consciously existentialist fables, it is, except for those imposing some parochial thesis about "American Black Culture" on the author, Wright's most interesting novel. Critical charges against it for melodrama, for passages of didactic abstraction and jargon and awkwardness, and for obsessive pessimism, correctly apply to all of Wright's books. Nor, as I have already suggested in discussing his work of a decade earlier, is the existential moral focus an imposition of the author's Paris days. As black boy from Natchez, as naturalist writer from Chicago, and as left-Negro militant from New York, Wright had always practiced the "literature of extreme situations," dramatized the "gratuitous act" of an "ethical criminal," centered on the isolation of American Raskolnikovs meditating on man's terrible freedom and compulsion, and insisted on revealing "the horrible truth of the uncertain and enigmatic nature of life." Black Wright was a birthright existentialist.

The dramatization in *The Outsider*—the name, says his biographer, was suggested by a reader of the manuscript—employs the melodrama usual to philosophically insistent literature, as in Marlowe, Dostoyevsky and Sartre, to highlight choice. The protagonist, ex-philosophy student Cross Damon, rebels against the humiliations of a resentfully aspiring black middle-class family, the tedium of a postal clerk's job, the sense of failure in sexual complications, the oppressive Protestant ethos of his milieu, and the whole complex of Negro-American "nonidentity." (The allegorical emphasis includes the demonic crucifixion suggested by the name of the hero and the parody of Søren Kierkegaard's use of the postman as archetypal Christian in *Either/Or* as well as novelistic sub-division into an existential pentad of "stages": Dread, Dream, Descent, Despair and Decision [i.e., death].) A fortuitous subway accident, in which a mangled black body with the wrong coat is misidentified as the dead Cross Damon, allows the protagonist to pretend to be dead and flee his past life. Damon attains the moral limbo of totally alienated freedom—a hugely appealing contemporary fantasy. In the following days he kills a "Negro clown" (his Jim Crow antithesis) who could identify him with his past, tricks several kind people whose pathos would impose obligations of his freedom, covers his masqueraded identity by burning the Selective Service office (it was, with appropriate irony, in the basement of a church), and, with moral impartiality, kills a fascistic racist and an exploitative Communist. Soon after, dreadfully free logic drives him to murder another suspicious political functionary. He attempts to achieve a sense of purpose in anguished love for the victimized wife of one of his victims (Eva, the primal sensitive artist) but she, confronted with knowledge of Cross Damon's past and amoral acts, commits suicide, leaving her Damon in ultimate loneliness and despair. Such is the dread of truth in others, and the price of truth for the self. Cross Damon's own death, at the hands of bureaucratic functionaries who must destroy him because they cannot understand him, simply closes the absurd rebellion to get "outside history," social morality, and the meaningless self.

Cross Damon's destructive acts, of course, also reflect psychological compulsions. He finally recognizes that he was partly in rebellion against his puritan mother: "It had been her moral strictures that had made him a criminal. . . ." His "ungovernable compulsions" to murder his enemies also reflect the social oppression and outcastness of those who "live in but not of the normal rounds of ritualized life." But Wright also wants to fuse these circumstances with the existential-outsider crux in which a man can propound gratuitous crimes, i.e, make a "free" selection of assertions by a "petty god" in a "Godless world." Like Raskolnikov, Cross Damon comes to treat people as "insects." A Dostoyevskian psychological policeman (Ely Houston, the "outsider" crippled District Attorney) points out the metaphysical logic of Damon's destructive actions, his reasonable but inhuman responses to a world losing its mythologies of values. The "logic of atheism," of total disbelief in man and men, cannot give sufficient shape to personal desires and promises in a meaningless universe. Recognized truth is not enough for life. Sadly, this outsider must also discover under his arguments the truth revealed by the earlier underground man: "the feeling that had sent him on this long, bloody, twisting road: self-loathing. . . ."

Can Wright sufficiently relate the dialectic about existential awareness and the compulsions of his black American? It remains problematic, perhaps because of inadequate artistry. Wright does show Cross Damon's mistake in letting "contingency" become "destiny" in some scenes. His purposes were insufficient and perverse, though it is not clear what else would have worked in a world dehumanized into Communists versus policemen. Partly because of his personal disillusionment in the forties with Communist manipulation (the detail appears in Wright's contribution to *The God That Failed*), he dramatizes his Communists, if not his policemen, as too cynical, as men inhumanly pursuing only the "sensuality of power" (the point may come from George Orwell). They all play in existential "bad faith" with "the far-flung conspiracy pretending that life was tending toward a goal of redemption."

Thus Wright's Cross Damon ends making demonic criss-crosses for the author, cancelling each lie with another lie, each crime with another crime. For non-political example, early in the novel Damon becomes estranged from his wife, Gladys, the epitome of the black bourgeoise, the predatory middle-class virtues:

> ... as he suffered her nagging, he felt increasingly walled off from her; but the more he felt it the more he sought to hide it, and finally there crept into his dealings with her a weird quality of irony. It first manifested itself in an innocent question: How could he help Gladys? And the moment he asked that question he knew he did not love her and perhaps had never loved her. ... She had become for him an object of compassion. He was now haunted by the idea of finding some way to make her hate him. Her hatred would be a way of squaring their relationship, of curing her of her love for him, of setting her free as well as himself.

In his ornately perverse "psychological attack" upon his wife, and upon himself, Damon draws upon his earlier aberrant behavior, upon a fluke episode, and comes home unexpectedly, walks in like a mute and mad stranger, hits his wife, walks out, and later returns at his usual time as if nothing had happened. This perversely ironic psychological dramatization drives him into the total alienation he demands and makes flight imperative. Thus "contingency" reveals "destiny," though one as destructive, and self-destructive, as the materials from which it is made. Here, perhaps with more irony than Wright intended, we find a naturalistic delineation of Sartre's maxim that "man chooses himself," which must include that man significantly desires to be that which has happened to him.

As in this representative episode, Wright's usual deployment of inverse and doubling emotions (hate as love, destruction as compassion, compulsion as freedom) ends in self-rejection since each insistently reversed self becomes unacceptable. But, we should note, this goes beyond Wright to characterize much of existentialism's analysis of man. Our doubts that Cross Damon's "weird irony" reflects freedom as much as self-hating compulsion also apply to the gratuitous murder and embracement of death by Camus' Mersault in *L'Etranger*. (*The Outsider* also parallels *The Stranger* several times in the inability at remorse, etc.) But the ambiguities between existential freedom and the compulsions to self-destruction appear not only in Wright and Camus but in Sartre, Genet, Bowles, Mailer, and other self-consciously existential fabulists, and become crucially definitive of modern Western man's loss of positive myth and community. We might also note that, in spite of the usual arguments of traditional moralists, art can locate its insights in hatred as well as in love.

In profound ambiguity, Cross Damon serves as the hero and the victim of existential lucidity. While his choices of action and identity appear free, they also reveal "dark compulsions" in the three pathetic women he chooses, in the betrayals, the acts of violence, the self-confessions, the disguises, the flights, and the self-destruction. He insists, like many contemporary political leaders, nihilistic juveniles, and certain other criminals, that "no ideas are necessary to justify his acts." *That idea* is but another version of Raskolnikov's final dream in *Crime and Punishment* of the "new men," the amoralists of the totalitarian and apocalyptic age.

The existential scene in which Wright places his amoralist tends to only one tonality—an *a priori* blackness. His dark-skinned hero-victim moves solely through the dark wintry season, the black ghettos of Chicago and New York, the dark despair of the "literature of the irrational" (his favorite reading, which gives him away to the intellectual policeman), and even a black levity. The blackness, of course, provides practical images to embody the darkness of dread. Where Sartre in *Nausea* has some difficulty in reasonably presenting Roquentin's repulsion to the "viscous" horrors of his own body, Wright's Damon can more readily see, and treat, his black body as "an alien and despised object" because the white society in its Manichean fears does just that. To "stand outside the world" in the moral and social darkness, for Wright's protagonist, depends on the actual as well as metaphysical alienation of the black man from the white rationalizations of ordinary life and social order.

In his effort to find the "relationship of himself to himself," to escape from his "burden of nonidentity," Cross Damon diabolically takes on "the project of deception," which must finally mislead himself as well as others. Some of this anguished dramatization of the theology and self-defeat of living lies seems to draw upon Sartre's analysis of *mauvaise foi* (*L'Etre et le Néant*, Ch. 2). In both, the systematic bad faith used to hide inner emptiness becomes a bitter parody of the daily compromises and resentments of most men, though the lies and other deceptions American whites demand from blacks may be the most debilitating.

The deceptions and ambiguities and inversions so crucial to the existentialist unfolding of human behavior rest in a desperate romantic irony: enlightenment perversely requires a descent into the darkness. Only thus does one get "outside" not only the usual history and ideas but mere control by circumstances. For Wright's figure, however, very little can be found down and out. Damon's repeated existential maxim, "Man is nothing in particular," shows a greater sense of futility than its source, Sartre's "Man is a useless passion." Is embittered blackness the source of the difference? For Wright's Damon, anyway, there remains after the descent no irreducible value of the human individual. His desperate individualistic assertion of free value ends treating men as "insects," "meaningless obstructions," "nothings," including himself. Wright has carried the existential quest to a dead end.

Perhaps there is a peculiarly American insistence here, and not just in the obvious mockery of our pious idealistic and manipulative optimisms.

Where Kierkegaard's "single one" could fall back before the horror of the arbitrary absolute on a humble moral identity (the familial postman in Deer Park), or more atheistic and anti-bourgeoise European existentialists establish themselves in honorific identities (as traditional artistic and political rebels), the American outsider cannot achieve an adequate role for his metaphysical pathos. Wright is aware that when one is being nothing in particular, passion spent, an amorphous appearing society presents "no form or discipline for living." The apparent mobility, the patently fortuitous order, the lack of heroic patterns, the chameleon styles, of American mass society do confuse even negative limits. Though a victimized black, a Cross Damon has apparent access to much; he can borrow money, travel first class, anonymously shift places and take on deceptive roles. He can even make an elliptical confession of his crimes to the inquisitor and go technically free, though to little purpose and satisfaction. The slightness of American community and identity make concrete his apocalyptic existential question: "Could there be a man in whose mind and consciousness all the hopes and inhibitions of the last two thousand years have died?" It receives the Nietzschean answer in the final chapter of *The Outsider:* "The real men, the last men, are coming." The sloughing off of the old consciousness and culture threatens to be soon and complete in America.

The rage of disbelief in anything, heightened by Wright's angry sensibility, whiskeyed and bitter black intellectual, and black-and-white winter urban world, takes unfortunate political focus. It may be, though I doubt it, appropriate to show the rise of "valueless men" in the guise of power-longing and manipulative political figures, Communist functionaries. But the didactic and obsessive debating with them, by Damon-Wright, turns out to be more than a heavy artistic failure since it also contains no political resolution. The nineteen-fifties politics of leftist disillusionment leaves only a total *a*politics. In his, and the decade's, last years Wright sometimes prophetically yearned to go beyond it by identifying with a Third World Politics of the oppressed. But in *The Outsider* the political rhetoric reveals larger intellectual and moral inadequacies. For instance, the disenchantment with all political ideology and idealism does not acknowledge the need for most men to rely on faiths in order to act. Wright quite obscures the differences in his characters' convictions, allowing no significant conflict of views between Christian and Communist and cop, or anyone else. All come out as pathetic victims "playing god." All those "suspending ethical laws" get mashed together even though criminal, Communist, cop, artist, lover and existentialist do and mean something rather different. Wright, like his protagonist, descends only into negative belief even though he aims to bitterly expose that failure.

Why did Damon commit his crimes? Intellectually, it was because "I don't *believe* in anything." The lies, the murders, the flight, the self-destruction, are the "ludicrous protest" of an "inverted idealist." He "wanted to be free" to find out "what living meant." And he has broken through to the answer: "Nothing."

But not quite nothing. The insight of *The Man Who Lived Underground* has been in several ways extended in *The Outsider:* "Men hate themselves and it makes them hate others." Like Wright, Cross Damon could shed much of the white middle-class American way imposed, at best, on the black American, but not the hatred and self-hated. He didn't finally get "outside." Cross Damon's last words, "I'm *innocent.* That's what made the horror . . . ," simply completes the "underground man's "plaintive demand, "I'm guilty." Neither bring justice. Guilt and innocence have lost meaning. Thus the restatement of Nietzsche's prophecy for our Age of Nihilism: "The myth men are going. . . . The real men, the last men, are coming."

In this existential anti-existentialism, Wright can see, but not present, the resolution of the failing outsider quest for meaning: "Alone a man is nothing." Wright re-enforces that existential discovery with the rages responsive to the unjust and false American social order and the anxieties responsive to the heroic theology of Protestant atheism. He dramatizes that attempts to live by isolated moral logic, such as killing men who "deserve" to be killed, ends in nothing. Neither the logics of salvational ideologies nor the rebellions against repressive circumstances can create authentic being. Wright's half-hearted asides calling for a humanized scientism and benevolent moral idealism also seem quite inadequate for any community of genuine and humane being.

Even the crucified atheist criminal, the modern form of the saint, cannot sufficiently transcend our destructive compulsions and emerge with trust in the other and with the passion and richness of *unjustified* life. And the very texture of Wright's art cannot present a sufficient positive sense of living, adequate scenes of tangible life. *The Outsider,* then, considerably fails, though it does achieve some wisdom. Existential awareness, we are reminded by Wright, provides an extreme exploration into truth but no mythos to live by. Its insights may be considerable but remain alienated from a full sense of life, maintaining themselves only by endless self-purgings and demonic catharsis. To attempt to be outside reveals black truths about those inside but is no sufficient escape from them. A heroic negativity, primarily critical, and diagnostic, existential explorations display the limits of rebellion, defiance and perversity. That black awareness, I have argued along with Wright, is true but won't do. It intensifies individual understanding but won't further the mutuality we need.

Such heroic nothingness does provide devastating insights into the covert nihilisms of most contemporary social, scientistic, and religious as well as political ideologies. The black writer like Wright who courageously, however falteringly, refuses to conceive himself writing just for and of blacks, and who purges his black self-hatred, reaches towards our better purposes. Black writing can only be fully serious and pertinent when it goes beyond being black, both ethnically and philosophically. It must, even in the Age of Nihilism, come inside and find a "new man" who cannot only transform violently guilty self-hatred but achieve a community of joyous acceptance of self.

Richard Wright in a
Moment of Truth

by Blyden Jackson

Many people, if not most, perhaps never associate Richard Wright with the state of Mississippi, which is another way of saying that they do not associate him with the South. He was, however, a Mississippian, a Southerner, and to call him that is not merely to demand due recognition for the statistics of his birth and residence during his plastic years, but also to recognize a fact of the utmost importance in understanding the growth and peculiarities of his artistic imagination. Richard Wright still remains best-known as the author of the novel *Native Son*. Four years before *Native Son*, however, he had published a novella which he called "Big Boy Leaves Home." It is of this earlier and relatively unnoticed novella that I wish to evangelize.

"Big Boy Leaves Home" is a story which proceeds from beginning to end as a simple, straight-line narrative. Mechanically, at least, it is assembled like a play, detachable into five episodes, each as clearly discrete as a scene in a formal drama, and each along the time-scheme of the novella, placed somewhat later than its immediate predecessor, until the action, at the point which in a theater would ring down the final curtain, conveys Big Boy, the story's titular protagonist, northward toward Chicago, secreted in the covered back of a truck.

The first episode breathes something of the atmosphere of a rural Eden. On a clear, warm day in Mississippi four self-indulgent Negro boys are discovered in a wood on the outskirts of the little town in which they and their families reside. The boys are Big Boy and his constant companions Lester, Buck, and Bobo. It becomes quickly obvious that Big Boy is the natural leader of the four and the constant recipient of hero-worship from the other three. It becomes equally obvious that the four should not be where they are, for it is a school day and they are decidedly of school age. They are, then, young rebels giving full vent to some of their rebellious

"Richard Wright in a Moment of Truth" by Blyden Jackson. From *The Southern Literary Journal*, 3 (Spring 1971), 3–17. Copyright © 1971 by the Department of English, University of North Carolina. Reprinted by permission of the Department of English, University of North Carolina at Chapel Hill.

tendencies. And yet it does not appear that they are criminally inclined. They are, rather, healthy and high-spirited cousins-german of Huck Finn, with a proper ambivalence of attitude toward the queer world of adults and a proper interest in enjoying their youth while they still have it to enjoy. They are not, it must be confessed, altogether nice by the standards of a Little Lord Fauntleroy. Their language, for example, runs to words not used in polite child-rearing circles. Their sense of fun expresses itself too often in the sadistic exploitation of some defenseless victim's physical discomfiture. They know, too, about sex, and not through programs of sex education. Even so, they cannot be classed as juvenile delinquents. Nothing about them stamps them as young practitioners of vice and violence. But just as undeniably they cannot be classed as adults. To recognize this is of the utmost importance in a reading of their story. They like to try to act like grownups. What normal adolescents do not? Nevertheless, as adults, they are actually only innocents, actually only ingénues uninitiated into most of what are often called the facts of life. To be classed as adults, they have still seen far too little of the scattered and extensive middens of corruption which tend to separate in a most decisive manner prototypical adulthood from even the latest phase of non-adulthood. Their innocence does not make them as pure as the driven snow. But it does permit them still to think and act like irresponsible children. And it is as irresponsible children, out for a children's lark, that they suddenly, and capriciously, decide to quit their wood—one is strongly tempted to say their enchanted forest—and go swimming, trespassing on the land and the pond of Ol Man Harvey, a white man noted for his lack of love for Negroes and, not incidentally, noted especially to them for his aversion to their swimming in his pond.

The second episode takes them, consequently, from their open wood to Ol Man Harvey's pond. For a golden moment it is as if they had not left the wood, as if they are still, as it were, in the innocent world of their enchanted youth. They swim, appropriately for innocents, in the nude. They have, at least temporarily, abandoned swimming and are sunning themselves, still in the nude, on the beach of Ol Man Harvey's pond when they look up and find, fixedly regarding them from a spot on the pond's opposite bank, a white woman whom they do not know and who does not know them. Abruptly their story has changed worlds. It has crossed a line. The woman watching them clearly is already virtually on the verge of hysteria. They try to prevent an apparently all too impending disaster, to assure the strange white woman, who looms between them and their clothes, that all they want is to get those clothes and depart the pond in peace. But this woman is not part of the world of the beginning of their story. She belongs to the world controlled and interpreted by adults. In that world, at least when "Big Boy Leaves Home" was written, all Negro males, even young and with their clothes on, were potential rapists. And so this woman screams, and screams again, for someone named Jim, and Jim himself, a white man from her world, comes apace, with a rifle in his hands. He asks no questions and pauses not at all to profit from a single bit of rational analysis. Instead, he fires and kills two of the potential rapists, Buck and Lester, instantly. But Bobo and Big Boy, in a manner of speaking, have better luck. They survive the white man's initial barrage. Swiftly a moment of violent confusion ensues, and then ends, with the white man's rifle somehow in Big Boy's hands. Unable, as he sees it, under the circumstances to resort to any other method of deterrence, Big Boy shoots to death the white man and he and Bobo, with their clothes and the now expendable garments of Buck and Lester, vanish in the direction of the town.

The third episode changes the setting from a white adult world to a black. Big Boy has managed to make his way home to his own house. Presumably, so has Bobo. At Big Boy's house his parents and his sister now are told about the terrible thing which has happened at the pond. Hastily they summon, for advice and counsel, a handful of the respected elders of their local black community. The elders summoned decide that Big Boy perforce must hide himself for the evening and the night in one of a set of pits dug for kilns on the side of a hill overlooking a main highway known as Bullard's Road. Word is to be sent to Bobo to join Big Boy in hiding there. At six in the morning Will Sanders, a son of one of the counseling elders, will pick the two boys up. By a fortuitous coincidence Will is already scheduled, just after the approaching dawn, to drive a load of goods to Chicago for his employers, a trucking company.

In the fourth episode Big Boy does reach the prescribed hill safely and does conceal himself deep within a chosen pit. He is waiting now for Bobo. Darkness comes, but no Bobo. What does, however, arrive at last, direfully impinging itself upon Big Boy's consciousness, is a mob that gathers on a hill directly across the road from the one in which he is concealed and from which he can hardly fail to see as from a seat within the mezzanine of a theater or concert hall, virtually any atrocity that the mob may intend to perpetrate. And the mob does perpetrate a major atrocity. It has captured Bobo and it brings him to its hill. As Big Boy watches, helpless to intervene or withdraw, it proceeds there, on its hill, to tar and feather Bobo, and to burn him at the stake. Then, as a rain begins to fall, the mob, its baser appetites assuaged, melts away in small groups into the night.

The fifth, and final, episode is muted and brief. Morning comes, and with it, unobtrusively parked on Bullard's Road, Will Sanders' truck, into which, collected from his night-long perch, Big Boy is safely stowed and thus spirited away to Chicago, famished and thirsty, and bereft forever of the kind of innocence which had still been largely his before the incident at Ol Man Harvey's pond.

"Big Boy Leaves Home" was accepted for publication in the spring of 1936. It seems to have been actually written down in the summer and fall of 1935. It seems also to have a discernible pre-history to which I wish now to allude, for reasons that I trust will appear as I proceed.

Richard Wright fled the South in 1927, two months after his nineteenth birthday. He came directly to Chicago, where, by 1932, led by his enthusiastic attachment to a John Reed Club, he had become a Communist. His Communist affiliation brought him eventually into association with a fellow Communist who, like himself, was a Negro born and bred at a considerable distance below the Mason and Dixon Line. Wright speaks of this black fellow-Communist, under the almost certain alias of Ben Ross, in Wright's version of his own experience of communism, which he originally contributed, under the title. "I Tried to be a Communist," to the *Atlantic Monthly* in 1944. This so-called Ross, who had a Jewish wife, the mother, by him, of a young son, interested Wright deeply. Wright saw Ross as "a man struggling blindly between two societies," and felt that if he "could get . . . Ross's story, . . . he could make known some of the difficulties in the adjustment of a folk people to an urban environment."[1] Therefore, he persuaded Ross, in effect, to sit for a pen portrait. On occasion he interviewed Ross for hours in Ross's home. Meanwhile, however, the Communist command in Chicago had become cognizant of Wright's interest in Ross and had begun to view this interest with mounting concern. Once aware of the Party's apprehensions, Ross ceased to speak freely to Wright either of his life or of himself. This inhibition of Ross's responsiveness sabotaged Wright's original hopes. Through Ross, moreover, Wright had met some of Ross's friends and, expanding on his original plan, had conceived the notion now of doing, with Ross and Ross's friends all in mind, a series of biographical sketches. Now, however, not only Ross but all of Ross's friends as well had become afraid to talk to Wright as Wright had once had ample reason to suppose they might. Wright consequently altered his intentions. In virtually Wright's own words, after he saw that he could do nothing to counteract the effect of the Party's powerful influence, he merely sat and listened to Ross and his friends tell tales of Southern Negro experience, noting them down in his mind, and no longer daring to ask questions for fear his informants would become alarmed. In spite of his informants' reticence, he became drenched in the details of their lives. He gave up the idea of writing biographical sketches and settled finally upon writing a series of short stories, using the material he had got from Ross and his friends, building upon it and inventing from it. Thus he wove a tale of a group of black boys trespassing upon the property of a white man and the lynching that followed. The

---

[1]"Richard Wright," in Richard Crossman, ed., *The God That Failed* (New York, 1949), p. 115.

story was published eventually under the title of "Big Boy Leaves Home."[2]

Corroboration of Wright's direct testimony in "I Tried to Be a Communist," and some further suggestions concerning the genesis of "Big Boy Leaves Home," are supplied in Constance Webb's recent biography of Wright.[3] This biography, it is of some significance here to note, bears the character of an official life. Indeed, in the book's "Introduction" Miss Webb so defines the nature of what she has done in no uncertain terms. In this "Introduction," that is to say, she first makes specific allusion to her personal friendship with Wright and his family which began, she tells us, when Wright was at work on *Black Boy* in the earlier 1940s and lasted until his death. She cites the many materials, such as notes, letters, telegrams, manuscripts, and ideas for new books which, from the time of her decision in 1945 to compose a study of him and his work, and in full knowledge of her plans, Wright delivered to her over a period of fifteen years. She also refers to her many long hours of conversations with Wright in New York City, on Long Island, and in Paris; to her continuing relations with Wright's wife after Wright's untimely death; to the assistance provided her by Wright's brother, Alan, Wright's close boyhood friend, Joe C. Brown, and Wright's literary agent, Paul R. Reynolds, Jr.; to the aid given her by an impressive number of Wright's fellow authors and others of Wright's acquaintances who were in a position to speak of Wright with some authority; and, finally in this present context, to the access granted her by Wright and his family to hundreds of letters from Wright to Wright's editor, Edward C. Aswell.

With these credentials, which are not to be summarily dismissed, Miss Webb positively identifies the pseudonymous Ben Ross as one David Poindexter, a black member of the Communist Party, who had been born in southwest Tennessee in 1903 and had come North when he was seventeen. The family attributed by Miss Webb to Poindexter is the same as that attributed by Wright to Ross. In all the other details which she stipulates, moreover, including Poindexter's status as the original of Big Boy, Miss Webb's assimilates Poindexter to the person whom Wright, conceivably in order not to expose a friend and benefactor to possible jeopardy, named as Ross in "I Tried to Be a Communist." But when she reports directly on the genesis of "Big Boy Leaves Home"[4] Miss Webb does not parrot what Wright had once said about his determination, if he could, to use Poindexter, or Ross, as an instrument by means of which he could make known some of the difficulties attendant upon the adjustment of a folk people to an urban environment. In this context, as a matter of fact, she makes a statement which would seem to contradict Wright's

[2]*Ibid.*, pp. 119–120.
[3]Constance Webb, *Richard Wright* (New York, 1968).
[4]*Ibid.*, p. 125.

own about the folk. She says, instead and unequivocally, that in his first series of short stories, *Uncle Tom's Children* (the series of which "Big Boy Leaves Home" became a part), Wright set himself a conscious problem, the explication of the quality of will the Negro must possess to live and die in a country which denies him his humanity.[5] Furthermore, applying her statement to "Big Boy Leaves Home" specifically, she asserts, within her analysis of that story, that "Big Boy Leaves Home" represents this quality of will as being "only that of the most elemental level—the ability to endure,"[6] for, she finally adds, the lesson to be extracted from Big Boy's experience is the dependence of his survival "upon the communal nature of the black community which planned, aided, and organized an escape."[7]

When she says that Wright, in creating "Big Boy Leaves Home" and the other stories in *Uncle Tom's Children*, "set himself a conscious problem," the significant word is *conscious*. She has left no doubt, as already indicated here earlier, of her conception of her relationship with Wright. He made of her, according to her implication it is clear, an *alter ego* privy to virtually all of himself that he could communicate to her or anyone. Furthermore, although the word *conscious* does not appear in her declaration that Big Boy's story was planned to demonstrate how his community rallied round him to ensure the preservation of his life, it seems unmistakably clear that here she speaks, too, as a medium who is reporting not only what was in Wright's mind, but also what she would contend he knew was there. Here, then, is testimony, much of it of a hearsay nature indeed, but nevertheless purporting, in its general trend, to have the value of evidence which Wright himself could not have failed to give had he ever had to speak about the intended function of "Big Boy" under solemn oath in a court of law. It reveals, to repeat for emphasis, that Wright had chosen a definite thing to do when he wrote "Big Boy Leaves Home," and that he was not confused as to the nature of that thing. It seems to argue also Wright's own belief that he had substantially achieved his conscious intent.

Writers, however, sometimes belie their own intentions. Sometimes, moreover, what they do actually may well seem better than what they thought they had intended. No one, I think, would argue seriously for a reading of "Big Boy Leaves Home" as an account of an adjustment by an agrarian folk to an urban setting, deeply though Wright once indicated that he was interested in Ross-Poindexter and drenched though he once was in Ross-Poindexter's life and history. If then, however, "Big Boy Leaves Home" is to be read primarily as a parable about the quality of will necessary for the Negro to solve the major problem which he faces in his American environment, and if the message of such a parable centers

[5] *Ibid.*, p. 157.
[6] *Ibid.*, p. 159.
[7] *Ibid.*, p. 159.

in an account of the manner in which one Negro community expressed the quality of its will through its capacity to save some of its own, then neither the form nor the content of the parable is aesthetically impressive. "Big Boy Leaves Home" becomes then only an exercise in the depiction of a failure. Its focal point, if not its climax, must then be found to be in its third episode, for in this episode the representatives of the Negro community do gather, in Big Boy's home. The preacher, Elder Peters, is there, and Brother Jenkins and Brother Sanders, with Big Boy's parents and his sister. They commune with each other. But with what results? Big Boy's father can only berate Big Boy on the folly of his disobedience to his mother's injunction to go to school. The women in the house can only watch the men gathered there in virtually unbroken silence. No one can respond affirmatively to the distressed father's plea for financial aid. The sister has done some service in bringing to the house the three outside counsellors. The mother gives Big Boy simple food to take with him when he leaves. Still, it is chance alone and Big Boy's own animal excellences which pave the way for his escape from certain death. No effective aid reaches Bobo. No account is taken of provisions to safeguard Big Boy's family, who, as Big Boy later overhears in his kiln, are burned out of their modest dwelling. The most that can be said when all is done is that Big Boy did elude his would-be slayers and that a fellow Negro, who happened to be going in that direction anyhow, drove him North.

But to read "Big Boy Leaves Home," whatever Wright's original conscious aims, in accord with the form dictated for it by its own development, and to sense its content shaping itself to match that form, and its function emerging as the strong, inevitable concomitant of both, is to witness what well may be one of the three or four finest moments in Negro fiction. Of this inherent form and content it is now high time to speak.

It will be remembered that Big Boy's story is shaped into five episodes, five scenes conducting a flow of action and related meaning from a point of attack to a conclusion which should round out and justify the whole. This form, at least in its handling here, is flexible as well as fluid. It permits variations of pitch and tone and atmosphere which all contribute to the story's total impact. At the beginning the pitch is moderate. The tone and atmosphere are genial, almost sweet. The function of the content is expository. The identity of the protagonist is established and the condition of all four of the boys made known. And beyond all this a theme is adumbrated. For these boys are scholars out of school. They have interrupted their vocation for a holiday of their own making. Still, the fact is clear. They are young, much untaught, and at an impressionable age. To learn, to grow, in other words, in one way or another, is their *métier*. It is hard to see how they should live through any single day without acquiring some new knowledge. In what they are reside the germs of what this tale must be. Then comes the first progression, bringing with itself a proper set of changes. At the swimming hole the white world intrudes. The mood of the first episode is shattered by the killings. In a swirl of strident sound and emotions at high pitch and harshly tuned, with corresponding action that is equally cacophonous, a motif of pain and mystery, the ugliness of racistic custom is introduced. Then comes an interlude with a reduction in pitch and a moderation of tone, but without a return to the relative serenity of the introduction, as Big Boy spends a moment with his own kind in his father's house. But this interlude is also prelude, and a fitting one, to the big scene of the story. This big scene, as the logic of the story would demand, is the lynching on the hill, the spectacle of Bobo coated with hot tar and white feathers, burning in the night. This, as we shall see in terms of content, is the moment of truth in the story, It is also the very peak of the wave of form, when pitch and tone and atmosphere all coalesce at their highest points. The story cannot end at such a level of crescendo and fortissimo. It does not; it declines to the low key of its final episode when Big Boy, all passion spent, drifts off to slumber on the bed of the truck that bears him away to the North. But let us return to the lynching on the hill.

I have said that for this story it is the moment of truth. And it is. It is the moment when Wright, whether wittingly or not, gathers up the essence of that which he is struggling to express and stores it all into one symbol and its attendant setting. For the spectacle of Bobo aflame at the stake does constitute a symbol. It is a symbol, moreover, the phallic connotations of which cannot be denied. Indeed, the particularity of its detail—the shape of its mass, its coating of tar, the whiteness of the feathers attached to its surface or floating out into the surrounding air— are almost all too grossly and gruesomely verisimilar for genteel contemplation. Whether Wright so intended it or not, the lynching of Bobo is symbolically a rite of castration. It is the ultimate indignity that can be inflicted upon an individual. Such an indignity strips from a man his manhood, removes from him the last vestige of his power and the last resort of his self-respect. In the lynching of Bobo, thus, all lynchings are explained, and all race prejudice. Both are truly in essence acts of castration. It is not for nothing that the grinning darky, hat in hand and bowing low, his backside exposed as if for a kick in the buttocks, seems so much a eunuch. He has accepted in his heart the final abasement, the complete surrender of his will, and so of his citadel of self, to anyone with a white skin. He has capitulated to the most arrogant demand which one human creature can make upon another. This, then, is the true anatomy of racism. It makes no difference where or how it prefers its claims, whether in an apology for its own being so adroitly composed as the novel *So Red the Rose* or in the blatant conduct of the old-style sheeted Ku Klux Klan. What racism demands is that every white man should be permitted to reserve the right to visit, with impunity, upon any Negro whatever, any outrage of that Negro's personality the white man chooses to impose. This, then, is the symbolism of Bobo's burning body on the hill. But around that symbolism clusters another set of facts put into another pregnant image. For, as Bobo burning illustrates the essence of one indispensable aspect of racism, the mob illustrates another. It is an efficient mob, a homogeneous grouping. Yet no one has really organized it. It has no officers and no carefully compiled manual of behavior. Still it operates like a watchmaker universe. Its members know what they are supposed to do, and they do it, as if they were performing the steps of a ritual dance—which of course they are. For that is the real secret of the people gathered around Bobo on his Golgotha. They are responding not only to xenophobia and to an obscene lust for power. They are responding also to an urge equally as neanderthal in its origins. They are acting tribally, even as every lodge brother, black or white or yellow or red, who ever gave a secret handshake and every Babbitt who ever applauded a toastmaster's feeble attempts at jollity at the luncheon of his service club.

To belong, to conform, and thus to avoid the existentialist nightmare of exercising the prerogative of individual freedom of choice; to be able to contribute all of one's own release of foible and malice to custom that must be followed for the good of the community; to accept the myth that at some time in the misty past a voice, as it were, from some local Sinai spoke to the elders of the tribe and told them how certain things must be done and what prescribed rites must be followed to avert the anger of the gods; thus to be exempted from a sense of guilt at one's own evil; thus to hallow the meanest of the herd instincts; thus to institutionalize mediocrity's hatred of the indomitable spirit and its envy of strength and beauty: this is the pathos, and yet an important part of the explanation, of the capacity to endure of the tribe. This is also as much a part of racism as its lust for power. The castration and the tribalism complement each other. Without either, racism would not be at all exactly what it is. To perceive them, to really take them in, is, as Henry James might say, to see and know what is *there*. And it is part of the excellence of form in this story that Big Boy does see them, that by the story's own handling of its arrangements he is put in such a position that he cannot do otherwise. For, as this story so manages the sense of form which shapes its episodes to place its big scene right, it regulates concurrently another element of form, its control of its own point of view, to the end that at the proper point in the narrative's development the impression it conveys of who is doing the seeing will be as right as the prominence and the substance of what is to be seen.

Thus at the beginning of the story we are aware of, and share, to some extent, in the consciousness of all the boys. But this is Big Boy's story. It is really he whose loss of innocence, as it were, and compulsory education under special circumstances embody all that this story has to say. And so, increasingly, as the story moves from the open country to the lynching on the hill, Big Boy's consciousness becomes the sole point of view. Yet this constriction and this concentration are really the ultimate outgrowth of a rather delicate continuous maneuver of adjustment. Throughout the bulk of his story Wright's handling of his point of view is as dramatic as his separation of his matter into scenes. We watch the characters perform. We hear them talk. From outside their consciousnesses we infer their thoughts and feelings. Yet we identify increasingly with Big Boy, if for no other reason than that we see nothing which he cannot see and hear nothing which he cannot hear. But after Big Boy bids adieu to his parents and their friends and, successfully negotiating his sprint through hostile territory to Bullard's Road, comes to bay at last crouched deep within his kiln, we become more and more intensely one with him. We wonder with him why Bobo has not come, share with him his reverie as he relives the events of his day, mourn with him for Buck and Lester, regret with him that he did not bring with him his father's shotgun, and finally, in fantasy, imagine with him that he is blasting away with that shotgun as he withstands a mob. As white men searching for the Negro "bastards" drift down *his* hill we share, too, his fear, and finally, as the lynch mob gathers, our senses become, like his, preternaturally acute, to watch with him in anguish and extreme distress the torture and destruction of the last of his close boyhood friends. Thus the heightening and the concentration of the point of view join with the elevation of the episode and the power of the symbolism and the imagery to speak in blended voices acting in mighty concert of the inner nature of racism and to trace its roots deep down into the past of human psychology and custom.

It is not a quality of the Negro will which this story explicates, nor is it anything to do with folk adjustment in a city. Far from either. It is, rather, the psychology, and the anthropology, of American racism. It is a lesson given to Big Boy and through him to the world at large. It is a lesson, moreover, which rounds off beautifully both the form and substance of "Big Boy Leaves Home." For the plot of this story represents a progress, not a conflict. Its succession of vignettes combine to form a curious kind of sentimental journey in which Big Boy does leave home; does lose, that is, his relative state of innocence; and does experience an illumination, an exercise in education, that provides him with a terrible, but richly freighted, insight into the adult world.

It has been rather customary not to think of Richard Wright as a Southern writer, except, of course, by the accident of birth. I cannot share that view. A writer belongs, I would argue, in the final analysis, to the country where his artistic imagination is most at home. Wright clearly supposed that this country, for him, was not the South, just as he supposed that in "Big Boy Leaves Home," in spite of the resemblances between Ol Man Harvey's pond and the pond in Jackson, Mississippi, around which

Wright had played in his own youth, he was writing about Ross-Poindexter and, in a philosophic vein, either about a folk people seeking a new adjustment in a setting alien to their past or struggling for self-gratifying survival against a powerful outer world hostile to their hopes. Indeed, in one of the major episodes of *Black Boy,* his own account of his youth and early manhood, Wright tells of his last encounter with his father, an encounter that occurred after twenty-five years of absolute separation between the two, as well as, also, after Wright had published *Native Son.* He meets his father on a Mississippi hillside. He tries to talk to him and then he says, "I realized that, though ties of blood made us kin, though I could see a shadow of my face in his face, though there was an echo of my voice in his voice, we were forever strangers, speaking a different language, living on vastly different planes of reality." On one level of interpretation Wright here does speak true. Between him and his father time and experience had fixed an impenetrable gulf. But the possibly implied symbolism of the confrontation is false. Deep at the core of his own being, whether as a person or as an artist, Wright always remained his own Big Boy who never did leave home, and it was always true that the closer he could get to the homeland of his youth, which was also the homeland of his creative skill, the happier he was in the fiction he was able to produce.

Wright's last considerable essay into fiction was his final novel, *The Long Dream.* In startling ways it reproduces all the significant elements of "Big Boy Leaves Home." Its setting is a Mississippi town and, incidentally one which, for all of his obvious intentions to have it otherwise, he does not update from the Mississippi which he quitted as a youth. Its protagonist is a Negro boy as exceptional among his peers as Big Boy is among his. Moreover, this boy too is in the process of growing up, for *The Long Dream,* like "Big Boy Leaves Home," is an initiation story. Fire figures prominently in the drama of *The Long Dream.* Indeed, fire repeatedly plays a mythopoeic role in Wright's important fiction, as in the furnace of *Native Son* or the collision of electrically driven monsters in the subway wreck of *The Outsider.* The Negro elders of "Big Boy Leaves Home" reappear in the protagonist's father, the doctor, the madam, the mistress, and the father's helper of *The Long Dream.* They are no more potent in the latter work than in the former. They have neither the grace nor the glory of the father in "Fire and Cloud" or the mother in "Bright and Morning Star." The strange white woman who precipitates catastrophe for the protagonist of "Big Boy Leaves Home" precipitates catastrophe also for the protagonist in *The Long Dream.* And, as at the end of "Big Boy Leaves Home," Big Boy is headed for another life in another world, so at the end of *The Long Dream* its protagonist is on a plane *en route* to Paris. The real difference, indeed, between "Big Boy Leaves Home" and *The Long Dream* is in the relative quality of the art of each. James Baldwin, whose attitudes toward Richard Wright are much too complex for quick definition, once referred, with complimentary intent, to Wright as a "Mississippi pickaninny." In so doing Baldwin directly was comparing Wright with the Existentialists amongst whom Wright, in his later life, found himself consorting in Paris, and was thus paying genuine respect to a capacity in Wright to see life as it actually is and not according to some evanescent theory, which Baldwin thought he could divine in Wright, but not in Sartre and his disciples—and which, additionally, Baldwin, in pensive mood, attributed to the lessons Wright had learned during Wright's rough-and-tumble existence as a boy and precocious adolescent in the Delta South. I think the phrase is apt, especially since it is clear that through it Baldwin intended no racial slur. For Wright was a child of his own youth. Out of that youth he derived not only his practical sense of hard reality but also the home country for his artistic imagination. Thus in much more than the mere statistics of his place of birth is he a Southern writer. When he follows his home country North, as he does in the first two books of *Native Son,* he is still on his native ground. When he tries to return to it, as in *The Long Dream,* seeing it through other eyes than truly his own, he has deserted the one source of his greatest strength. He has become, that is, in all too sad a consequence, his own Big Boy away from home.

The Art of Richard Wright's Short Stories

by Edwin Berry Burgum

Richard Wright is the first Negro novelist to gain a wide audience of white readers and to be accepted by that audience as one of our distinguished authors. Without feeling any need for a separate category because of his color, we spontaneously mention his name along with Hemingway or Steinbeck or whom you will. At the same time, paradoxically, we cannot fail to be aware that he criticizes his white audience more trenchantly than any other Negro novelist has done. Our acceptance of him under such circumstances does not merely testify to the serious attention problems of racial discrimination today compel; it is a tribute to the quality of his writing. It is evidence that he belongs with those among us who express themselves with distinction.

The choice of a controversial topic, of course, is no guarantee of good writing. On the contrary, it has often distracted both author and reader from a proper attention to it. Unless it is well executed, the popularity of such a novel is likely to be more ephemeral than the issue on which it is built. *Uncle Tom's Cabin,* which was widely read before the Civil War, is said to have intensified the demand for Negro emancipation. But it has survived only as melodrama for children, despite the increasing importance of its general theme. The chief reason, probably, for its failure to hold its public is not the parochialism of the story, but its technical deficiencies. Written in the same decade as some of the best work of Poe and Hawthorne, it shows no sign of kinship in technique. It hardly suggests Mrs. Stowe's better work of a decade later in *Oldtown Folks.* In place of the quiet realism of this latter work, *Uncle Tom's Cabin* utilizes the methodological clichés of the Sunday School tracts of the period. Perhaps its loose narrative structure, its sentimental definition of character, the perils which pursue the innocent Eliza are esthetic proof that its theme was really premature, that, as has often been said, the Civil War was actually fought for the expansion of northern industry and involved the emancipation of the slaves in only a superficial way. If this is true, the superior quality of *Native Son* might be taken as evidence that the question of Negro rights has at last become a central issue for the development of our national society. At all events, unlike its predecessor in theme, *Native Son* is not isolated by its style of writing from the prevalent contemporary techniques.

At the same time, it is not an example of the best of them. Though superior to our ordinary novels, *Native Son* does not possess the characteristics of our most careful craftsmanship. Not only does the author include minute dissection of the motives behind the action and the dialogue, but these explanations are spun out after the manner of one feeling his way into a difficult subject. Grammatically, to take an instance, this means a participial construction left hanging at the end of a sentence where it qualifies a clear statement or leaves a conclusion tentative or ambiguous. It is the method of Dreiser's *American Tragedy*. But since Wright's plot is more complex, the effect is not that of mere padding but of a too conscientious endeavor to get to the bottom against all obstacles. It is at opposite poles from the bright competence of a Proust among the nuances of human motivation. These deficiencies show that Wright, though sensitive to the techniques of the psychological novel, has not yet been able to apply them with a sure hand. Fortunately the short story permits only a limited documentation; and it is upon the quality of his short stories that Wright's reputation as a stylist, at present, rests. *Native Son* widened his audience to include the average reader. But the reader who is sensitive to style will continue to prefer the short stories.

Awareness of the esthetic limitations of Wright as a novelist should not, however, obscure our admiration for the extraordinary qualities of these stories, whether written before or after *Native Son*. If he has not yet conquered the problem of detail in the novel, it is precisely in the handling of detail in his stories that his distinction is to be found. The "classical" short story was conspicuously lacking in this respect. From the pioneer work of Poe to Maupassant and Stevenson, it might achieve a powerful effect of melodrama or surprise ending. It might be witty and allusive, but it was never characterized by a profoundly moving plot and an abundance of significant detail to assure plausibility. What accumulation of detail there was was generally employed for superficial ends. It either provided a well-knit but flashy plot, as in Maupassant, or merely furnished a background of atmosphere to an even simpler plot, related to it only by the pathetic fallacy, as in Stevenson. There has since then grown up a story of quite the opposite type, in those of Chekhov and Katherine Mansfield and Hemingway, where nothing but nuance falls into some sort of obscure relationship, which could hardly be called a plot with a conclusion. Their themes are smothered and lost sight of out of fear of the crudity of exposure in an open resolution. Such have been the two tendencies in the short story: the one affording the thrill of action without genuine insight into character; the other insight into character which aimlessly evaporates. To the literary historian, Wright's importance is that, by bringing both traditions together, he has moulded a type of story superior to either. When detail becomes significant by being significantly associated, the story not only gains direction and climax, but the flimsiness of a melodramatic climax is transformed into the unforgettable power of tragedy.

From the historical perspective, this, I think, is what Wright has accomplished. But I do not mean to imply that he has worked either directly or consciously with either of these traditions. Unimpeded by the requirements of a formal education, his bent for writing appears to have led him directly to authors of current reputation and the writers of the past who influenced them. He has assimilated from them what his developing talent needed, and taking place as it did without external compulsion, the assimilation has sometimes been so complete as to be fairly unrecognizable. I am told that the most powerful influence upon him has been Hemingway, whose pugnacious, independent temper seems to have appealed to him. From Hemingway doubtless came his objective attitude, his direct, unflinching vision, and the short, firm sentences, with their frequent change of grammatical subject, as the appropriate vehicle of expression. Wright's sentences are stript bare of all but the necessary adjectives and connectives. Each is a vigorous self-sufficient unit, which expels its pent-up meaning and willingly gives way to the next in line. But they all retire before the tense authority of dialogue. The dialogue itself is candid, the sort the character would have used in life, or the sort that aims to give such an effect.

> He saw the mob close in around the fire. Their faces were hard and sharp in the light of the flames. More men and women were coming over the hill. The long dark spot was smudged out.
> "Everybody git back!"
> "Look! Hes gotta finger!" [1]

If this passage does not remind one of Hemingway, it is because his style has been assimilated into a quite different personality, and used to such different ends that the relationship is disguised. This is partly owing to the fact that Wright is dealing with Negro dialogue, but mostly because his insights are richer and deeper than Hemingway's. For you will never find the passages of sentimental or sadistic writing in Wright that you will in Hemingway's work. If Wright has emotional conflicts in his short stories, they are dissipated by the act of composition. But Hemingway's emotional blocks are at the basis of his style, which does not resolve them but expresses them, transformed in various ways, as irony, or sentiment,

[1] Wright, Richard, *Native Son*, New York, 1940, by courtesy of Harper and Brothers.

or brutality, or the inconclusive ending; but always controlled by understatement.

> The world was not wheeling any more. It was just very clear and bright, and inclined to blur at the edges. I washed, brushed my hair. I looked strange to myself in the glass, and went downstairs to the dining-room.
> "Here is he!" said Bill. "Good old Jake! I knew you wouldn't pass out."
> "Hello, you old drunk," Mike said.
> "I got hungry and woke up."
> "Eat some soup," Bill said.
> The three of us sat at the table, and it seemed as though about six people were missing.[2]

Despite the appearance of directness of statement here, the actual emotional meanings are all transformed and controlled, even negated by the conscious surface of the personality. Both writers begin with objective description of the surface. Hemingway gives us only so much of the depth as the surface reveals, which, with his type of character, is very little. But neither does Wright desire nor are his characters sophisticated enough, to conceal from themselves and others what lies deeper within. So the two styles, technically so similar, are used to opposite ends—in Hemingway to distract attention from the confusions beneath, and in Wright to reveal a process that is going on to eradicate what confusion may exist, and therefore to promote a definite resolution of the action at the end of the story.

But Hemingway also did Wright the service of leading him to other authors. Passages, for instance, under the influence of Gertrude Stein are occasionally conspicuous in both writers. They are usually passages, like this from Wright, of interior monologue.

> Never in all her life had she been so much alone as she was now. Days were never so long as these days; and nights were never so empty as these nights.

From such open expression of melancholy Hemingway draws back into his habitual mood of cynical reserve. But Wright proceeds from them further into poetic prose which utilizes contemporary metrical cadences to convey pleasurable emotions, even though they be of hopes as yet unfulfilled. Not from Hemingway but from the Donne-Hopkins' tradition came a later wish of this same girl for "white bright days and dark black nights" (to which a rare new element has been added since "dark black" in this context cannot be taken as a sinister but only as a pleasurably mysterious phrase). More generally, such passages are closer to the fiction of Lawrence and Anderson.

[2]Hemingway, Ernest, *The Sun Also Rises*, New York, 1926, by courtesy of Charles Scribner's Sons.

> Again she felt his fingers on the tips of her breasts. She backed away,
> saying nothing this time. She thrust the gourd out from her. Warm fingers
> met her cold hands. He had the gourd. She heard him drink; it was the
> faint, soft music of water going down a dry throat, the music of water in a
> silent night. She sighed and drank again.

Here the mood and the meaning are close to Sherwood Anderson. But
there is wanting the slightly neurotic tempo of his cadences and his inter-
rogative appeals to the reader. The description of thinking (like Wright's
sentences occasionally) offers the enrichment of insight into aspects of the
immediate sensation not indispensable to the plot. In Anderson, such
sentences are typical, and their overtones accumulate into a general state
of narcissistic revery. But in Wright these impressions, though
immediately peripheral to the external action, furnish insight into the
character that has them, and so, in the long run, they feed into the course
of events, to increase the dramatic power and plausibility of the emerging
plot. But the most important stylistic influence hardly needs to be mentioned. For idiom, and cadence, and emotional attitude, Wright was fortunate in being able to use the tradition of Negro folk poetry after it had
been given polish and flexibility by two generations of sophisticated Negro
poets and prose writers. He could thus combine, without embarrassment
of fumbling, white and black traditions of craftsmanship of equal maturity.

His employment of these materials, however, to the attainment of a
significant plot must be ascribed to non-literary factors. Fundamental,
without question, was the nature of his childhood experiences, which he
has described in several autobiographical works. The hardship and cruelty
of his childhood set up reactions in him which must be ascribed to the
prevalence of a vague awareness of Negro rights in the environment and
which led to the personal search for more adequate understanding. He
picked his non-literary studies as unacademically as we have seen him
choosing his literary. Here again, he had the good fortune never to have
had a formal education with its clutter of useful and useless facts, of
tenable and fantastic theories. The sociology he chose substantiated his
experiential view that our reactions are conditioned by our environments.
His study of psychology, especially as illustrated in the psychological
novel, gave him a competence in understanding how complex these reactions to environment actually are. His study of Marxist philosophy, in
particular, enabled him to understand that these reactions, however complex, are only variants of class attitudes that are fundamentally the same.
By its emphasis upon class conflict it gave him the power to sense the
existence of plots in life, just as his psychology had enabled him to develop
them with lifelike and probable detail.

The theme, then, was at hand for Wright, as it had not been for either
Poe or Katherine Mansfield, and Wright was more fortunate than

Hemingway in being so circumstanced that he could pick it up without equivocation and efficiently transform it into art without distortion from any personal limitations. I do not wish to derogate the value of the work of these other writer... But it is all the same true that Poe was so circumstanced that he had only the sensational themes of decadence to build into a short story since his personal neuroses led him to the decaying feudal life of the old South. Similarly, Katherine Mansfield's precise but timid vision was too delicate to penetrate beyond the wisps of sentiment floating over the crumbling fabric of the Victorian heritage. Hemingway, on the other hand, tries to conceal from himself by a pugnacious front his identification with the social distemper he despises in the world of the prosperous around him.

Wright's theme, by contrast, is embedded in the structure of our present society, both north and south, and race riots and lynchings have exposed it uncompromisingly to both Negroes and whites. The conditions of his own life afforded him the capacity to sense its significance more sharply than any white man and many Negroes could. His gift for writing was encouraged by his awareness of this material craving representation. And he came at a time when the illiterate folk literature of the Negroes had already been taken over by educated Negro poets and become the dominant tradition of modern Negro literature. Under these circumstances Wright's application to it of the mechanisms of fiction, as established among white writers, was no longer a possible miscegenation, but deepened his penetration of his theme and enabled him to transfer it into the awareness of his readers.

The illuminating contrast here, where the short stories are concerned, is not with Hemingway who becomes the more resentful the further he gets from his normal association with sophisticated people. It is rather with an author like the Irishman Synge who, when he sympathizes with the tragedy in the life of the poor, turns it not into cynicism but pathos. Once more I cite for the purpose of definition rather than derogation. But, fine as *Riders to the Sea* is as a sad drama of Irish folk life, its sense of gathering doom reminds one more of Maeterlinck than of Wright. The difference that, in the one case, the doom is understood to be imposed by the forces of nature and in the other by men is not a consequence of a difference in intention of sympathy but of insight into the reality of the situation, which was imposed by a difference in the experiential relation to it of the two authors themselves. Synge was a middle-class writer who felt a genuine middle-class sympathy for the poor Irish fisherpeople. He tried to write like one of them, indeed, so genuinely that he lived among them. Though he had assimilated their dialect, he was unable to assimilate the nuance of psychological meanings this dialect was capable of conveying. Furthermore, unlike Wright's Negroes, these back-country Irish were too benighted to understand the real cause of their misery, which surely lay more in their superstitions, their lack of education and machines, than in the implacable cruelty of the sea. Synge seeks to sympathize not only with their misery but with the superstitions they invoke to explain it, which he would never have accepted to explain anything on his own bourgeois level. Thus, instead of clarifying their psychology through presenting a more valid perspective upon the social factors that determined it than they themselves possessed, he actually increased its ambiguity. These people were too foreign to his habitual attitudes, and as a result his diction has more of vague 'atmosphere' than nuance, and his plot becomes dependent upon a mystical naturalism, depicting an ineffectual resistance to obscure irresistible forces, rather than a conflict of recognizable elements which is capable of a solution.

Wright, on the contrary, was born and brought up in the midst of his material. His education, instead of alienating him from his past and its loyalties, was assimilated into already determined attitudes and merely enabled him to express them more adequately than Synge's sincere but external intention of sympathy could do. Nor should it be overlooked that these individual divergences between writers who both shared the same general aim, were magnified by the fact that this aim was interpreted differently by the different milieus of which each was a part. Synge's Ireland was witnessing the rise of the bourgeoisie into self-consciousness with the usual trappings of vague proletarian sympathy, whereas Wright was part of a larger context of the rise of the American proletariat into self-consciousness with overtones of hostility towards the middle class. Synge's spontaneous attitude towards the Irish populace is seen in *The Playboy of the Western World,* where the meanings of idioms and plot are quite clear since he makes no pretense of greater sympathy than is involved in the good-natured exposure of shiftlessness and eccentricity.

The difficulties which Synge encountered in *Riders to the Sea* are analogous to Wright's in *Native Son.* But under the changed circumstances, these latter were not such as to be insoluble this side of mysticism, but were solved, rather, with awkwardness and hesitation to the sacrifice of esthetic quality. In *Native Son,* in other words, where Wright took the larger circumference of black and white, bourgeois and proletarian society, as his milieu, he had to comprehend a comparatively unfamiliar and a predominantly hostile environment. But in the short stories, his locus is the black world of the South where he felt completely at home, and where he had only to articulate the misery and revolt of the black man. Both his plot and his style were implicit in his theme, which naturally sought the direct expression of dialogue in the folk idiom. His knowledge of the white literary tradition was necessary only to enable him to evoke the more perfectly what was latent within. At the same time he knows that his particular subjects are not direct representations of his own experience. He follows Eliot's law of the objective emotional correlative. Because he comprehends it so distinctly and feels its validity so genuinely, he appears dominated by his theme. He seems to forget himself in its expression and follows his own story as breathlessly as any reader. He thus, as a stylist, possesses the assurance that is typical of the writer of distinction, who seems to be merely articulating, by means of his craft and his insight, the significant experiences of his fellow men.

Wherefore Wright can take over the *mot juste* of literary tradition, and can use it with an ease forbidden to the inventor of the term, because he is not expressing an alien and supercilious attitude, but only fulfilling the intention of his people in a refinement of their natural cadence and idiom. His selection of words is that normal to the tradition of good writing, not primarily because he is steeped in that tradition, but because good writing, as Eliot's law suggests, recognizes its fealty to the living situation, and uses 'traditions' only as tools to achieve its clarification. His choice of diction, dictated by the needs of the situation, therefore, follows a middle course betwen the underprecision of mystic or romantic escapism and the overprecision of the rationalistic. It maintains a balance between the expository and the emotive aspects of words. It meets the demand for the "right word" because the "ends," since they are adequately understood, can determine the "means." His words are not chosen so that attention is distracted from the theme (the "end") and kept centered on the complexity of the immediate sensation or activity (the "means"). But they are selected, instead, with such judiciousness and economy that suspense is created, and the present scene calls forth its successor until a significant plot has been completely woven. The use of diction in this way is possible only when the social sphere proffers a theme which is not paralyzed by paradox or ambiguity, and which the author's social point of view enables him to recognize.

These comments are applicable to literary forms generally, and their emphasis upon plot does not imply that Wright's stories are virtually one act plays. They do make use of an unusual amount of dialogue, in order to intensify the validity of the action and the degree of emotional response. But they are not open to the usual objection to the one act play, that it does not have space enough for significant accomplishment. Because they are short stories, they can employ other mechanisms besides dialogue, and accomplish more in less space. Though Wright never obtrudes obiter dicta, by employing a certain amount of description and a considerable amount of stream of consciousness, he avoids the limitations of the dramatic form.

How Wright achieves these ends can be illustrated by reference to *Long Black Song*. In this story he builds his climax with extraordinary discretion and subtlety. Beginning with a comparatively simple situation, both action and characterization grow more complex as the narrative unfolds. The characters change as a result of the action. They learn through critical experience. There are therefore two aspects of every situation, since each has an effect both upon the nature of the personality and upon the externalization of its nature in the action. For the most part, of course, it is a new facet of a persistent character structure that the new situation discloses. But at moments of climax the personality is dialectically changed, and its outward expression redirected, although this can happen only to the principal character since he alone is principally engaged in the action. Thus in *Long Black Song,* the wife of the poor Negro farmer is the principal character at the start. Her romantic but entirely legitimate longing for a better life follows the familiar American tradition and affords the story a congenial orientation within which the failure can unfold. Her seduction by a white youth only sets the theme into motion. She then retires, keeping the same character structure and the same accompanying ideals. She becomes a chorus upon the action, through which we remain aware that the dream of a better life is frustrated by the inability of men to co-operate, which to her means, first, the conditions of marriage that led her to seek out a Negro lover, then the war that took her lover away, and now the interracial fighting that proceeds under her own eyes. For, after her husband returns and discovers her seduction by a white man, he takes over the story. The external action, though the tension becomes intense, is easily described. The Negro kills the white salesman when he comes back for the Victrola he had left the night before (symbolic both of the wife's dream and of her downfall). A posse gathers to lynch him. But after killing as many of them as possible, he prefers to die in the flames of his own house rather than surrender to their vengeance.

What gives this story its vitality and its individuality is the fact that its action is associated with an inner revolution in the character of the protagonist. It is this element that distinguishes it from the short story of tradition. The poor farmer had been an exceptional type of Negro. He had been neither easygoing after the old manner nor in conscious revolt like so many of the metropolitan Negroes of the present day. On the contrary, to his wife's discomfiture, he had assimilated the practical version of the American way as completely as any respectable poor white farmer. He had believed that if he worked hard, adding to his little property by depriving himself and his wife of casual comforts, above all, if he could acquire a hired man, he would have won all the self-respect and social standing a man requires. Thus, as usual in Wright, although his plot is on the surface sheer race conflict, the deeper implications transcend race, apply equally to whites, and only become the clearer through their more intense representation in Negro material. For here, any reader, black or white, conservative or radical, can agree on the diagnosis: that such a belief, though it looks practical, is actually more fantastic than the wife's romantic dream.

Racial feeling becomes the device through which the Negro farmer rejects a point of view that is not racial at all (but bourgeois), and attains a heroism which transcends its racial stimulus (since it is now shared by all those who have a valid belief in democracy). When Silas learns that his wife has been unfaithful with the salesman, he feels at first that she has been traitorous both to him and to their race, and ruined his lifetime of effort. He soon comes to see that her disloyalty to him is permitted by the white bourgeois code he has accepted in other areas. It is the prototype in personal relationships of his stupidity in the economic. Her error has permitted his discovery of an inconsistency in his philosophy of life. So he reorients his attitudes. His hatred turns away from his wife, whose offense he now sees has been imposed upon her by the social system he had accepted and expected to profit by. But instead of letting his hatred turn inward upon himself for having been misguided, his poverty and his race buttress what had been healthy in his bourgeois attitude. His self-reliance guarantees that his energy continue to be directed outward, but towards a new objective. It gives him the courage to kill the white offender and to fight against the posse as long as he can. On the surface this new aim may look like simple uncontrollable desire for revenge. And part of his motivation also is without doubt a continuation of his old ambition for property. But when he retreats within his own house to die there in the flames, he is doing more than protecting his property to the bitter end. His principal motive, I believe, is to withhold from the posse the satisfaction of their sadism in killing him. When dying must be, he wishes to control his own dying and make it an assertion of his new sense of values. To have fought against the posse until the degrading end of their final overpowering him would have been to have continued on another level the old bourgeois fallacy of free competition. His governance of his own death is his application of a new standard for living. In his final act he is already tasting the freedom of the better life of which his wife had dreamed.

Though Silas' revenge is violent, it is based upon a valid conviction and not a fantasy. The conviction is, of course, that men ought to defend themselves when frustrated of their legitimate expectations from life by continual repression. When this defense, though it benefits the personality, results in outward disaster, this conviction has evoked a tragic theme. It is, in fact, the tragic theme of our time. And as such, it should be distinguished from the many themes tangential to it, that have flourished in the recent past, and which are, by contrast, the themes of pathos. Negroes, as they become sophisticated, might conceivably have adopted any number of these bourgeois attitudes, which involve irony or pathos in place of tragedy. In the poetry of Robinson Jeffers, after a life of violent inner and outer conflict, death becomes the desired passage into inert anonymity. For Thomas Mann, sin and suffering, through the violence of war, become therapeutic devices of purgation by means of which we

automatically recover our lost perception of the virtuous life. As in Dostoievsky, the act of violence automatically sets up its opposite; a different
consciousness is created spontaneously by the mere course of events. In
Wright, a learning process is basic. The reciprocity between developing
events and the changing personality involves more than the emergence of
different orders of intuition. Part of the reciprocity is between the individual's reason and his emotions. The process, thus conceived, assumes
the emerging control of the consciousness, both over one's emotions and
the external event. In such a process the end is tragedy when the improved
personality, though it deserves to be successful, is defeated by the particular order of events concerned. Wright's characters are, strictly speaking,
illiterate. Yet they illustrate better than Mann's characters, for all their
rumination, this sort of learning from experience, this growth of a more
authentic awareness of the individual's relationship to the outer world.
Errors in its verbal statement and vacillations of mood are evidence that
the awareness is only forming in the consciousness. But it comes through
occasionally, and these occasions are reliable clues by means of which we
may understand the unuttered internal meanings behind the hero's overt
actions. "Ah'm gonna be hard like they is. So help me, Gawd, Ah'm gonna
be hard. When they come fer me Ah'm gonna be here. 'N when they git
me outta here theys gonna know Ah'm gone." The statement is in terms
of mere resistance, but it is nevertheless the clue to an inner life, which
is expanding on a new basis, with a sense of competence and co-ordination
to a valuable end. Silas is turning against his oppressors the principle
they pervert but which, all the same they taught him: the principle that
a man should stand up for his rights. Justified, unperverted as he accepts
it, it becomes for him a new ideal of manhood, and death is taken as only
the means to achieve it, when there is no other way.

The nature of the theme and the psychology of the heroic personality
are the same everywhere in the modern world. The same need to die
rather than suffer the inner degradation of slavery and bitter oppression
is the note of anti-fascist literature everywhere. It reappears with only
minor changes of emphasis, whether the locus be Spain or China with
Malraux, the Soviet Union with Ehrenbourg, occupied France with
Pozner, fascist Germany with Anna Seghers, or this account at home of
Long Black Song. Everywhere, also, in Wright's stories, it is the underlying
attitude. Other stories more deliberately than *Long Black Song* define its
political implications. There is a community of aim and attitude in the
opponents of fascism everywhere, which transcends differences of race and
class and nation; so that readers sense this community even when members of their own group seem to be attacked. This distinction Wright
makes explicit in *Bright and Morning Star*. In this story he makes you hate
the lynch mob with a contempt and ferocity only equalled in Soviet stories
of the Nazi invaders or American accounts of Japanese atrocities. He

makes you hate the white informer within the sharecropper's union. But he is careful to introduce other white members of the union whom the Negroes trust because of their character and their willingness to suffer. But the protagonist is an old Negro mother, and the emphasis of the plot is upon her expiation of her error, which has betrayed her son to the mob. Under her son's eyes, before they are both beaten to death together, she avenges herself and him by taking the life of the stool-pigeon she had trusted. But this sequence of external events has been accompanied by changes within her personality. Her awareness of betrayal has been the start of a process of inner development. From a passive, old-fashioned Negro, with misgivings about her son's union activities, she has learned from error, and now, instead of wailing and submitting, she turns to action. Her intense identification with her son, no longer merely maternal, becomes the greater since she can now in a measure identify with his values in living. Her view of the world has become more complex because she has learned that people are not always what they seem. Though she is not yet certain of the criteria for trust in other people's actions and ideas, she has at length learned to trust herself. Under these circumstances, revenge is only the negative aspect of an awakening self-respect, and the fact of her own dying is driven out of consciousness by the fact of successful action in behalf of her son and the ideals they now hold in common. She has become capable of the same order of heroism as Silas.

The heroic theme in Wright takes the dramatic form of physical conflict. Through the action, the reader becomes aware of changes within the personality of the hero. But the hero's attention is never centered, as it is in Malraux, introspectively upon himself. At the same time, unlike most of the definitely antifascist fiction, unlike *Native Son* as well, the short stories deal with rigidly limited situations. They do not involve any broad picture of social conflict. They are so written that the reader will fit them into the larger frame by himself. Wright's characters are part of that larger frame, but they are too unlettered to be aware of their symbolic roles. They fight generally in isolation, or as a little isolated band, with the intensity and at times the morbidity of those who must fight alone. Somehow, dimly, and quite unverbalized, a faith in democracy animates them so that they seem at times to presage those guerilla fighters so common in Europe during the Second World War. But this isolation of Wright's characters, if it seems politically a proof that the stamina needed to build an organization precedes organization itself, esthetically it permits a plot that, by stressing conflict of individual wills in place of social forces, gains in dramatic intensity.

But this conflict of wills can exist only when there is a valid conflict between reaction and democracy within society. The writer who can believe in the progressive extension of democracy will be able to recognize the conflict and squarely face it. Its recognition, by making possible the construction of a plot, both removes the taint of pathos or sentimentality or melodrama (which are the stylistic evidences of the failure to recognize the conflict or to evaluate it), and restores high seriousness to the tragic action. It must not be forgotten that Aristotle's definition of tragedy was determined by his belief in the dominance of clear-cut moral laws, and that our loss of the capacity to create the tragic plot in the modern world is the result of our pluralism and negation of belief. The difference between plot as defined by Aristotle and as Wright uses it is owing to a difference in the nature of the beliefs the plots subsume. In Aristotle it is an eternal proscription which a superior man unwittingly violates. When he becomes aware of his violation, he accepts outward penalty and physical suffering with inward resignation as justified. But in Wright the belief is one created by man, which unfolds, grows richer in content and greater in extension, by the cumulating pressure of man's exercise of his own potentialities. In tragic action under these conditions, it is not the hero who sins, but his opponent. The hero is a common man who is made to suffer because he has got in touch with reality, because his awakened potentialities have brought him into conflict with the forces of reaction. His suffering, consequently, though it is physical as well as mental, is accompanied by an inner state of feeling which is the opposite to submission, one of active, exalted conviction of self-fulfillment.

In these short stories the tragic action ceases to be a mechanism for preserving the status quo by showing what happens to those who violate it. It becomes the price one may have to pay for the satisfaction of living according to one's ever-expanding convictions, of challenging what one has come to know to be evil, and promoting what is for one's own good because it is for the common good. It becomes the present sacrifice men are willing to make for an awareness of the better life within them. A tragedy, then, as a literary form, consists of a conflict in the objective world, through which a contradiction develops, between the external circumstances of the hero's life, which ends in a death imposed by his opponents, and his internal state of feeling, which becomes a sense of fullest living. This contradiction is promoted by his discovery through action of an error of judgment, and ends, through the right use of that discovery, in what is actually the satisfaction of the better integrated personality, even when unlettered Negroes are only aware of the surge of mother love or the obligation their dignity as human beings has laid upon them.

Richard Wright: The Man Who Lived Underground

by Michel Fabre

I

Always interested in new ideas and conscious of his responsibilities as a black intellectual, Richard Wright must nevertheless be considered, when one delves into his fiction, primarily as a storyteller for whom a good narrative is valid for what it relates as much as for what it signifies. One constantly finds traces in him of the poor black child who owes his spiritual survival in racist Mississippi and, in part, his vocation as a writer to detective stories, popular fiction and dime novels. Indeed, he was always drawn towards stories in which truth is stranger than fiction; and after bringing unlikely events into his novels, he took a sly pleasure in disclosing the authenticity of episodes which his bewildered readers had taken for wild fabrications.

We can easily imagine his delight when he came across, in the August 1941 issue of *True Detective*, "The Crime Hollywood Couldn't Believe," written by Hal Fletcher from the account given by Lt. C. W. Gains of the Los Angeles Police. One night in November 1931, the sub-manager of the local branch of the Owl Drug Company had deposited eleven thousand dollars in the safe of his store; and, on opening the intact safe the following morning, the director had not found a trace of the money in it. As the two men were above all suspicion, and there was no sign of burglary, the mystery remained unsolved. Two weeks later, the safe of a clothing store—to which only the owner possessed the key—was emptied in the same way. Then there was an epidemic of thefts; linen, jewelry, typewriters, food, blankets, books, etc., disappeared by magic always in the same neighborhood. In the spring of the following year, the field of these mysterious thefts was transferred a few streets. Incredibly enough, the manager of the Baker Shoe Company, who had left two thousand dollars and twenty-

"Richard Wright: The Man Who Lived Underground," by Michel Fabre. From *Studies in the Novel*, 3, No. 2 (Summer 1971), 165–189. Copyright © 1971 by North Texas State University. Reprinted by permission of *Studies in the Novel* and the editor.

six cents in his safe one fine night, found the two thousand dollars there, but no sign of the twenty-six cents. Police rounds and surveillance produced no results until the following year, when, at the end of nine consecutive nights of watching in a store, a policeman saw an arm coming up out of the floor to turn the lock on a trapdoor. The arm disappeared when he tried to grab it, but this time a search of the basements revealed a hideout which was well furnished with blankets, canned goods, and alcohol. At last in February 1933 the police arrested Herbert C. Wright, white, thirty-three years old, and from a good family. He had seen sewermen at work and had decided to solve his problem of unemployment by building his world from their underground universe. He did not harbor any particular grudge against society, the magazine specified, and was perfectly sane.

Intrigued, the novelist immediately became interested in the motives of his strange namesake, who was still serving a ten-year sentence in the penitentiary. On October 27, 1941, he asked the governor of California for the record of prisoner number 55836, the details of which did not make the situation any clearer. The thief claimed to have been guided at times by his dead mother's voice when undertaking his burglaries and was seemingly proud of the names given to him by the press ("the human mole," "the tunnel burglar"). But he had done his best to help in returning the stolen objects and had not incurred any punishments in the penitentiary.

With these facts in hand, Richard Wright set to work, using as his guide the account in *True Detective,* which stressed the ingenuity of the burglar and the fact that he was perhaps motivated more by challenge than by gain, and which delighted in using images of dripping, dark labyrinths. In the autumn of 1941, he rapidly wrote 150 pages of a novel—since it was then a brief novel and not a short story—which he immediately turned over to his agent and friend, Paul Reynolds. On December 13 he wrote thanking him for having looked through the manuscript and emphasized the fact that it was "the first time [he had] tried to go beyond stories in black and white."

At that time, the narrative included a first section of seventy typewritten pages which have remained unpublished: on his way home one Saturday night, a black servant finds himself arrested by policemen who drive him to the police station, take away his money, and by all sorts of brutal means and tortures try to make him confess to the murder of a Mrs. Peabody. Fred Daniels can think only of his wife, who is about to have a baby, and of his great weariness. He signs a confession at dawn despite the fact that he is innocent. After the so-called reconstruction of the crime, he is brought back home where his wife, who is surprised and terrified, must be taken to the maternity hospital. Fred is taken there as well, and that is where he manages to escape through a window, running in the rain, hiding in entrance-halls until the providential opening of a manhole cover leads

him to the underground world. Then followed the pages which make up
the short story in its present form.

Reynolds attempted in vain to find a spot for the narrative in several
magazines after Harper and Brothers had found it to be too short for a
novel. In the spring of 1942, Wright allowed his friend Kerker Quinn to
publish two excerpts of about ten pages—describing the scene in which
Daniels papers his cave with dollar bills, rings, and watches—in *Accent,*
a little magazine he was launching. Edwin Seaver, after trying to interest
Harry Scherman of the Book-of-the-Month Club in it, finally published
"The Man Who Lived Underground" in his anthology *Cross Section* in
April of 1944. But it was then a novella of forty-six pages rather than a
novel. The first two chapters and a part of the third had been cut out in
order to have the story begin under rather mysterious circumstances after
the descent into the sewers. The narrative was most likely cut down in
that way to enable it to fit into the format of the anthology, but we do
not know who cut it. Wright does not refer to this alteration in his correspondence, and Edwin Seaver confesses that he no longer has any recollection of it. The novelist was probably not opposed to this cut, since the
symbolic significance of the narrative "beyond stories in black and white"
was heightened by deleting the police brutalities inflicted on the innocent
Negro.

The critics generally saw this short story as the most striking one in
Cross Section, though not as the best. Sterling North wrote in the *Chicago
Sun* of June 4, 1944 (sec. 5, p. 2): "As an enthusiastic Wright fan of several
years standing I may perhaps be permitted to point out that Wright is
still doing variations on the same theme and is dangerously near J. Farrell's cul de sac." In the *New York Times* of May 28, 1944 (sec. 1, p. 14),
Thomas Lyle Collins emphasized, without giving an opinion, "the morbid
and disturbing analogy between the way white oppression forces the Negro
psyche underground and this frightening narrative." Harry Hansen, who
was more discerning, observed in the *New York World Telegram* of May 31:
"No doubt Richard Wright had more in mind than the story of a criminal's
escape. His Negro had a symbolical mission in his wayward flight from
the inevitable. . . . But, he adds, Wright is not a symbolist and [his] story
stands or falls on the narrative, not on the suspected implications."

A large majority of the newspapers echoed the review by the American
Negro Press in which the critic saw the short story as a "denunciation of
the white race" which he thought was to be found in Wright. The importance of the short story in Wright's career as a novelist was not felt at the
time, partly because of the publication of *Black Boy.* This work created an
image of Wright that was to become popular in the United States. His
existentialism as it existed in the short story was neglected, and when it
strongly reappeared in *The Outsider* in 1953, it was then considered, and

wrongly so, more as being taken from the European literary fashion than as an original and strong tendency of Wright's. "The Man Who Lived Underground," which was reprinted once in 1945 and twice in 1956, had to appear in *Eight Men* in 1961 to reach a wider public which was capable of considering it in its true perspective.

II

The short story is therefore situated in the heart of a culminating period in Wright's production, between the adaptation of *Native Son* and the composition of the unpublished novel *Black Hope* and *Twelve Million Black Voices* on one hand, and the birth of *Black Boy* on the other. All of these undertakings were more or less intermingled in Wright's mind at that time, and we can find slight or strong traces of these preoccupations in the short story. Thus, Daniel's employment as a servant and his relationship with his employer were certainly inspired by the research carried out for *Black Hope* in employment agencies or at the Domestic Workers' Union. The Clinton Brewer case afforded Wright with details of police brutality. Several elements seem to be drawn from *Native Son*: the running from the police, the feelings of the hunted man, the importance of food, the symbolic role of the rat and of the religious hymns, the basement furnace, the newspaper in which the fugitive reads about his case, his imitating the way people act in the movies, his precarious victory which is expressed as a defiance, and his final need to establish contact with the outside world. The dream about the drowning woman and baby the protagonist is unable to rescue is taken from the unpublished *Tarbaby* and is perhaps the echo of personal phantasma similar to those depicted in *Black Boy*. There is too close a resemblance between the jewelry shop and the optical company where Wright was humiliated by the white workers for the diamond theft not to seem like a transposed revenge. The situation of the underground man also comes from the satirical episode entitled "What You Don't Know Won't Hurt You," which expresses the bitter segregation experienced by Wright as an employee in the Michael Reese Hospital in Chicago in 1933.

Apropos of this experience of the underground, one wonders if Robert Bone is justified in seeing Dostoyevsky's *Notes from Underground* as one of the sources of this short story and of Ralph Ellison's *Invisible Man*.[1] Wright was familiar with the Russian novelist's work; nevertheless any influence from Dostoyevsky's narrative proves to be negligible and limited to the situation of the man underground in the case of his short story. The

[1] *The Negro Novel in America*, rev. ed. (New Haven: Yale Univ. Press, 1965), pp. 201–2. See also R. Bone, *Richard Wright* (Minneapolis: Univ. of Minnesota Press, 1969), p. 26. See n. 3.

Dostoyevskian figure is endowed with acute sensitivity, and he is consumed by a burning hate at the memory of the humiliations he had suffered, but his dreams of revenge crumble because he is certain they are doomed to fail. Fred Daniels could not be characterized in this way, and Wright never uses his hero as a mouthpiece against the industrial society, nor does he consider him to be mad. The Dostoyevskian man withdrew from the world out of spite; Wright's escapes from it by accident and wishes to return. He experiences no resentment at the memory of the cruelties he has suffered, but rather a feeling of superiority which is awakened in him by his metaphysical discoveries underground. Instead of seeking revenge, he tries to share them with his tormentors in an outburst of generosity. As for the situation of the man underground symbolizing that of the Negro in American society (and here Wright refers to his own experiences), the novelist has painted it in a perspective which is exactly opposed to Dostoyevsky's: rather than brooding over past humiliations, he sees his exclusion more as an opportunity to scrutinize his culture from the outside.

Therefore, the underground rather clearly represents the marginal character of the black man's existence and his ambiguous rapport with American civilization. The short story stands at a kind of philosophic crossroads in the evolution of Wright's thinking, midway between *Native Son* and *The Outsider*. This appears in the intrigue as much as in the resonances of the narrative: Fred Daniels runs away from the police as does Bigger Thomas, and, in this sense, he does not voluntarily withdraw from society. But he prefers to "stay away" for the duration of the story in the same way as Cross Damon, when accidentally liberated from his past, chooses to remain on the fringe. And the gesture made to return is identical in both cases: Daniels does not succeed any more than does Bigger in securing the ties which anchor him to society. Nor will he succeed any more than Cross Damon who, on his deathbed, proclaims his fear of complete solitude. "The Man Who Lived Underground" has many features and details in common with *The Outsider*: their existentialist philosophy; the symbolic role of the church; the theme of the innocent victim; the criminal who needs the policeman, and their deep resemblance; and, above all, man's feeling of horror when, like Kurtz in *Heart of Darkness*, he examines the depths of his soul and his mortal state.

III

Out of the authentic adventure in *True Detective* Wright has retained, along with the general plan, the disconcerting details which take the narrative out of the commonplace and not just the characteristics which would heighten its interest as a detective story. The novelist borrows the vicissitudes, suspense, and violence from this genre, but he transforms the questioning of the system which the theft represents into something more basic than questioning the aspects of ownership. Daniels is not a common thief. When he sees a trembling hand slip a roll of bank notes up a sleeve, he becomes indignant because "he felt that his stealing the money and the man's stealing the money were two entirely different things. He wanted to steal the money merely for the sensation involved in getting it, and he had no intention of spending a penny of it; but he knew that the man who was stealing it was going to spend it, perhaps for pleasure" (p. 132).[2]

The thief who wants to get rich quickly conforms to widely accepted social imperatives, breaking certain rules at the same time. But Daniels is a kind of revolutionary since his action is aimed at breaking social conventions. In this and many other passages, Wright's commentary sets the narrative in such a perspective. The action unfolds as in a detective film, but it is entirely different from a cops-and-robbers story, since the supposedly guilty person (not a criminal, only an amateur burglar) has discovered a new metaphysical rule in the social game which enables him to define himself as being neither more nor less guilty than other men, who are often mere amateurs in comparison.

Such are Daniel's reactions to the punishments that his own malfeasance brings to other persons. He has absolutely no scruples about letting the shopboy be accused instead of him; at most he feels a vague contemptuous pity for him: "Perhaps the beating would bring to the boy's attention for the first time of his life the secret of his existence, the guilt that he could never get rid of" (p. 144).

It is the same for the watchman who "was not guilty of the crime of which he had been accused, but guilty just the same, had always been guilty" (p. 145). Thus the watchman appears as a reflection of Daniels, who felt guilty not only for having given in to the police brutalities, but for an original crime as well, for the same sin as the congregation singing in the basement church:

> He felt that their search for a happiness they could never find made them feel that they had committed some dreadful offense which they could not remember or understand. He was now in possession of the feeling that had gripped him when he had first come into the underground. . . . It seemed that one was always trying to remember a gigantic shock that had left a haunting impression upon one's body which one could not forget or shake off, but which had been forgotten by the conscious mind, creating in one's life a state of eternal anxiety (p. 143).

Here we reach the heart of Wright's metaphysical anxiety, the feeling of precariousness, of a diffuse and obscure guilt which he has strongly

---

[2]All references to "The Man Who Lived Underground" are from *Black Voices,* ed. Abraham Chapman, Mentor Books, 1968.

experienced since his childhood, and which he constantly seeks to interpret through the tools of Marxism or psychoanalysis.

In the framework of the narrative, we discover that this guilt is not within the province of the police or the law; on the contrary, it is such a basic psychological fact that it represents (in the Kantian sense) one of the forms of the human mind, the mark of our condition.

The terrestrial universe and the world underground are in fact posed like two sides of the same reality, separated by the thickness of a wall, a partition, or even a clouded window. We cannot suppose for an instant that the fugitive will be able to organize his universe independently of the other, nor that the everyday world will escape his searching look. Alone in his cave, Daniels tries to elaborate his universe in an ironical antithesis to what is considered the normal world. He would simply have to take it apart and invert the relationships. But whether he takes apart or reconstructs, Daniels is nonetheless prisoner of the preexisting relationships, because reversing a signification implies accepting its priority. It is impossible to create *ex nihilo*, to attain an independent, asocial perspective; the individual cannot elude his human and cultural heritage, since the metaphysical reality of the human condition seems to deny solitary existence.

After the lyrical episode where the cave is transformed by Daniel's artistic imagination and culminates in an assertion of his autonomy and defiance against society, the protagonist finds himself unsatisfied, burning with a strange fever, and prompted to return to the world. For the first time, he feels smothered by the walls which protect him from others. He has understood the necessity of human solidarity, not as much from a pragmatic or moral point of view as from a philosophical or existential perspective. This interdependence is the foundation of personal identity. Indeed, life on earth is absurd, and it confuses appearances with a rational order. Its habits replace authentic perceptions to such a point that identity is continuously mistaken. A similar kind of logic leads the policeman to consider the night watchman's suicide as proof of his guilt. The truth of the imagination or of the unusual is constantly rejected, and Lawson (the son of the Law) concludes that it is necessary to shoot Daniels and "his kind. They'd wreck things" (p. 160).

The polarization of the two universes and their complementary elements thus functions on the moral and metaphysical levels simultaneously. From the first episode in the church a change is operating on the hero's values. At the beginning of his action as a voyeur he feels embarrassed and guilty. But why? The juxtaposition of the foul-smelling sewer and the worshippers seeking God suggests a revolting contrast. Wright uses the term "obscene." There is an obscenity in the disparity between the actual situation of man and his aspirations, between the beast and the angel.

By going down into the sewer, Daniels was freed from his past. He was a victim, an innocent man who was declared guilty by the police and the law. Down below, through his gradual experience of irresponsibility associated with the invisibility which makes him omnipotent, he has, paradoxically enough, a deep feeling of guilt. He feels guilty for existing like any other man, but he is also guilty because he is apart and unable to remain a superman, beyond good and evil. Thus his return to the world above ground is justified on the moral level.

On the metaphysical level, his progress reflects a difficult acquisition of identity and poses the problem of the definition of man. We can see how gradually this identity appears. At first, the protagonist is designated simply as "he" by the omniscient narrator. His appearance is slowly defined; his race is given by contrast to the white man who looks at him; his physical strength is measured against the water's; his composure is seen against the sights he encounters—the rat, the dead baby, and the filthy sewer; he gives us his name by writing "freddaniels" on the typewriter; finally, when he returns above ground, his image appears in a mirror. However, a name has no meaning in the world underground, and the hero forgets his so completely that he is unable to state his identity when he turns himself in to the police. He has literally lost it, thereby becoming "the man who lived underground," a modern version of Everyman.

The identity that Daniels was seeking was neither personal nor racial but rather a definition of man as a member of the human family. This is even more important than the rather obvious symbolism of the rebirth of man. We can surely find the myth of the old man and the new which is transposed into images of childbirth. The sewer resembles the womb with its dripping dome and its multiple drains into which body fluids spout forth, and the newborn baby is carried. Returned to the maternal womb, man is recreated, charged with a new force, and then ejected. The image of man as the son of the earth remains less essential, however, than his definition as a gregarious animal. Daniels can acquire his identity only through others. A reflection of himself is not sufficient, nor is the fugitive replica found in the figure of the watchman. Daniel's one-sided view is ineffective, like words without dialogue. As Cross Damon says, man must "throw bridges between men." Even though we have deliberately held off from using the term until now, this is a brand of atheistic existentialism. Wright will bring it more clearly to light in *The Outsider*. He will explore its concepts in his introduction to *Black Metropolis*, borrowing from William James the notions of an "unguaranteed existence" and of hell as the supreme punishment because of its complete isolation. By this indirect manner "The Man Who Lived Underground" is related to *No Exit*. Sartre's words "Hell is others" are literally reversed, since, for Daniels, damnation is the absence of others.

Here we should point out the secondary nature of the racial situation. The protagonist's race most certainly plays a part in the plot. If his skin had not been dark, Daniels would not have been arrested and falsely accused, and, at the end of the story, the policemen would not have treated him in such a scornful manner. However, as in *The Outsider,* Wright is less interested here in the condition of the American Negro than in that of the individual in modern society. It is true that in the eyes of many the Negro is thought to be one of the last incarnations of authentic individuality and that the two categories tend to blend together. Nevertheless, an essentially racial interpretation of "The Man Who Lived Underground" as a fable of the Afro-American situation strikes us as being if not exaggerated, at least too restrictive. Robert Bone starts correctly with the marginal situation of the black man but interprets too exclusively the sights viewed by Fred from behind the scenery as a series of vignettes depicting this racial situation. He sees the black congregation as representing religious segregation, the dead baby as the Negro rejected by American culture, the dead body on the embalmer's table as the black man emptied of his substance and transfused with the stereotyped vision of the white world.[3]

Wright is careful, however, not to indicate the race of the baby and the corpse, and it seems to us that such visions express, primarily and respectively, the irrational and shameful aspect of any religion, and the purely materialistic values of a pitiless society which kills its children and turns death into an industry. It is above all the situation of Daniels himself, who is followed and chased in a dark world (a dirty, evil-smelling character such as the white man imagines the Negro) and who is finally eliminated by the oppressive system, which is a parable of black life in America. Everything he sees constitutes more a view of Western civilization from behind the scenes than a picture of the black segregated world.

This is tantamount to saying that the protagonist's situation remains constantly existentialist as opposed to that of the other characters—existentialist because it is situated in the middle ground where the critical and exterior viewpoint merges with direct, immediate access. Excluding the black man from American society or putting Daniels between brackets in the sunless world places them in this situation at the outset. Here, the lower or underground position is less important than the exclusion or marginality. Setting the individual apart allows him to pass judgment in a more detached and perhaps objective manner on whatever he is excluded from. At the same time, it implies a certain invisibility of the individual whose personality is unrecognized. If he is not actually seen, he does not exist. The metaphysical bearing of this image of the black outsider is thus double. It presupposes superiority in his vision over the common vision, also the agony in his exclusion and the necessity to return, as Ralph Ellison in his turn admirably asserts in *Invisible Man.*

[3]Bone, pp. 26–29.

IV

Without stretching the structure of the narrative, we can easily construe the underground adventure of Wright's hero as an existential parable, but also as a quasi-mythological quest that uses certain techniques such as are found in myths or folk narratives. We find obstacles to be overcome, a "sesame" or magical instrument, a guarded treasure, infractions and punishments, adverse destiny and protective divinity, going beyond the human condition and the fall that occurs after such hubris. It is even possible to show how certain episodes relate to the weird vision of the future as found in science fiction. The story makes us think, for example, of the beginning of H. P. Lovecraft's *Demons and Wonders*: by entering the cave, the imprudent person risks entering a different world where time takes on another dimension and whose rules defy those of his own. Here, the detailed, careful description of certain happenings (such as the slow burning of a match or the description of a hymn as a "feathery cadence") is enough to make everyday events appear out of the ordinary: this type of description is also effective in creating a constant state of suspense, the latter being more a question of feeling outside the natural sphere and incessant bewilderment than of intrigue. We often find ourselves on the other side of the mirror and think of Lewis Carroll; sometimes an insidious metamorphosis brings us even closer to Kafka. In this obscure world, eyes can no longer see but fingers take on sight in such a way that Daniels's "fingers toy[ed] in space like the antennae of an insect" (p. 120). This abnormal perception of an environment which seems unnatural to man further increases the general impression of strangeness. Indeed, there is something monstrous, something fascinating, about the surroundings, such as the many-colored, muddy slime that swells up like boiling lava on another planet. Similarly, faced with the rites of the underground world, the spectator finds himself becoming vertiginously mesmerized by a vision of bottomless obscenity. In this world, the human voice is insignificant: the baby floating in a foamy halo that has blossomed out like a sinister bouquet utters a silent cry. However, on the other hand, things can speak. Thus, the objects hanging on the wall of the cave convey an angry message. In the end, the distraught man can no longer even understand the meaning behind his own desires and sensations: "His mind said no; his body said yes; and his mind could not understand his feelings. A low whine broke from him and he was in the act of uncoiling. . . . Like a frantic cat clutching a rag, he clung to the steel prongs . . ." (p. 147). The unnameable has reduced the rational being to a mere animal.

Strangeness, bewilderment, the supernatural—most of the elements of the fantastic are combined in this narrative. It would only require striking out several descriptions that are too explicit for us to imagine ourselves on another planet. But, just when we find ourselves being attracted to and summoned by the unreal, the author reintroduces realistic notation which prevents us from going off into an imaginary world. He compels his hero to rationalize things, to bring what seemed bizarre back down to familiar ground. When Daniels discovers a metal pole, some sewerman had to abandon it for its presence to be justified. When he finds himself in what he thinks is a cave, it is just an old, unused sewer. We might expect that the author was disciplined for too long a time in the realistic tradition to be able to free himself from it, but then, after reading several pages, we understand that the appeal of the narrative lies in this continual alternation between the mysterious and the commonplace (and an examination of the writer's successive drafts reveals, moreover, that such was his intention). Once we have accepted this imaginary world, we are not shocked by the strangest of episodes. Because we are continually obliged to question whether the fantastic is taking place, our sense of criticism cannot let up; Wright uses this tension to lead us to question the familiar, something we would refuse to do when reading a dreamlike tale.

V

Thus, the narrative, having hesitated on the edge of the fantastic, wanders away from it. There is only one world, not two; what appeared at first to be out of the ordinary is really, on closer view, just the reverse side of the everyday and made out of the same material. Clearing up the mystery amounts to the same thing as creating the world, and, by this indirect means, the underground exploration represents the process involved in developing a culture. This makes us think of Robinson Crusoe, for, after his drowning fall, Daniels resembles the castaway equipped with a few matches and his own ingenuity who first ensures his own survival and then builds up a civilization. Like Crusoe, Daniels is a kind of pioneer, a *homo faber*, the latter owing to the fact that tools are the key to the evolution of man: a metal pole, which becomes the extension of his arm; a rusty pipe, which turns into a crowbar and drill; and finally the precious toolbox, which he discovers in a basement. By way of engaging in conversation, Crusoe had his parrots; Daniels has a radio. Crusoe trimmed his quilled pen; Daniels steals a typewriter. Increasingly entranced by his mechanical skill, Daniels patiently learns the necessary, ritualistic movements so that he eventually masters the technique well enough to type a single sentence. By typing this line, he has reinvented language and literature. Typing, here, represents more artistic creation than functional writing, for solitude allows one to do what one wants in a life which, in the beginning, consisted of merely ensuring one's survival and making use of the resources of one's surroundings. Daniels experiences both a Machiavellian and an innocent delight when handling precious objects: dollar bills smelling of fresh ink; the watches, now just something to look at because the hands no longer point to any real time; the rings, glittering in the light cast by the bulb; and the diamonds, sparkling like stardust fallen to the ground. Like a potentate and aesthete, Daniels enjoys a luxury that represents more than just the eccentricities of a millionaire, for he has forgone his desire to possess things in a world rid of economic value.

Thus, the hallucinatory scene in the cave, which is the climax of the short story, can be seen as the epiphany of artistic creation. Our underground Robinson Crusoe plays a game of scattering the diamonds by kicking the heap in which they are arranged in order to feel equal to God; mathematical certitude tells him that, as he walks back and forth in measured and blind pace, his shoes will, at a moment determined by the law of probability, hit the heap—hence demonstrating a freedom contingent on chance. Looking down in all his glory upon his universe, he reminds us of Bigger, the successful murderer, contemplating Chicago. But this Nietzsche-like Crusoe, who finds himself metaphorically on the opposite side of the starry dome above, has already made a tour of his island and its possibilities. Alone in his eerily lit cave, he mumbles the fateful words "Anything's right." Whereas Crusoe clung to the laws of the country he had lost, Daniels breaks all ties and comes to the conclusion that there is no providence. However, his solipsism horrifies him to the point that he will eventually return to civilization and expose himself to its dangers.

VI

Whether studied as a detective story, myth, fantasy, or history of the creation of human values, this short story, owing to its cyclic, uncoiling action in which each projective stage calls for a similar retrograde stage, presents us with the same humanist message that says that man acquires his identity from other men. Alone, the individual can superimpose various masks and define himself by his aptitude in leading a protean type of life and in histrionics; however, he would not know how to define the criteria necessary to differentiate reality from roles and appearances. He plays his parts in succession. When the occasion arises, the hero, from his well-positioned perch, contemplates not only the nudity of the corpse but the nudity of souls as well. He is continually the invisible, transparent man. Eyes are so used to looking at him without seeing him that one person mistakes him for someone else and another can distinguish no more than his outline. When the couple comes into the grocery store, he sells them grapes and his guise as salesboy hides him. He is the ghost that the young girl thought she saw. In the jewelry shop he becomes a thief. Finally, in the cave, he is actor and artist, listener and spectator, poet and God. But he plays his role so well and is so good at becoming or staying invisible that he is reduced to a mere apparition, and even his most creative ventures cannot give it form. The shift between what is real and what is imaginary lasts so long that we no longer know if reality actually exists or if it is reducible to a succession of appearances. Perhaps the ultimate question that Wright wanted to ask is not "Does man survive outside a society which forms and defines him while all the same oppressing him?" but rather "Does a reality exist in each person which is eternal and unalterable and which some call God?"

In this interplay of illusions, the story in all its ambiguity seems to be at the same time both its own subject-matter and an aim in itself. Appearing as a parable representing man's identity, the writing in fact becomes its own story and its reality exists as it unfolds before us. Almost everything that "The Man Who Lived Underground" relates about the nature of mankind could be applied to the nature of literary works. Just as Daniels needs a spectator in order to exist, so does fiction need a reader. Likewise, an individual reaches out towards his fellow men, and a written work towards a public, and also towards all works in general, for it is by relation to them that the individual work is defined. It is at the heart (literally the geometric center and dramatic climax) of the narrative that we find a work written "en abyme." The short sentence "It was a long hot day," correctly and neatly typed, seems to be chosen out of the air, but it takes up again the beginning sentence in the first unpublished version of the novel and creates a strange feeling of infinitude by suggesting that a fictitious character writes his own fiction, creates his own being. Just the simple fact that man's assertion as an artist has been placed at the center of the work would be enough to prove how important the creative process and the result (here the short story) by which he becomes incarnate are in the eyes of Wright. Daniels's expedition is a literary trajectory "par excellence." His transformations and wanderings underground reflect the winding becoming of a work in the subconscious. Constrained by time, both come to find solipsism, which shatters their existence and hurls them towards others in order that they may exist. "The Man Who Lived Underground" thus also appears to be a parable of a literary work, since its narrative becomes a discourse on the narrative in general and, by implication, a discourse on literature in general. It is woven of this fluctuation between the known and the unexplored, so well illustrated by the protagonist's scuttling route. Like his acts, the work is gratuitous and disputable; like them, it bursts into fireworks and iridescently burns away as each facet sends out flashes that answer other flashes. Like the underground labyrinth, it is made up of uneven surfaces and reversals in direction, of obstacles and sudden illuminations, of premonitory visions and imperceptible cadences, of the familiar and the fantastic.

Above all, it is like a periplus that comes around back to itself after being unwound by thin, successive and transparent layers which reveal converging perspectives, unwound until alpha coincides with omega and a perfect circle is formed. While making this short circular journey, the narrative is being symbolically written—not as a genesis, but as a brief fulguration between life and death. Fred Daniels literally exists the duration of a short story, the span of a reading of forty-odd pages. During this passage of time, the various levels of the narrative are superimposed upon each other and mirrored ad infinitum. Then everything returns to the sphere of potentiality. The story ends with the image of man unjustly vanquished, carried away into the solitary entrails of the earth, like a dead, wandering planet. But we have only to again start reading for the narrative to resume its fleeting existence. And thus "The Man Who Lived Underground," owing to its splendid polyphony of meanings and its balanced precision, may be said to represent Wright's richest short piece, one woven of the same exacting perfection as a poem.

Chronology of Important Dates

1908	4 September: Richard Wright born on a plantation at Roxie near Natchez, Mississippi, to Ella (Wilson) and Nathan Wright.
1910	Birth of brother (Leon) Alan.
1911	Family moves to Memphis.
1913	Nathan Wright deserts impoverished family.
1915	Richard and Alan briefly in an orphanage.
1916	Briefly attends Howe Institute, Memphis, Tennessee.
1916–17	Lives with his mother, brother, and aunt in Elaine, Arkansas; uncle is murdered.
1917–18	Lives in West Helena, Arkansas; his mother's health worsens.
1919–25	Lives in Jackson, Mississippi, with his grandparents.
1920–21	Attends the Seventh-Day Adventist School in Jackson, Wright's first full year of schooling.
1921–23	Enrolled in Jim Hill School, Jackson.
1923	September: enters the Smith-Robinson School, Jackson.
1925	29 May: graduates from Smith-Robinson Junior High, valedictorian; this was the end of Wright's formal education. Leaves Jackson for Memphis, Tennessee; begins to read H. L. Mencken, Theodore Dreiser, and Sinclair Lewis.
1927	December: leaves Memphis for South Side of Chicago, where he finds early jobs in a delicatessen and cafeteria and as a postal clerk.
1931	Publishes "Superstition" in *Abbott's Monthly Magazine*.
1932	Attends the First National Conference of the John Reed Club, Chicago; works in Michael Reese Hospital, Chicago.
1933–34	Early poetry published in *Left Front,* which he later co-edits.
1934	Joins the Communist Party (perhaps as early as end of 1933).
1935–36	Works with the Illinois Federal Writers Project; attends the Congress of the League of American Writers in New York as a delegate; contributes to *New Masses*.

1936   September-November: publicity agent for Chicago Federal Negro Theater.

1937   June: moves to New York.
              Collaborates with Dorothy West and Marian Minus on *New Challenge*; becomes Harlem editor of the *Daily Worker*; publishes "Blue Print for Negro Writers."

1938   February: wins the *Story* magazine contest with "Fire and Cloud." *Uncle Tom's Children: Four Novellas* published by Harper & Brothers.

1939   Marries Dhimah Rose Meadman (whom he leaves the following year); receives a Guggenheim Fellowship.

1940   *Native Son* is published by Harper & Brothers, a Book-of-the-Month Club selection and best-seller; receives Spingarn Medal from NAACP; *Uncle Tom's Children: Five Long Stories* reissued by Harper with the addition of "Bright and Morning Star" and "The Ethics of Living Jim Crow [an introductory essay]."

1941   March 12: marries Ellen Poplar.
              Twelve Million Black Voices: A Folk History of the Negro in the United States published by Viking Press; dramatic adaptation of *Native Son* (with Paul Green) on Broadway with Canada Lee as Bigger Thomas, John Houseman producer, Orson Wells director; first meetings with Dr. Frederic Wertham marked the beginning of Wright's psychoanalytic concerns.

1942   First version of "The Man Who Lived Underground" published in *Accent*; first daughter, Julia, is born 15 April.

1944   Published "I Tried to Be a Communist" in the August issue of the *Atlantic Monthly*; leaves the Communist Party; enlarged version of "The Man Who Lived Underground" published in *Cross-Section* edited by Edwin Seaver.

1945   *Black Boy: A Record of Childhood and Youth,* published by Harper & Brothers, is another Book-of-the-Month Club selection and best seller.

1946   Meets Jean-Paul Sartre at the home of Dorothy Norman in New York; on May Day leaves for a visit to France at the invitation of the French government; received in Paris by Gertrude Stein.

1947   After a short stay in New York, Wright returns to Paris to establish permanent residence; meets George Padmore, who has a great influence on his ideas about Africa.

1947–48   Collaborates with Leopold Senghor, Aimé Césaire, and Alioune Diop in the establishment of *Présence Africaine*.

1949   Rachel, the Wrights' second child, is born in Paris on 17 January.

1949–50   Spends time in Argentina making the film version of *Native Son* with Pierre Chenal and playing the leading role; trip to Haiti.

1951   On his return to Paris founds the French-American Fellowship.

1953   *The Outsider,* published by Harper, is not well received by the critics; leaves in June on the Elder Dempster Line for Accra, Gold Coast (Ghana); spends the summer in Ghana collecting materials for a book.

1954   *Black Power: A Record of Reactions in a Land of Pathos* published by the World Publishing Company; *Savage Holiday,* published by Avon Books, a novel ignored in U.S. although the French version (*Le Dieu de mascarade*) receives considerable critical attention; August-September: tour of Spain.

1955   Travels through Spain and to the Bandung Conference in Indonesia; *Bandoeng, 1.500.000.000 hommes* published in Paris by Calman-Lévy; English edition published following year by World Publishing Company as *The Color Curtain.*

1956   *Pagan Spain* published by Harper & Brothers; Wright collaborates with Louis Sapin on a play, *Daddy Goodness* (produced 1959).

1957   *White Man, Listen!* is published by Doubleday.

1958   *The Long Dream* is published by Doubleday.

1959–60   While recovering from amoebic dysentery experiments writing haiku.

1960   February: dramatic adaptation of *The Long Dream* (by Ketti Frings) opens and closes on Broadway.
    28 November: dies at the Clinique Eugène Gibez of a heart attack; cremated at the Père-Lachaise Cemetery, December 5.

1961   *Eight Men* published posthumously by Pyramid Books.

1963   *Lawd Today* (begun as early as 1931) published posthumously by Walker and Co.; "Five Episodes from an Unfinished Novel" appears in *Soon, One Morning: New Writing by American Negroes,* edited by Herbert Hill (New York, 1963), pp. 139–164.

1977   *American Hunger,* a continuation of *Black Boy,* published posthumously by Harper & Row.

Sources for Chronology:

Michel Fabre, *The Unfinished Quest of Richard Wright* (1973) and Constance Webb, *Richard Wright* (1968).

Notes on the Editors and Contributors

RICHARD MACKSEY, Professor of Comparative Literature and for a decade Director of the Humanities Center at the Johns Hopkins University, has written on a range of European and American authors, including Sterne, Keats, Dostoevsky, Ruskin, Proust, Kafka, Stevens, and Williams; he has also published essays in film criticism, hermeneutics, intellectual history, and mathematics. He is the editor of *The Structuralist Controversy* and *Velocities of Change* and has contributed to three other volumes in the Twentieth Century Views series.

FRANK E. MOORER, a former student of Richard Macksey, has been Director of the Library at Wilberforce University and a member of the English and History Departments there. He has published on Richard Wright, Flannery O'Connor, Ayi Kwei Armah, and William Attaway. He is presently completing work for a Ph.D. in Afro-American and American Studies at the University of Iowa and also teaches in the Core Literature Program.

MARGARET WALKER ALEXANDER is a poet, novelist, and Professor Emeritus of English at Jackson State University. She is the author of *For My People* and *Jubilee*. She knew Richard Wright when both were living in Chicago during the 1930s.

The late EDWIN BERRY BURGUM was an editor of *Science and Society* and taught at the New School for Social Research. He is the author of *The Novel and the World's Dilemma* (1947; 1963).

MICHEL FABRE, a graduate of the Ecole Normale Supérieure, is Professor of American and Afro-American Studies at the Sorbonne. He is the author of *The Unfinished Quest of Richard Wright* and is presently preparing a volume of Wright's letters for publication.

The late NICK AARON FORD was Professor of English at Morgan State University. His critical essays were published in *College English*, the *English Journal*, *New England Quarterly*, and the *CLA Journal*.

DONALD B. GIBSON is Professor of English at Rutgers University. He is the author of *The Fiction of Stephen Crane* and *The Politics of Literary Expression* and is the editor of *Five Black Writers*.

BLYDEN JACKSON is Professor of English at the University of North Carolina at Chapel Hill. He has published widely on Afro-American literature and is also the author of *The Waiting Years*.

ESTHER M. JACKSON is Professor of Theater and Drama at the University of Wisconsin, Madison. She has published articles on Shakespeare, Faulkner, and Ellison and a book, *The Broken World of Tennessee Williams*.

GEORGE E. KENT, Professor of English at the University of Chicago, has published studies of Baldwin, Ellison, Faulkner, Jean Toomer, and Gwendolyn Brooks. He is the author of *Blackness and the Adventure of Western Culture* and is working on a study of black autobiography.

KENETH KINNAMON is Professor of English at the University of Illinois, Urbana. He has published articles on Baldwin, Hemingway, and Langston Hughes and a book on Richard Wright, *The Emergence of Richard Wright: A Study in Literature and Society.*

HAROLD T. MCCARTHY is Professor of English at the University of Massachusetts. He has published on Henry James, Mark Twain, Hemingway, and "the expatriate experience."

MARIA K. MOOTRY, Assistant Professor of Black American Studies, Southern Illinois University at Carbondale, has published articles in *Black World*, the *CLA Journal*, and the *Massachusetts Review*. She is currently editing a volume of critical essays on Gwendolyn Brooks.

HORACE A. PORTER is Assistant Professor of English at Dartmouth College. He has published in the *American Scholar* and the *Journal of Negro History*. He is presently completing a critical study of James Baldwin.

NATHAN A. SCOTT, JR. is Commonwealth Professor of Religious Studies at the University of Virginia, where he is also a member of the English Department. He was for many years Shailer Mathews Professor of Theology and Literature at the University of Chicago. His numerous books include *The Broken Center, Negative Capability, The Wild Prayer of Longing, Three American Modernists,* and *The Poetry of Civic Virtue.*

PAUL N. SIEGEL, Professor Emeritus of English at Long Island University, has published books and essays on Shakespeare as well as studies of Isaac Bashevis Singer and Leon Trotsky.

DARWIN T. TURNER is an Iowa Foundation Distinguished Professor in the English Department and Chairman of the Afro-American Studies Department at the University of Iowa. He has published articles on Jean Toomer, Shakespeare, Melville, Twain, and Hawthorne. He is the author of *Three Afro-American Writers and Their Search for Identity* and has edited *The Wayward and the Seeking: A Collection of Writings by Jean Toomer* and *Black American Literature.*

KINGSLEY WIDMER has written widely on modern literature including books on D. H. Lawrence and Henry Miller; he was formerly a member of the English Department at the University of Wisconsin, Madison.

Selected Bibliography

This is a selected bibliography of critical and biographical materials on Wright. Several of the books listed contain fuller bibliographies. For the serious Wright student the following bibliographies are essential: Michel Fabre and Edward Margolies, "Richard Wright (1908–1960): A Bibliography," *Bulletin of Bibliography*, XXIV (Jan.–April, 1965), 131–33, 137; John M. Reilly, "Richard Wright: An Essay in Bibliography," *Resources for American Literary Study*, I, no. 2 (Autumn, 1971), 131–80; Jackson R. Bryer, "Richard Wright (1908–1960): A Selected Checklist of Criticism," *Wisconsin Studies in Contemporary Literature*, I (1960), 22–33; and most recently, Michel Fabre and the late Charles T. Davis, *Richard Wright: A Primary Bibliography* (Boston: Hall, 1982). Several journals have devoted entire issues to Wright: *Negro Digest (Black World)* XVIII (December, 1968); *CLA Journal* XII (June, 1969); *Studies in Black Literature*, I (Autumn 1970); and *New Letters* XXXVIII (December, 1971) (later reprinted by the University of Michigan Press, 1973, as *Richard Wright: Impressions and Perspectives*, edited by David Ray and Robert M. Farnsworth).

Abcarian, Richard, ed. *Richard Wright's "Native Son": A Critical Handbook*. Belmont, Calif.: Wadsworth, 1970.

Algren, Nelson. "Remembering Richard Wright." *Nation*, CXCII (January 28, 1961), 85.

Avery, Evelyn. *Rebels & Victims: Richard Wright & Bernard Malamud*. Port Washington, N.Y.: Kennikat, 1979.

Baker, Houston, ed. *Twentieth Century Interpretations of "Native Son."* Englewood Cliffs, N.J.: Prentice-Hall, 1972.

Bakish, David. *Richard Wright* (Modern Literary Monographs). New York: Ungar, 1973.

Baldwin, James. "Many Thousands Gone." In *Notes of a Native Son*. Boston: Beacon, 1955, pp. 24–45.

——————. *Nobody Knows My Name: More Notes of a Native Son*. New York: Dial Press, 1961. (Contains "Alas, Poor Richard," "Eight Men," and "The Exile.")

Baron, Dennis E. "The Syntax of Perception in Richard Wright's *Native Son*." *Language and Style*, IX (1980), 17–28.

Barton, Rebecca Chalmers. *Witness for Freedom: Negro Americans in Autobiography*. New York: Harper & Brothers, 1948, pp. 254–68.

Bone, Robert. *Richard Wright*. Minneapolis: University of Minnesota Press, 1969.

—————. *The Negro Novel in America*. Rev. ed. New Haven: Yale University Press, 1965, pp. 140–52.

Brignano, Russell Carl. *Richard Wright: An Introduction to the Man and His Works*. Pittsburgh: University of Pittsburgh Press, 1970.

Brivac, Sheldon. "Conflict of Values: Richard Wright's *Native Son*." *Novel*, VII (1974), 231–45.

Brown, Lloyd W. "Stereotypes in Black and White: The Nature of Perception in Richard Wright's *Native Son*." *Black Academy Review* I (Fall, 1970), 35–41.

Burgum, Edwin Berry. "The Promise of Democracy and the Fiction of Richard Wright." *Science and Society*, VII (Fall, 1943), 338–52.

Butterfield, Stephen. *Black Autobiography in America*. Amherst: University of Massachusetts Press, 1974, pp. 155–79.

Charney, Maurice. "James Baldwin's Quarrel with Richard Wright." *American Quarterly*, XV (Spring, 1963), 65–76.

Creekmore, Hubert. "Social Factors in *Native Son*." *University Review*, VII (Winter, 1941), 136–43.

Cruse, Harold. *The Crisis of the Negro Intellectual*. New York: Morrow, 1967, pp. 181–89.

Davis, Arthur P. "*The Outsider* as a Novel of Race." *Midwest Journal*, VII (Winter, 1955–56), 320–26.

Davis, Charles T., "From Experience to Eloquence: Richard Wright's *Black Boy* as Art." In *Chant of Saints*, ed. M. S. Harper and R. B. Stepto. Urbana: University of Illinois Press, 1979, pp. 425–39.

Dickstein, Morris. "The Black Aesthetic in White America." *Partisan Review*, XXXVIII (Winter 1971–72), 376–95.

Ellison, Ralph. "The World and the Jug." In *Shadow and Act*. New York: Random House, 1965, pp. 115–47. (A response to Irving Howe's "Black Boys and Native Sons.")

Emanuel, James A. "Fever and Feeling: Notes on the Imagery of *Native Son*." *Negro Digest*, XVIII (1968), 16–26.

Everette, Mildred W. "The Death of Richard Wright's American Dream: 'The Man Who Lived Underground.'" *CLA Journal*, XVII (March, 1974), 318–26.

Fabre, Michel. "Fantasies and Style in Richard Wright's Fiction." *New Letters*, XLVI (1980), 55–81.

—————. "The Poetry of Richard Wright." *Studies in Black Literature*, I (Autumn 1970), 10–22. (Fabre also contributes an interview with Simone de Beauvoir and a letter from Dorothy Padmore to this special issue of *SBL*.)

—————. "Richard Wright and the French Existentialists." *Melus*, V (1978), 35–51.

——————. *The Unfinished Quest of Richard Wright,* trans. Isabel Barzun. New York: Morrow, 1973. (An essential biographical work; contains a useful bibliography.)

Felgar, Robert. *Richard Wright.* Boston: Hall, 1980.

——————. "'The Kingdom of the Beast': The Landscape of *Native Son.*" *CLA Journal,* XVII (March, 1974), 333–37.

Fishburn, Katherine. *Richard Wright's Hero: The Faces of the Rebel-Victim.* Metuchen, N.J.: Scarecrow Press, 1977.

Gayle, Addison. *Richard Wright: Ordeal of a Native Son.* Garden City, N.Y.: Anchor Press/Doubleday, 1980.

Gérard, Albert. "Vie et vocation de Richard Wright." *Revue Générale Belge,* XCVII (June 1969), 334–57.

Gibson, Donald. "Richard Wright: The Politics of a Lone Marxian." In *The Politics of Literary Expression: A Study of Major Black Writers.* Westport, Conn.: Greenwood, 1981, pp. 21–57. (This volume contains a bibliography on Wright.)

Gilenson, B. "Die 'zweite Geburt' von Richard Wright." *Kunst und Literatur,* XXVIII (1980), 95–103.

Glicksberg, Charles I. "Existentialism in *The Outsider.*" *Four Quarters,* VII (Jan., 1958), 17–26.

Gloster, Hugh M. "Richard Wright: Interpreter of Racial and Economic Maladjustments." *Opportunity,* XIX (1941), 361–65, 383.

Gounard, J. F. "La carrière mouvementée de Richard Wright." *Revue de l'Université d'Ottawa,* XLVI (1976), 520–43.

Graham, Don B. *"Lawd Today* and the Example of *The Waste Land.*" *CLA Journal,* XVII (March, 1974), 327–32.

Grenander, M. E. "Criminal Responsibility in *Native Son* and *Knock on Any Door.*" *American Literature,* XLIX (May 1977), 221–33.

Ground, Jean-François. "Richard Wright as a Black American Writer in Exile." *CLA Journal* XVII (March, 1974), 307–17.

Hand, Clifford. "The Struggle to Create Life in the Fiction of Richard Wright." In *The Thirties: Fiction, Poetry, Drama,* ed. Warren French. Deland, Fla.: Edwards, 1967.

Hill, Herbert, moderator. "Reflections on Richard Wright: A Symposium on an Exiled Native Son." In *Anger and Beyond: The Negro Writer in the United States,* ed. H. Hill. New York: Harper & Row, 1966. (Discussion among Horace Cayton, Arna Bontemps, Saunders Redding, and Hill.)

Howe, Irving. "Black Boys and Native Sons." *Dissent,* X (Autumn, 1963), 353–68. (Reprinted in *A World More Attractive: A View of Modern Literature and Politics.* New York: Horizon, 1963, pp. 98–122.)

Hyman, Stanley Edgar. "Richard Wright Reappraised." *Atlantic*, CCXXV (March, 1970), 127–32.

Isaacs, Harold. "Five Writers and Their Ancestors." In *The New World of Negro Americans*. London: Phoenix, 1964, pp. 231–87.

Jackson, Blyden. "Richard Wright: Black Boy from America's Black Belt and Urban Ghettos." *CLA Journal*, XII (June, 1969), 287–309.

Kinnamon, Keneth. *The Emergence of Richard Wright: A Study in Literature and Society*. Urbana: University of Illinois Press, 1973.

——————. "The Pastoral Impulse in Richard Wright." *Mid-Continent American Studies Journal*, X (Spring, 1969), 41–47.

Kim, Kichung. "Wright, the Protest Novel, and Baldwin's Faith." *CLA Journal*, XVII (March, 1974), 387–96.

Kostelanetz, Richard. "The Politics of Unresolved Quest in the Novels of Richard Wright." *Xavier University Studies*, VIII (Summer, 1969), 31–63.

McCall, Dan. *The Example of Richard Wright*. New York: Harcourt, Brace and World, 1969.

Margolies, Edward. *The Art of Richard Wright*. Carbondale: Southern Illinois University Press, 1969.

——————. "Richard Wright: *Native Son* and Three Kinds of Revolution." In *Native Sons: A Critical Study of Twentieth-Century Negro American Authors*. New York: Lippincott, 1968, pp. 65–86.

Nagel, James. "Images of 'Vision' in *Native Son*." *University Review*, XXXVI (1969), 109–15.

Redding, Saunders. "The Alien Land of Richard Wright." In *Soon, One Morning: New Writing by American Negroes, 1940–1962*, ed. Herbert Hill. New York: Knopf, 1963, pp. 50–59.

Reilly, John M., ed. *Richard Wright: The Critical Reception*. New York: Burt Franklin, 1978.

Rickles, Milton and Patricia. *Richard Wright* (Southern Writers Series). Austin, Tex.: Steck-Vaughan, 1971.

Riesman, David. "Marginality, Conformity, and Insight." *Phylon*, XIV (1953), 241–57.

Scott, Nathan A., Jr. "Judgment Marked by a Cellar: The American Negro Writer and the Dialectic of Despair." In *The Shapeless God: Essays on Modern Fiction*, ed. Harry J. Mooney, Jr. and Thomas F. Staley. Pittsburgh: University of Pittsburgh Press, 1968, pp. 139–69.

——————. "Search for Beliefs: The Fiction of Richard Wright." *University of Kansas City Review*, XXIII (1956), 131–38.

Sanders, Ronald. "Richard Wright and the Sixties." *Midstream*, XIV (1968), 28–40.

Smith, Sidonie Ann. "Richard Wright's *Black Boy:* The Creative Impulse as Rebellion." *Southern Literary Journal,* V (1972), 123–56.

Stepto, Robert B. "'I Thought I Knew These People': Richard Wright and the Afro-American Tradition." *Massachusetts Review,* XVIII (1977), 525–41.

——————. "Literacy and Ascent: Richard Wright's *Black Boy.*" In *From Behind the Veil: A Study of Afro-American Narrative.* Urbana: University of Illinois Press, 1979, pp. 128–62.

Walker, Ian. "Black Nightmare: The Fiction of Richard Wright." In *Black Fiction: New Studies in the Afro-American Novel since 1945,* ed. A. Robert Lee. New York: Barnes & Noble, 1980, pp. 11–28.

Ward, Jerry W. "Richard Wright's Hunger." *Virginia Quarterly Review,* LIV (Winter, 1978), 148–53.

Webb, Constance. *Richard Wright.* New York: Putnam, 1968. (A biography based on a twenty-year friendship with Wright and material made available by his widow.)

Wertham, Frederic. "An Unconscious Determinant in *Native Son.*" *Journal of Clinical Psychopathology,* VI (July, 1944), 111–15.

White, Ralph K. "*Black Boy:* A Value Analysis." *Journal of Abnormal and Social Psychology,* XLIX (1962), 149–63, 187.

Williams, John A. *The Most Native of Sons.* Garden City, N.Y.: Doubleday, 1970.

Winslow, Henry F. "Richard Wright: Destroyer and Preserver (1908–1960)." *The Crisis,* LXIX (1962), 149–63, 187.

Wright, Ellen, and Michel Fabre. *Richard Wright Reader.* New York: Harper & Row, 1978. (A comprehensive survey of Wright's work, containing some essays and letters not previously collected.)

Index